CRISIS MAN
A SPIRITUAL APPROACH

SOLVING LIFE PROBLEMS FROM THEIR SPIRITUAL ROOTS

PRAYER BANK, WORD BANK AND TEARS BOTTLE!

Written By
APOSTLE MARK EXCEL

Edited By
AKEH KUFUMNAUKE

Reviewed By
DR. ENE I. ETTE (PhD. FCCP)

Where There Is No Christ, There Is Crisis

Crisis Management: A Spiritual Approach
Solving Life Problems From Their Spiritual Roots.
by Apostle Mark Essien Excel

Printed in the United States of America

ISBN 9781613799406

This hand-book is an effective weapon for those who desire freedom from the powers of darkness and are involved in daily Spiritual warfare. It contains strategies for victorious Christian living.
By Apostle Mark E. Excel

For information on Voice of Freedom International Ministries, Inc. or Apostle Excel,
Contact us at: P. O. Box 899, Brentwood, NY 11717, or 631-428-1432; 631-630-6245, or ciemw@vofim.org, voiceoffreedom_ministries@yahoo.com
Website: www.vofim.org

Published by: Xulon Press

AssociateEditors
PASTOR ANN EXCEL
PASTOR ENO-OBONG SIMON-ETIM
DANIEL FAZZINA

www.xulonpress.com

Dedication

This book is dedicated to all intercessors, prayer warriors and those involved in daily spiritual warfare.

I pray that the Lord grant them the grace needed to defeat our arch-enemy, the devil, in Jesus' name. Amen.

Table of Contents

Acknowledgements

I thank God for the wonderful opportunity afforded me to teach His Word.

I say a big thank you to Bishop Carlton Brown for his contribution to our wellbeing in this mission field. My special thanks go to Apostle David Buchanan whom God used to pilot me for two months suffering mosquito bites with me as we slept in an open field ty and strength.

May the Loogether. Many thanks to Rev. Charles and Virginia Pitts who saw Apostle Buchanan and me sleeping in a gas station and took us home and provided a home and comfort for us.

Again my thanks go to Dr. Michael and Ann Aliquo and their three precious girls who vacated their room to give accommodation to my family for a year and a half and cared for all our needs.

What can I say to Rev. Scott and Dianne Cuoco whom the Lord has continued to use until now to sustain us? Many thanks. Furthermore, I will not fail to mention Ministers Harold and Lilian Butler who do not hesitate to deny themselves in order to provide for our needs. Also I will not forget to say many thanks to my name sake, Pastor Mark and Lora Dellosso of the Heart of Worship Fellowship Center.

I say a hefty thank you to Minister Rick Jordan, my TV producer who put me on TV for the first time and has produced my programs over seven years without charge. I offer many thanks to you, Pastor Veama Braithwaite of Faith, Love and Charity Ministries for your love, contribution and driving skill that you used to help us when we needed help most. Much more so do I say a big thanks to Deacon and Deaconess Craig and Yvonne Neal whom God put in my life and have one family with mine for their continuous love, support and fellowship.

Again I say a big thank you to Deacon Tom and Elizabeth Budny for their support and hospitality. Special thanks to Bishop Brugard and Rev. Reyette Brutus of the Remsen Church of God for their support. And a big thanks to Rev. Dr. Cheryl Ault for all her support, provisions and love. Again, big thanks to Evangelist Caroline Udenze (Noni) for her connecting prowess and love.

I will not forget to say a big thank you to Pastor Enobong Simon Etim for opening the door of her house for our ministry and Pastor Bassey Ekpenyong whom God has used both as an assistant and a blessing to our ministry, and Pastor Florence Ekpenyong who is blessed with the gift of encouragement and Pastor James and his wife, Evangelist Charlene LeBrun who hold up my left and right hands in ministry.

My special thanks go to all friends, supporters and well-wishers that I cannot, for space, mention by name whose contributions and support have been invaluable.

Above all I say thank you to all the students and teachers of Voice of Freedom School of Ministry, both old and new, and my editor, Brother Akeh Kufumnauke of the Creative Artist Inc., Dr. Ene I. Ette and Dr. Usukumah whose contributions are immeasurable and through whom this work is made possible.

Finally, my special thanks go to my precious wife and a true help meet indeed and my wonderful children who are my joy and strength. May the Lord bless you all.

FOREWORD
BY
BISHOP CARLTON BROWN

Apostle Mark Excel is a man of *integrity*, *vision*, and practiced faith, who has now set his experiences in spiritual warfare to print for the purposes of furthering the Kingdom message in an age of dull spiritual perceptions, and dysfunctional ministry performance.

His writings have been composed while on divine assignment from his native country of **Nigeria**, to minister here in the **United States**, a land that once served as the bastion of religious freedom and responsible spiritual teaching. Sadly, too many of our ***watchman on the walls*** have failed to heed the lessons of our brothers and sisters in Europe, and hence a nation whose masses were at one time thankful to God for His manifold blessing, has now become dismissive of the principles upon which our freedom and prosperity have been founded upon.

The great satanic deception is to convince his victims of his own incompetence, insignificance, and better still, his non-existence. Thus rendered as impotent or invisible, he is facilitated in the devastating erosion of human kind's spiritual insight and moral posture. Unfortunately, this negative effect is not only being played out on the secular stage, but the drama also has found a prominent placement on the altar of our numerous denominations, including the once vibrant and course-correcting pulpits of the Pentecostal/Charismatic movement.

Is it not interesting the significant numbers of nominal Christians who confess to believing in Heaven, but have serious doubts about the reality of Hell who are attending most of our churches today? Certainly, many non-believers will boldly declare that hell is what we experience in the world today, where its fires and torments end with the peace we will all equally share once deposited in our graves. How unfortunate the scarcity of voices in our pews that will venture forth from the church to boldly differ with such deceptive, and distressful musings.

Our dearth of conviction and divine enlightenment leaves, at times, even the most ardent church attendee to be victimized by the hordes of Satan's "principalities and powers", to wreak havoc in our pursuit of divine purpose, with the gates of our spiritual and natural counsel operating bereft of the divine wisdom and demonstrative power that are the prerequisites to our achieving the ultimate success found only in the center of God's will.

Apostle Excel's book brings light to the circumspect manner in which a believer is to walk in order to master the Christ life, and repel the negative forces that are directed against his or her fulfillment of divine destiny. Apostle Mark deftly achieves his purpose to cause his reader to think *out of the box*, by raising our awareness and evaluation of how we perceive the world around us, and then connecting the power of our faith to those revealed conditions through a blanketing of the pointed, purposeful and powerful prayer language he catalogues in this book.

Some readers will no doubt raise question with the multiple varieties and characteristics of the warfare prayers he will suggest to us. However, when these categories are coupled with the many illustrations on how this knowledge and execution of prayers have resulted in the advancement of Kingdom purposes and deliverance of Kingdom participants, then the question will also be explored... *when is too much prayer ever a bad thing?*

I believe you will find this book to be at times ***challenging***, at other times ***comforting***, and in the final analysis ***critical*** to the upgrading of your spiritual values regarding the taking of territories from the enemy, as you sustain a spiritual journey that will effectively classify you as "*more than conqueror*" in the divine economy.

Bishop Carlton T. Brown
Senior Pastor,
Bethel Gospel Assembly, Inc. New York City

Chairman
Bethel Gospel Global Assemblies International
& Urban Global Missions Alliance

Author -" Until Death do we S.H.O.P"

PREFACE

On the fateful morning of Sunday the 30th of December, 1973, my father called me as early as 6.00 a.m. and directed me to get ready because he had a place he wanted me to go and represent him. "Today," he said, "you are going to the headquarters of our church at Abak Ukpom to represent me. Pay attention to the messages given there, write the announcements down and come back with the necessary information for our branch." I thought about it. I was still a teen and men and women from all walks of life, from more than two hundred villages, would be there, as it was an annual convention. But why would my father send me, a young man of seventeen? This was an affair for grownups. Am I not too young for this assignment? I contemplated all these points in my young mind. But it was an abomination to tell one's father, "No!" Up on my feet I got and began my journey towards Abak Ukpom.

I enjoyed every bit of the service at Abak Ukpom. Hundreds of people were in attendance. I watched and noted every speech and carrying-on by the dignitaries, pastors and deacons present at that big convention. At the end I began my trip back home satisfied that I had carried out my father's bidding to the best of my abilities. Upon arriving back home my father was in continuous meetings with different groups of people. I wanted to give him the report of what went on at the convention at Abak Ukpom, but he was occupied continuously. It was like the Last Supper, I remember thinking. People were filing in as if they were paying their last respects. Yet no one was dead or dying!

Before I had time to talk to my father, it was night time and the moon had already appeared. Traditionally during this season, young children would gather under a tree and tell folktales and play various other children's games, especially hide and seek, to fully take advantage of the bright moonlight. My friends and I, young boys and girls soon congregated under a big tree in the compound and we began a rigorous game of hide and seek. We continued in our night play until past mid-night when I heard my step mother's voice ring out my name. I excused myself from my friends and reported to her.

"Your father is calling you." she said. I immediately ran to my dad. When I stood before him, he looked at me and saw the heaving of my chest. He knew that I had been playing and he said to me, "Where is the information that you brought back from the church convention and why have you not informed me up till now? I replied, "Tete, (an affectionate name I normally called my dad), since I got back I had sought an opportunity to speak with you but you were too busy; one group would leave and another one would arrive." But Tete was not satisfied with my explanation. He knotted up his brow and offered these words of wisdom: "Remember to always do first things first, stop postponing things to your own convenience. Do not let obstacles stand in your way and divert you from your assigned goal. When you become a man of God, when do you think will be a good time to talk to God? Do you not know that all over the world there is no single time that people do not talk to God? Will you like to wait for a free time to talk to God?" What Tete was saying was that the fact that visitors had gathered to see him should not have prevented me from my goal. I should have pressed ahead. In the future I should not let obstacles and diversions becloud my judgment and divert me from my stated goal. I did not know that he was giving me his last message that will help me through life on earth. These words sank in to my spirit then and have remained there to this day. These simple words also have helped me to be who I am today. Tete blessed me after his words with me and told me to come to bed after playing with my friends. By the time I came to bed Tete was reading his Bible. He spoke to me again and also blessed me a second time as I slept off within a minute or two.

In the morning, I woke up to a funeral wail-Tete was gone. He had passed away during the night. More of this will be found in my yet to be published book: "Journey Through Life." Today I have come to understand what Tete was talking about. Many have left first things to pursue after vain things, temporary pleasures, and frivolous undertakings. Many also, including God's ministers, have pushed God's assignments to a second place embarking on building their houses first while the Ark of the Covenant of God has no place to rest. Some have embarked on vain undertakings without an understanding of their rightful priorities. This leads to unending procrastinations and eventual failure in life.

This is how Jesus put it: *But seek ye first the Kingdom of God and His righteousness: and all these things shall be added unto you.* **Matthew 6:33**

************ ************************** ************

September 10 1989, as I lay on my bed with my wife by my side after a beautiful Sunday service where I had preached, the Lord appeared to me and said to me, "Come with Me." All I remember is following Him with my two hands on my head crying: "See how I go very lonely, see how I go very lonely," as He led me through a tunnel to an unknown destination.

It was indeed a lonely road, as just the two of us were making the trip. As I cried the more, the Lord turned back to me with these two questions: "Can you go back and get your wife and your child?" My answer was, "No." A second question came: "Can you go back and get your money in the bank?" I answered again, "No." Then He said onto me, "Go and preach the Word." Again he said to me, "Follow me," and I followed Him weeping. That trip with the Lord took us to a place reserved for the wicked called ***hellfire.*** I was conducted around three different compartments of burning furnaces to witness multitudes in great torment with the only word coming out of their mouths being an unending cacophony of screams for water, water, and more water!!! I also remember seeing a young man from my village who died during the civil war walking close to the door and saying to me, "Go and tell my parents where I am."

Afterwards, the Lord took me through a narrow path as though we were ascending a hill and at the end a mighty gate was opened and we ascended into heaven. The Lord showed me the purpose of true life in Christ Jesus, and what true worship was like as the saints who made it there were in constant worship of the King of kings and the Lord of lords. This went on as multitudes of angels dressed in golden white with all kinds of trumpets provided the music as they marched in a way that no man has ever done on earth. I then understood that true joy and true glory was possible only in the Lord's abode.

Little did I know that the Lord was getting me prepared for a later appearance and commissioning as a missionary to the nations, a calling which began a few years later when the Lord sent me to be His ambassador in Togo. My upcoming book, "Journey to Hell and Heaven" will delve deeper into the experiences I had and the activities that occur in hellfire and in heaven.

Even though my spirit left me as my wife awoke the next morning and met a dead husband on the bed by her side, my knowledge of the vision is still very fresh in my memory. I have taken it upon myself as my life's mission and primary responsibility the reply that the Lord gave to me when I said to Him, "I want to remain herein heaven" when I saw the glory and the beauty of heaven. My request He politely turned down by ordering me to: "Go and tell the world what you have seen, deliver a message from Me and train my end-time army." He said to me again, "Many will believe you, many will not. Many will receive you many will not. But go ahead and do that which I send you."

It is therefore my desire to travel to wherever He sends me to deliver the message of hell and heaven and to train today's believers to do first things first by answering the call of God and being involved in God's end-time army. A good messenger does not speak his own words but the words of his master and ultimately returns to his master with the feedback.

It is my desire to impart spiritual knowledge through spiritual information and education and the strategy which could help the church of Jesus Christ to defeat the plans of the devil and to quench all the fiery darts of the wicked as I was instructed by our Lord Jesus Christ. I will use all scriptures given by the inspiration of God for reproof, correction and instruction in righteousness, and to exhort and warn as I was instructed. It is also my desire to help in building and structuring effective prayer mechanisms that would stop the infiltration of witches in local assemblies. As a revivalist, I will throw my weight behind leadership of the church for internal revival of the membership of the Body of Christ. It is also my desire to carry out global evangelization and soul winning and the deliverance of those souls in prison whose physical bodies are in the church. Finally, it is my desire to help resolve conflicts and doctrinal differences which are the major causes of division in the church of our Lord Jesus Christ.

These desires have motivated me to write this book.

Apostle Mark Essien Excel.

CHAPTER 1

INTRODUCTION

This book is written as a balancing tool in the hands of all believers who may have read books on prayer or who may have sought to know more about how to pray with results.

It is written by someone who has a practical knowledge of deliverance ministry and has been involved in various organs of praying ministry: intercessory, warfare, devotional, corporate and personal or private prayer. I spend a good deal of time on my knees during quiet time and in meditation, and I am also a strong believer in the family altar.

A strong Christian is not known because of the number of times he goes to church in a week, or how much offerings and tithes he gives. A strong Christian is known by his ability to weather the storms of life that sooner or later come to try his faith in Christ.

The fact remains that many of the deliverances those deliverance-seekers receive do not last long due in part to the absence of some follow up programs or "after deliverance plan..." the last state of such persons become even worse than the beginning.

"When the unclean spirit is gone out of a man, he walketh through dry places, seeking rest, and findeth none. Then he saith, I will return into my house from whence I came out; and when he is come, he findeth it empty, swept, and garnished. Then goeth he, and taketh with himself seven other spirits more wicked than himself, and they enter in and dwell there: and the last state of that man is

worse than the first. Even so shall it be also unto this wicked generation." **Matthew 12:43-45**

In line with the above scriptural citation, this book addresses important aspects of prayer in crisis management, as well as components and terms of effective prayer.

WHAT IS CRISIS?

A crisis is a stressful event or unexpected situation that pops up in our daily life with potential to maim or destroy our ultimate happiness. When unanticipated negative occurrences challenge our survival ability, we are psychologically thrown off balance. A crisis may at times be expected at some point, but the magnitude and effect are under estimated, hence the term "crisis" rightly applies. It should be noted that every crisis that occurs in the physical arena has already taken root in the supernatural world. In other words, the physical manifestation is an expression of its spiritual reality.

GENESIS OF CRISIS

And the LORD God called unto Adam, and said unto him, Where art thou?
And he said, I heard Your voice in the garden, and I was afraid because I was naked; and I hid myself. And He said, Who told thee that thou wast naked? Has thou eaten of the tree, whereof I commanded thee that thou shouldest not eat? And the man said, The woman who thou gavest to be with me, she gave me of the tree, and I did eat.
Genesis 9-12

This was the first recorded crisis in human history. Adam's disobedience and rebellion against God led him to flee from the presence of God and to forsake divine fellowship with Him. That episode in Eden was the mother of all crises which gave birth to all subsequent crises in human history because it introduced sin, suffering and inevitable death that comes in all types of unforeseen circumstances.

Crisis is an opportunity for God to "process the man in crisis" so as to qualify him for a lift and to catapult him to his destiny with an abundance of opportunities. Whoever went through crisis in the Bible came out on top: Abraham, Isaac, Jacob, Moses, David, Daniel, Jesus Christ, Paul the apostle, etc. Some of these individuals and their crises will be discussed in the next few chapters.

CLASSIFICATION OF CRISIS

Personally generated crisis:

- Family Crisis: involving spouse, children, relatives or friends
- Crisis with the Authorities
- Financial Crisis

Disasters:

- Natural crisis – tornados; earthquakes; floods; sickness; death; etc.
- Man Made crisis – war; fire; theft; accident; failure; and all human hostilities.

Spiritual Crisis

- These may result from not being able to pray as you ought to.
- Loss of vision, inability to remember dreams when they occur;
- Not being able to hear from God or understand when God speaks.

Since most people do not really anticipate a crisis, only a small percentage of people are normally prepared for one when it occurs. Some believers are not prepared for eventualities. They usually begin to fast and pray as soon as an event has already been announced, but often by this time it is too late and the event proceeds to fruition because it had already taken root in the spirit realm.

To understand how to deal with crisis, one must first understand the following terms.

1. Prayer Bank
2. Tears Bottle and Prayer Record
3. Word Bank
4. Counseling
5. Crisis Management

PRAYER BANK

To understand what a prayer bank is we must first understand what a physical bank is and the role that a bank plays in the society.

A bank is a place where money and other valuable items such as gold, diamonds, important documents, wills, etc. are stored for safe keeping until they are needed. Individuals go to the bank and open accounts based on their needs. There are checking accounts, savings accounts, money market accounts, etc. Each account is operated in accordance with the purpose that it was set up for. It is your ability to operate your account effectively with your bank that will enable it to grant you easy credit or loans. If you fail to operate your accounts for an extended period of time, those accounts could turn dormant.

A prayer bank therefore is a bank where you store up your prayers **spiritually, topically and specifically** for future use**.** The stored up solicitations readily make answers available to meet your unexpected needs when events occur in the future, or even prevent evil occurrence altogether.

A prayer bank is a preparation made against rainy days; some future necessity of life or spiritual provision in anticipation of what may or may not happen. It is a stitch in time that saves nine!

Scriptural support

Watch and pray, that ye enter not into temptation: the spirit indeed is willing, but the flesh is weak.
Matthew 26:41

Jesus told His disciples, and by extension us, to watch and pray so that we enter not into temptation. It therefore means that temptation is ahead and we have to watch: take precaution, observe and resist, then attack those forces that want to drag us into temptation. If we do not watch and pray in advance of the temptation, we then fall into it unexpectedly.

He is actually telling us to store up our prayers in our prayer bank to help us overcome the temptation ahead of us. He could as well have said to us to watch and pray against accident, or sickness or any unforeseeable occurrences. The prayers in our prayer banks help us walk through temptation if it occurs at all and prevents us from falling into it.

The fact that we pray in advance of temptation does not mean that we will not pray in the midst of the temptation, after all, the Bible says, "pray without ceasing." Invariably we do not have to wait to be attacked before responding with equal force. If Jesus Himself advised us to watch and pray, then this implies depositing prayers in our prayer banks in our preparatory sentinel phase. It is better to fight off the enemy who is sure to attack, than to wait to be attacked before responding.

For example, Joshua sent spies to Jericho in advance before he launched an attack against the land. Moses did a similar thing in his days. A prayer bank is a kind of spiritual spy sent to search, investigate, monitor and reveal the hidden plans and plots of our enemies against us.

Prophet Elisha acted in that capacity for Israel in their battle against Syria.

Then the king of Syria warred against Israel, and took counsel with his servants, saying, In such and such a place shall be my camp. And the man of God sent unto the king of Israel, saying, Beware that thou pass not such a place; for thither the Syrians are come down.
2 Kings 6:8-9

God will never send anyone on an errand or to a battle without first getting them prepared. In whichever way you look at it, advance preparation is needed before we step into battle. A prayer bank is a Christian necessity!

THE PARABLE OF THE UNJUST STEWARD

There is another incident in the Bible that is worth mentioning. This is a story about an unjust steward who worked for a rich man. When the steward knew that there were some accusations against him of how he wasted his master's resources, he began a process of making some provisions for the future. It is not that what he did was upholding, but the wisdom in what he did gives us a clue as to what prayer banks are all about. The Bible says that the Lord commended the unjust steward, not because he was pious but because of his wisdom in thinking about his future and making preparations for the unforeseen. The story says:

There was a certain rich man, which had a steward; and the same was accused unto him that he had wasted his goods. And he called him, and said unto him, How is it that I hear this of thee? Give an account of thy stewardship; for thou mayest be no more steward. Then the steward said within himself, what shall I do? For my lord taketh from me the stewardship: I cannot dig; to beg I am ashamed. I am resolved what to do, that, when I am put out of the stewardship, they may receive me into their houses...And the lord commended the unjust steward, because he had done wisely: because the children of this generation are in their generation wiser than the children of light.
Luke 16: 1-8

Do the children of light really care what might happen in the future, like an epidemic, death of children, war, tornados, etc.? Should the children of light behave like the goat, which while tethered to the stake, continues to eat blissfully the grass provided by his executioner while his fellow goat is being slaughtered right before his very eyes? His slaughter is assured and is next, yet he is blissfully unaware of this danger and or is resigned to it.

He only begins to bleat and kick and protest at the very last minute when the executioner removes the tethering rope and leads him to the butchering table. But surely the intelligence of modern day Christians should be greater than a pair of goats at the slaughterhouse. Yet we would be hard pressed to find a Christian who considers the inevitability of death seriously. We blissfully chew the curd of material existence enjoying the pleasures that the material world provides while all around us, people are suffering and dying untimely deaths at the hands of witches. It never occurs to us that we will sooner than later suffer the same fate and to store up prayers and provisions for this inevitable fate that all of mankind must someday suffer.

Truthfully, in every war there are people that profit from it and there are those that die from it. God uses important historical events to promote His children and simultaneously to bring down the wicked. Therefore God expects all of His children to be prepared; to have an account ready for eventualities.

HOW THE PRAYER BANK WORKS

And He spoke a parable unto them to this end, that men ought always to pray, and not to faint; Saying, There was in a city a judge, which feared not God neither regarded man; and there was a widow in that city; and she came unto him, saying, avenge me of my adversaries. And he would not for a while: but afterward he said within himself, though I fear not God, nor regarded man; yet because this widow troubleth me, I will avenge her, lest by her continual coming she weary me. And the Lord said, hear what the unjust judge said. And shall not God avenge His own elect, which cry day and night unto Him, though He bear long with them? I tell you that He will avenge them speedily. Nevertheless when the Son of man cometh, shall He find faith in the earth?
Luke 18:1-8

Each time you deposit a prayer into the bank, you are keeping account with the King of all kings and the Lord of lords. And a record is kept as though you deposited money into your bank account.

..A devout man, and one that feared God with all his house, which gave much alms to the people, ***and prayed to God always****. He saw in a vision evidently about the ninth hour of the day an angel of*

God coming in to him, and saying unto him, Cornelius. And when he looked on him, he was afraid, and said, What is it, Lord? And he said unto him, ***Thy prayers*** *and thine* **alms** *are come up for* ***a memorial before God.***
Acts 10:1-4

Can my prayers and alms and your prayers and alms go up before God for a memorial? Yes that can happen if you have stored up the prayers backed by good works, already. It is not too late, begin now to store up your prayers against that day! Store up your prayers to be eligible for a memorial before the Almighty God. And back your prayers up with other Biblical injunctions: faith, love, forgiveness, giving, etc.

We are not suggesting that you pray one prayer ten or twenty times before God can hear or answer you. What we are saying is that you must have a prayer stored up in your prayer bank. That prayer will stimulate your faith and cause you to believe God that your prayer has been answered. What you hope for must have a substance and produce the evidence that you have not yet seen. The substance or assurance is that prayer that you deposited since you did it by faith according to the will of God. But if you have no substance of things hope for, there will likely be no evidence of things not seen. It will end up as blind faith.

TEARS BOTTLE AND PRAYER RECORD

Thou tellest my wanderings: put thou my tears into thy bottle: are they not in thy book? When I cry unto thee, then shall my enemies turn back: this I know: for God is for me.
Psalm 56:8-9

Here the Psalmist gives a picture, a type of metaphor, of what it was for one to get immediate protection in the hand of the Almighty God from his enemy's persecution. It is as if God has a bottle whereby He collects and measures all the tears that fall from the eyes of His servants who cry to Him daily. He also has a book in which He records how many times one makes an inquisition unto Him concerning a particular need.

As David cried daily and made supplications unto God for protection from his archenemies, the Philistines, he was asking God to measure his tears that were in his tears bottle to see if the tears had reached the measure whereby God could defend him from his enemies. Simply stated, he was asking God this question: "Lord, have I cried enough to deserve your mercy? Is the quantity of my tears in my tears bottle before You full enough to move Your hands of compassion toward me? Are the records of my daily devotion before You okay?" The answer will come from God when He looks into the bottle to measure the weight of David's tears in the bottle, or when He checks the record of his devotion and supplications before Him. **Therefore tears bottles or prayer records are likened to what we refer to as prayer banks, and serve the same purpose.**

As we have stated before we repeat it again that the prayer of faith is now. Whenever you ask God in faith believing that you receive, then you have it. In **Isaiah 30:19**, God promised to be gracious to His people Israel if they would forsake running to Egypt for help and return to Him. He said, when He would hear their cry, he would answer it, there must first be a cry for Him to answer. Moreover **Isaiah 65:24** enables us to know that there will come a time when His elects will not even need to call, because before they call, He would answer. But as we make our supplications and prayers unto God by faith, we have to believe we have our petition even though there is no physical manifestation and continue with thanksgiving and praise unto His name. **Mark 11:24.**

WORD BANK

As in a bank, there must be something of monetary value to be used in opening an account or making the deposit: cash, treasury bills, gold, wills, etc. It is all contingent on what type of account one is trying to operate or for what purpose the account is being opened. Therefore the nature of the account determines the type of collateral deposit. The same goes for the spiritual bank, the cash, treasury bills, gold, wills and other monetary instruments for use in operating our spiritual bank is the *Word of God***.** One cannot begin to operate his spiritual bank except he first gathers the words necessary to meet the needs of the operation of that spiritual bank account.

Example: Although a lady might be thinking of getting married and becoming fruitful as soon as she is married, she does not have to wait to be married before beginning to ask God to bless her with the type of children she would like to have. While she is depositing prayers in her prayer bank for a husband, she can as well be depositing prayers in another bank for children. What she does is to key into the promises of God concerning fruitfulness and child bearing and even the rebuke of barrenness, and select those words of covenant that God makes with His children, and personalize them and claim them and build up a word bank (word storage) with them.

Example

Psalm 127:3-5
Genesis 1:28
Genesis 9:1, 7
Psalm 128:3, 6
Genesis 17:6
Exodus 1:19
Exodus 23:26
Song 6:6
Deut. 7:14

This word selection or compilation is to be used in our prayer by reminding God that He did promise to do it, as it is written:

Put me in remembrance: let us plead together: declare thou, that thou mayest be justified.
Isaiah 43:26

So shall my word be that goeth forth out of my mouth: it shall not return unto me void, but it shall accomplish that which I please, and it shall prosper in the thing whereto I sent it.

Isaiah 55:11

Then said the LORD unto me, Thou hast well seen: for I will hasten my word to perform it.
Jeremiah 1:12

Therefore the selection or compilation of appropriate words from the bulk of Words in the Bible to meet the operation of a particular spiritual bank based on a subject matter to be used as a deposit into your prayer bank is termed, "Word Bank."

There are about **788, 280** words in the King James Version of the Bible, and it is difficult if not virtually impossible for anyone to memorize all the verses of the Bible. However to be of help to oneself, it is essential to make a collection of essential scripture passages based on their themes to be used for your bank deposit.

What are some of the future life events that you think might happen that you do not have complete control over? Try as much as possible to identify and connect with a life event listed in this book. Utilize the essential verses provided and regularly deposit your devotion through the sample prayers and you will see the power of our God in action. After regularly depositing these inspired prayers in your prayer bank you will come to agree that God is not a man that He should lie, neither will He go back on His promises.

For further explanations please refer to chapters four, five and six for more on word bank and prayer bank.

COUNSELING

Counseling is getting advice, instruction or direction on how to deal with an emerging situation or crisis. A man who gives the advice is called "a counselor." The depth, weight and strength of wisdom, knowledge and advice derived from counseling are based on the depth of wisdom and knowledge the counselor possesses. Jesus alone is the true Counselor. Even before His birth, He was named a Counselor.

For unto us a child is born, unto us a son is given: and the government shall be upon His shoulder: and His name shall be called Wonderful, Counselor, The Mighty God, The everlasting Father, The Prince of Peace.
Isaiah 9:6

Many professing counselors today are deficient and ineffective. Some who are counseling married couples today are themselves divorcees. They use the spirit of enticement, academic knowledge and good speeches to buy the hearts of their captives whereas the foundations of the problems remain untouched. Their counsels become the venom of separation because they do not have any spiritual foundation. Instead of submitting themselves to the Master Counselor, Jesus, they choose bigger titles: "Doctor of Philosophy", Psychotherapist", "Marriage Counselor", to entice the populace. This is what the Lord says about these counselors:

Either make the tree good, and his fruit good; or else make the tree corrupt, and his fruit corrupt: for the tree is known by his fruit.
Matthew 12:33

The LORD bringeth the counsel of the heathen to nought: He maketh the devices of the people of none effect. The counsel of the LORD standeth for ever, the thoughts of His heart to all generation.
Psalm 33:10-11

Counseling could precede an event, or take place in the midst of a crisis or after crisis. Through the prayer bank, God reveals to a lot of people what danger is coming ahead and also counsels them on how to go about handling it. Elijah and the Syrians, Joseph and Pharaoh in Egypt, etc. are good examples.

In the midst of a crisis God counseled Prophet Elijah to go and hide by the brook Cherith so as to drink from the brook, and also commanded ravens to feed him. And afterward, God directed him to a widow at Zarephath who sustained him with her last meal. As crisis became more severe for Prophet Elijah, God also increased opportunities by directing His angel to cook and serve him. The double rations of heavenly meal that Prophet Elijah ate from the angel of God helped him to walk forty days and forty nights to Mount Horeb for the Word of the Lord.

After the temptation of Jesus in the wilderness, God sent His ministering angels to go and comfort Him.

Godly and spirit-filled counsels are therefore needed before, during and after crisis.

WHAT IS CRISIS MANAGEMENT?

Secular people will define crisis management as the process of dealing with crisis. But what they will not be able to do is break down what that process entails and the contents of the process from a spiritual perspective. Since all crises have a spiritual foundation it becomes imperative that we manage crisis not only from a material understanding but also with spiritual tools. Crisis management is laying a solid foundation or building a strong platform based on God's Words and promises which one could stand on in dealing with all crises that come his or her way. This foundation or platform involves procedure or mechanism, design, tactics or strategy for fighting crisis.

It involves the putting together of all the tools mentioned above: word bank, prayer bank, tears bottle or prayer record and counseling to defeat crisis and the plan of the devil against us. See chapter four for further discussion on how to manage crisis.

CHAPTER 2

CRISIS EVENTS IN BIBLICAL AND CONTEMPORARY TIMES

We have already stated that crises first take root in the spirit before they manifest in the physical. Crises are of different categories, we have natural and man-generated crises. These could further be classified into national and international crises such as war, famine, epidemics, and natural disasters due to environmental changes. Others include, family, church, personal, domestic, government, financial and relationship problems. Most times, when crises occur, there are opportunists who profit or benefit from them and there are those who pay dearly with all their investment or even their lives. No matter what type of crisis, advance preparation is always helpful in minimizing the effects of the disaster.

HURRICANE KATRINA

Hurricane Katrina was one of the worst natural and national crises in American history. It claimed about 1,836 lives and caused damages worth more than $81 billion US Dollars. Today many are still feeling the after-effect of such a deadly disaster. But if such a disaster had occurred in some developing countries, it might take more than 100 years to recover while some countries might even come to an abrupt end. If with the modern infrastructure available in the United States and with well-trained personnel at alert as well as people dedicated to community service, yet such losses occurred, what would have happened if there was no preparation at all made before it happened? It is clear that government's slow response marginally contributed to a few more dead, but the truth is that there were serious efforts in the part of the government and the people to help especially in rebuilding. It makes one wonder what could have happened in those countries without infrastructure and manpower. It is therefore appropriate to say that the rate of preparedness could limit the effect of a disaster or crisis.

One more thing to note in managing crisis spiritually is that the spirit that controlled the hurricane was not tamed in advance of the disaster. For instance, if the government had called for a national prayer to avert the hurricane from happening when the forecasts were made, most of the dead would likely be alive today. But the government was acting like King Saul, who destroyed all the witches in the land but sent to consult with the only one left in Endor when he was in trouble. The government being afraid of what people might say due to separation of church and state by not calling for national prayer to avert a predicted natural disaster chose the path of hypocrisy because after disasters like the Katrina, priests were invited to come and pray at the funerals of the souls killed during the disaster. If these priests and spiritual leaders had been invited prior to the crisis, the event could have been minimized or averted entirely. Banning of prayer in public places makes no sense since the same phenomenon is seen whenever a president, senator or top government official or one of those who legislate against public prayers dies; a priest is invited to officiate the funeral as a mark of respect, which makes one wonder the wisdom in banning public or national prayers at a time every society needs it most.

WITCHCRAFT CONVENTION

Recently, it was reported that witches were having a town-hall meeting in a particular hotel in Long Island. The churches in the Island were caught unprepared even though there was an awareness campaign and announcements made to that effect. A sister tried to contact some pastors in order to bring them together to pray and prevent such an event from taking place, but was told by a pastor that it would be impossible for the pastors to come together because, according to him, "we are not united." He was right because "a house divided against itself cannot stand." The witches had an undisturbed week long convention, cavorting around, polluting the entire land and moving from one corner of the Island to another casting their spells. And as soon as they finished their convention and left, a few churches sent letters out calling for prayers. The churches actually went and rented the same hall that the witches had used to hold their counter prayers. There was something wrong with this approach; what was wrong was that the "church" had heard the announcements on the radio, television, and other news media that the witches' convention was going to be held there, and the church leaders did nothing about it. Thank God for the few sisters that went around and cried to God, it might have been worst today than what we are seeing.

One does not wait to be attacked by illness before one begins to fight back. If one knows a way to prevent the illness in the first place, it is better to do so than to wait to be attacked first before seeking out a solution. To be proactive is better than to be reactive. But how can believers who should be prepared at all times be taken unawares? Perhaps it is because we as believers do not take seriously the biblical injunctions, "pray without ceasing", and "watch and pray." Many believers seem to be always late to the party. The witches came, had a party and the believers arrived to clean up afterwards!

The effect of that meeting is still being felt today in Long Island. Whether you believe it or not, the Island is suppressed by some evil powers. If you travel out of the Island for a while and come back, if you are spiritually sound, as soon as you step into the Island, the atmosphere changes. One begins to sense the presence of some oppressing powers. In addition to that, many have lost their jobs; unemployment rates have soared in their wake, cancer rates have been on the rise shortly afterwards, particularly among women. A host of other social ills have plagued the Island like gangs and drug activities in the wake of their convention.

I know of a man of God in Nigeria who organized a prayer meeting to stop witchcraft convention from being held in his State when he heard the announcement, and God honored him. He brought leaders of all the churches in that community together and declared a fast; it was during the fast that God spoke that the witchcraft meeting would not hold in that city. The cancelation was announced a few days before the day of the convention. I still believe that if the leaders of churches in Long Island had united and acted fast enough with authority in the name of Jesus and with fasting and prayer, the Lord would have prevented the witches from holding their meetings in that hotel. Or God would have neutralized the power and the after-effect that their meeting had on the people and the community. That is one of the functions of the church; to fast and pray so that evil will not take over the society.

Thanks be to God through Christ Jesus who strengthened few hands to be in constant intercession for the Island as recent reports show that things are beginning to function well again. I pray more people, particularly church leaders join in intercession for the land.

CHURCH PLANTING

I still remember several years ago planting a church in a location that was a witches' stronghold. All kinds of strange religions and worshippers of divers gods populated the street on which the young church was built. They used all forms of implements and condiments to worship their gods and idols. While some would be out very early in the morning half-naked, dancing and burning incense and consecrating the street with assorted demonic oils, others would be casting their spells in dark alleys, making incantations and calling down the devil himself. The place was ominous and dangerous. By 5.00 pm at sunset, the street would be completely deserted. One could scarcely see a single soul walking that street after that hour. There was an unspoken code of law; a curfew enforced by fear around the neighborhood. Armed robbers would begin congregating at sun down to plan where they would carry out the night's robbery.

I knew what I had gotten myself into when I chose this diabolically potent location to plant my new church. I took to heart what the Holy Spirit taught me. Each time I waited upon the Lord, I was taught to stay awake and pray in the middle of the night before evil men have the opportunity to block me and my prayers at dawn. My teacher once advised that if I ever buy land in such a demonic stronghold, I should not allow the idol worshippers to wake up before me and cast their spells, because if I allow them, I would go through a serious struggle throughout that day. Taking his advice I would remain at alert all night praying. From mid-night, I would be up praying, calling on the name of Jesus and pleading the blood of Jesus and calling down the fire of the Holy Spirit upon the area. This would neutralize all the powers of the false gods, false religion and false worshippers.

This sort of program was very effective as I almost paid with my life. One night for over two hours a winged skeletal creature fought me trying to slit my throat unsuccessfully. God stood by me and gave me final victory in that battle. He gave me complete victory over the demons that used to come and pull down the walls of our new church building. Today, the blood of Jesus has redeemed that street. The government has even recognized the street and has ordered it paved and is installing streetlights on a once dark, desolate and forsaken place. Praise the Lord!

It happened that when I would pray from 12.00 to 4.00 a.m. and lay down, these evil people would wake up to cast their spells, and their spells would not work. Today God has the glory, because both sides of the same street are prospering with more churches and residential buildings than ever before.

THE KILLING OF JAMES ZEBEDEE BY KING HEROD

The killing of Apostle James by King Herod is one of the events in the Bible that we have to consider carefully as an example of what the absence of intercessory prayer or prayer bank could cause. It seems the church was somewhat caught napping at the wheel when King Herod killed Apostle James, John's brother, and went further to arrest Apostle Peter.

Now about that time Herod the king stretched forth his hands to vex certain of the church. And he killed James the brother of John with the sword. And because he saw it pleased the Jews, he proceeded forward to take Peter also. (Then were the days of unleavened bread.)
And when he had apprehended him, he put him in prison, and delivered him to four quaternion of soldiers to keep him; intending after Easter to bring him forth to the people. Peter therefore was kept in prison: but prayer was made without ceasing of the church unto God for him.
Acts 12:1-5

The fact that there is no mention of the church in the whole episode leading to the death of Apostle James shows a church that was absent. It is similar to when parents are absent in the lives of their children and what happens to those children when they encounter a crisis. Such absence led to the sudden death of Apostle James. The church was in a serious crisis of persecution and lost sight of its primary responsibility, prayer.

As we may be aware, the church was going through a difficult moment at this time, even as the present day church is going through its own difficult time. Herod the King stretched forth his hand and vexed certain (individuals) in the church. While this shows that persecution is one of the worst types of crises one might have, it is also at this time that the Lord would show forth if we truly focus on Him and not on the problem. At a critical time of crisis, certain Biblical terms must readily be available for us: "trust in the Lord, stand firm, fear not, believe in God, hope in Him and have confidence and faith in God." But the sudden announcement of the death of Apostle James at the hand of Herod is troubling as there is no mention of the activities or the action of the corporate church. This suggests that the church might have focused on the persecution much more than on intercession. But when the church woke up to pray at the announcement of the arrest and detention of Apostle Peter after the death of James, he was released by an angel of God and saved.

What happened here is typical of what goes on in our daily lives, homes, and churches. We do not have to wait for any of our children to die, God forbid, for us to wake up and begin to pray for the protection of the rest. We do not have to wait until we marry before we start to pray for children or the types of children we would like God to bless us with, or even against miscarriages in our marriages. We do not have to wait until we take our final exams before we start to pray for jobs. We do not have to wait until we are employed before we start to pray to build a house or buy one. One can go on and on in all aspects of life, and this is why a prayer bank is necessary.

JOB AND CRISIS (TEST OF FAITHFULNESS)

Job was a faithful man that feared God and served the LORD with all his heart. Of Job the Bible wrote:

There was a man in the land of Uz, whose name was Job; and that man was perfect and upright, and one that feared God and eschewed evil.
Job 1:1

One day I was praying and meditating and it dawned on me to ask God why He allowed such a crisis to befall a man as Job who was faithful to Him. The answer that God gave me was beyond my imagination. The LORD directed me to a Bible verse for the answer:

The thing that hath been, it is that which shall be; and that which is done is that which shall be done: and there is no new thing under the sun.
Ecclesiastes 1:9

I still did not get it, and I began to wonder what God was talking about. One day the LORD brought to me the understanding of His Word. He said that He allowed the testing of Job by satan so that in the ages to come, believers who would be going through the fire of afflictions in the hands of their persecutors would not say, "We have not seen this before." But as Job was made to endure to the end, the believers of our days should not count their lives, children or material things as losses if they happen to lose them for the sake of the kingdom, but as gain which the Giver has preserved for them against the day of the Lord.

Secondly, it was to remind believers not to live the life of fear but of faith, hope and assurance. Job had spent every passing day of his life thinking about death. Although he had the fear of the Lord or respect to God and His Word, he did not let go of the fear of death. When death finally came he had this to say:

For the thing which I greatly feared is come upon me, and that which I was afraid of is come unto me. **Job 3:25**

Therefore carnally speaking, it was a great loss but spiritually speaking, it was a setting of precedent for today's believers to not allow fear of death to dominate or supersede the love of God in their hearts. And also to encourage those who would later lose everything for the sake of the gospel and even lay down their lives to not think of themselves as having lose anything. Job's first response was to worship God:

Then Job arose, and rent his mantle, and shaved his head, and fell down upon the ground, and worshipped, and said, Naked came I out of my mother's womb, and naked shall I return thither: the LORD gave and the LORD hath taken away; blessed be the name of the LORD. In all this, Job sinned not, nor charged God foolishly.
Job 1:20-22

Even when his wife charged him to curse God and die, he still did not accept to rebel against God.

Understanding is a key to Christian living. Without understanding we seem to settle in our hearts that we belong in this world, and everything in this world should be stored up for our children to the fourth and fifth generations after us. But do we really know what might happen after us? This is what a great wise man once reasoned:

Yea, I hated all my labor which I had taken under the sun: because I should leave it unto the man that should be after me. And who knoweth whether he shall be a wise man or a fool? Yet shall he have rule over all my labor wherein I have labored, and wherein I have showed myself wise under the sun. This is also vanity.
Ecclesiastes 2:18-19

The same wise Solomon had this to say in another place:

A good man leaveth an inheritance to his children's children: and the wealth of the sinner is laid up for the just.
Proverbs 13:22

What is this inheritance that a good man leaves behind? Is it checking accounts, numerous real estate holdings, riches, or worldly investment in knowledge? It is very important to note that as ages go by, influential families that did not know God or have God in their families begin to wind down in fame, wealth and influence. Why have historians not studied this phenomenon and documented it? It is only godly inheritance that will endure forever. Therefore the inheritance that a good man leaves for his children's children is the inheritance of God's Kingdom, Jesus Christ, and all the benefits: moral stability, goodness, continuity, etc. **Jeremiah 35.**

ABRAHAM AND CRISIS (FAITH AND FAMILY CRISIS)

Many people do not still see Abraham as a human being. They see him as a super human that once walked this planet earth. The man who later became the father of faith was just an ordinary man like you and me. He had his weaknesses and shortcomings. Getting to the land of Canaan and encountering famine, he ran, as I would have done, to Egypt. Being confronted with the reality of life, he told a lie. Therefore, the father of faith was a mortal being with many weaknesses like any of us.

The crisis of his obedience to God by having to depart from his land to a strange land that he did not know may not have been as tough as him having to send Ishmael away.

And Sarah saw the son of Hagar the Egyptian, which she had born unto Abraham, mocking. Wherefore she said unto Abraham, Cast out this bondwoman and her son: for the son of this bondwoman shall not be heir with my son, even with Isaac. And the thing was very grievous in Abraham's sight because of his son. And God said unto Abraham, Let it not be grievous in thy sight because of the lad, and because of thy bondwoman; in all that Sarah hath said unto thee, hearken unto her voice; for in Isaac shall thy seed be called.
Genesis 21:9-12

But in all these challenging crises Abraham was determined, strong, and willing to obey his God. He waited all his days to be blessed with a child at a hundred years. He willingly sent away the bondwoman and her son without much further complaints. He was later told to take the promised child, Isaac, to go and sacrifice unto the LORD and He never said no. That is the difference between Abraham and me or most of us. I would have looked for a way to bind the voice that whispered those words to me. I would have called on pastor friends to fast and pray with me. I would have searched out some verses of the Bible to support my stand, and I would have spoken in tongues to try to persuade God to change His mind.

Abraham had the understanding and quickly realized that, God who made the request had the power to bring his son back from the dead.

By faith Abraham, when he was tried, offered up Isaac: and he that had received the promises offered up his only begotten son. Of whom it was said, That IN ISAAC SHALL THY SEED BE CALLED: Accounting that God was able to raise him up, even from the death; from whence also he received him in a figure.
Hebrews 11:17-19

Abraham had to wait that long to mature and to align himself with God's Word on those matters mentioned above. It was not God's plan for him to wait that long, but that was how long it took him to get it right.

It is little wonder how people with understanding of the working of God have not allowed crisis to direct their actions and reaction during and after crisis, but order themselves according to the prescriptions offered by the Word of God in any given circumstance.

MOSES AND CRISIS (LEADERSHIP CRISIS)

And Moses said unto the people, Fear ye not, stand still, and see the salvation of the LORD, which He will show to you today: for the Egyptians whom ye have seen today, ye shall see them again no more for ever. The LORD shall fight for you, and ye shall hold your peace.
Exodus 14:13-14

It takes a man with a well-trained character to lead. Moses' problem with his people began when he saw an Egyptian fighting with a Hebrew and he killed the Egyptian and buried him in the sand. Leadership is not exerting your authority over people; they will eventually fight back and rebel. Leadership is submitting yourself to GOD who is the greatest leader so as to learn the concept of leadership which is being a good follower in the first place. No one who refuses to submit to another's leadership can be a good leader himself. Everything in this world is controlled by someone else in authority. There is nothing that exists that is not controlled. And if we begin to trace this authority systematically we will eventually come to the one who wields the ultimate authority. And that person is naturally God and there is no other authority over Him. He is therefore the ultimate leader and the ultimate authority. When we learn to submit to even the simplest authority we learn how to ultimately submit to God's leadership. A child may submit to his father or mother's authority. This is good training to submitting to his pastor's authority which is further training in submitting to God's leadership and authority.

God had to take Moses to the wilderness and keep him there for forty years in order to train him as to what leadership entailed. He had to serve Jethro and keep his flock. From there he learned the character of a sheep and a goat. He also learned how to serve, how to endure in the heat and cold, and how to deal with sick and healthy cattle. He learned how to make decisions and alter plans, how to defend and protect his cattle and how to be a good shepherd. Finally, he learned how to combine ministry and family: be a good leader, a good husband and a good father, all at the same time.

When God saw that he was now mature, he sent him back to Egypt to lead His people back to the Promised Land. Later in his life, the violent Moses who brutally killed an Egyptian was pronounced the meekest man on the face of the earth.

(Now the man Moses was very meek, above all the men which were upon the face of the earth.)
Numbers 12:3

The crisis of rejection at the beginning of Moses' life by his brethren led him to leadership school by God in the wilderness. When he graduated, he became a great but broken leader. Therefore crisis in our ministries and families can help us find our positions and use the experience of the crisis to help others better their lives. Moses was able to calm the children of Israel as seen in the quotation above when confronted with a critical situation in his leadership ladder. He knew that it was no longer him but the One who made him a leader who was leading. He learned a position of faith and understood how to deal with the weak and the strong amongst his flock.

THE WIDOW OF ZAREPHATH AND CRISIS (HUNGER CRISIS)

And the word of the LORD came unto him saying, Arise, get thee to Zarephath, which belongeth to Zidon, and dwell there: behold I have commanded a widow woman there to sustain thee.... And she said, As the LORD thy God liveth, I have not a cake, but a handful of meal in a barrel, and a little oil in a cruse: and, behold, I am gathering two sticks, that I may go in and dress it for me and my son, that we may eat it, and die. And Elijah said unto her, Fear not; go and do

as thou hast said: but make me thereof a little cake first, and bring it unto me, and after make for thee and for thy son.
1 Kings 17:8-13

This is a crisis of hunger, starvation and lack. It is a crisis that has made many to fall from grace and deny their faith and has made some to steal. This poor widow had concluded that her life and her only son's life had come to an end. She was gathering fire-wood to prepare her last supper when a strange man stood before her requesting to partake in her last supper. It is unimaginable how today's believers would have reacted to this strange man and his request.

The woman politely refused despite seeing his long dress, and knowing that this could be a messenger of God. Although God had told Prophet Elijah that He had directed a widow woman to feed him, God did not appear before this widow woman and say to her, "There is a man of God coming to meet you, feed him with your last meal." But God was ministering peace and understanding to her heart with His still and tender voice, so as to enable her comply with the message that the man of God would bring to her. It was the Spirit of God that spoke to the woman through her spirit. At the time of crisis, God wants us to be still and listen to Him ministering peace, understanding and direction into our hearts. But if we close the door of our hearts and shut Him out we stand to face the consequences of our spiritual insensitivity.

One thing about this story that makes me think and think again each time I read it is the insistence of the Man of God that the poor widow should make him a little cake first before making one for herself and her son. The man of God refused to buy into her fear, worries and complaints. He knew that he represented God and that he had the Word of God with and in him right there to solve the woman's anxiety problem, as it is written:

Where the word of a king is, there is power: and who may say unto him, What doest thou?
Ecclesiastes 8:4

Elijah wasted no time but to open the parcel that he brought from God:

For thus saith the LORD God of Israel, the barrel of meal shall not waste, neither shall the cruse of oil fall, until the day that the LORD sendeth rain upon the earth.
1 Kings 17:14

The prophet Elijah was telling her that if she would recognize God first despite her situation, the Lord would provide all her need according to His riches in glory by Christ Jesus, **Philippians 4:19**. He was telling her to "Be careful for nothing; but in everything by prayer and supplication with thanksgiving…" she should bring her requests to God trusting Him to provide, **Philippians 4:6.**

I do not know if today's Christians would have bothered to stop and listen to what message the man of God was bringing from God to them. My experience as a missionary in most of the places I have visited tells me that it would have taken extra signs by the man of God to convince today's Christians to listen. It is wonderful to know that the last meal that would have helped a poor widow and her son with strength to make their death beds brought much increase and life when used as a sacrifice unto God.

After the food problem was solved, the woman fell into a much deeper and bigger crisis; her only son and companion fell sick and died. But her yielded attentiveness and obedience to the word of God through the man of God led to a bigger miracle in her life: the resurrection of her only son and companion.

Your crisis may be similar to any of those mentioned, but the same God that worked with them to solve their problems is available to do the same to you in Jesus' name. Amen.

CHAPTER 3

WHY A PRAYER BANK?

MY SON'S EXPERIENCE

Recently my son in the Lord was booked for an event which he was to perform. He had been booked two months in advance of the day he was to perform. We began to deposit prayers in the bank against all the plans of the devil for the day of that event. A day before the event, his car that had never had any problems, suddenly broke down and had to be towed to the mechanic's workshop. This was a contract he had waited for a long time to come through. The enemy knew it and was also planning on what to do to disrupt the program. But because there were enough prayers in the bank to cover that day of the event from morning unto the evening, the enemy had to attack a day earlier. I remember vividly that each time he visited me we held hands and deposited a prayer. We prayed concerning the car, the weather, the equipment and the entire event, and because the enemy knew that the day and the event were heavily secured, he attacked a day earlier. My son had to use another car to get to the event. The event however went as planned and as we had believed God for; it was very successful. Consider this: What if his car had broken down on his way to the event? He would have missed the event he had invested so much in, both emotionally and financially and he would have been devastated.

As nature does not allow a vacuum, what we do not fill up with prayers must be occupied by something else; our enemy's wishes and desires.

Your manager may call to inform you that you are traveling tomorrow, that it is an emergency. That is fine. Your full account in the prayer bank has already taken care of any sudden travels that might come your way. It is not when you receive a sudden request to travel that you should call your church or prayer warriors to inform them that you have a sudden need to travel on behalf of your job. There is nothing wrong with that but the danger is that you might coincidentally be on the same bus or plane with someone that the enemy is targeting to kill through an accident. Two things might happen:

1. With prayers in your bank with God, He might cause a delay so that you miss your flight or bus and make alternate travel arrangements. The next day you might learn that the bus that you missed had an accident and many passengers died, one of which could have been you. It has happened many times.
2. You actually might make that trip and God uses your presence in the vehicle to stop the accident as in the case of Apostle Paul.

APOSTLE PAUL

The presence of Apostle Paul in the ship to Rome exemplifies this point. His presence on the ship saved everyone's life.

But after long abstinence Paul stood forth in the midst of them, and said, Sirs, ye should have hearkened unto me, and not have loose from Crete, and to have gained this harm and loss. And now I exhort you to be of good cheers: for there should be no loss of any man's life among you, but of the ship. For there stood by me this night the angel of God, whose I am, and whom I serve, Saying, fear not, Paul; thou must be brought before Cesar: and lo, God had given thee all them that sail with thee. Wherefore, sirs, be of good cheer: for

I believe God, that it shall be even as it was told me. Howbeit, we must be cast upon a certain island.
Acts27:21-26

MY TRIP FROM MY COUNTRY HOME

A similar incident happened once to me. I was traveling to my country home (village) to bring three of my nieces who were under my care to the city for their schooling. On my way back with the girls, our bus had a breakdown on a very bad spot on the highway. Many people dozed off inside the bus while others got off, the three girls with me were fast asleep and I also was asleep.

Suddenly, I felt a tap on my left shoulder; someone was calling me and commanding me to get up and pray. I opened my eyes and saw nobody. I closed my eyes again and went back to sleep. And again I felt a stronger hand shaking me with an even stronger command to "get up and pray!" I got up immediately and stood on my feet and called out, "Let us pray!" A few people were still awake discussing with their partners; a few were off the bus loitering around, while the majority was fast asleep including my three nieces. About two or three people joined me in prayer. As soon as I said "Father, in the name of Jesus..!" an oncoming bus at a very high speed had lost control and was heading directly for a head-on collision with our bus. Those who saw it coming screamed, everyone in my own bus that was asleep awoke, but as soon as I yelled, "In the name of Jesus…," that bus that was heading towards our own bus veered back onto the road and only struck our driver's side mirror and scraped off the lining on the side of our bus. It continued on its way without stopping.

I knew that harm was averted because of the prayer that I had stored up in my prayer bank. God sent His angel to wake me and because of my presence in the bus, everyone's life was saved.

OUR FIRST HOME

Again, I remember our first home as a newly wedded couple. We had a beautiful lace curtain around the four walls of our living room. I recall that at that time our senior pastor never failed to pray daily against fire disaster. One beautiful day I plugged a DVD player into a wall socket and left the house for church service. By the time we came back, we realized that the socket and the plug had started a fire and burned a circular hole in the curtain around where the socket was. When we returned from the church and opened the door, we could smell the fire and acrid smoke all over the house. We checked, and behold a small portion of the lace was burnt and the entire socket in the wall was burnt, but the fire went out on its own and the house was not burnt. This is what prayer banks can accomplish. My neighbors who witnessed it were amazed how fabric material all around the room would burn in a circle around the socket and the fire would go out of its own accord.

Since one person in your bus or plane can produce a covering for the preservation of life, one person also can be an instrument for disaster. So above and beyond the daily depositing of devotion into one's prayer bank, one must listen and obey the orders of God.

BUS ACCIDENT

As a young and newly married couple, my wife and I worshipped with a very strong Pentecostal Church. The Church was led by a very faithful woman who was assisted by her husband. Her main duty was prayer and fasting. We had such a strong prayer team that people who were afflicted by witchcraft powers were usually brought from other churches and places to our church for healing.

The woman of God had her own problem though; her own parents were into witchcraft and she refused to visit them for years. One day a so-called man of God traveled from the village where her parents were, to the city to see her. She had been warned in the words of prophecy about the coming of that man and was also warned never to accept to travel with him to see her parents because, according to the prophecy, God had not yet permitted her to go see her parents. She was also told that the visiting man of God was an agent who would undertake to bring her to be killed by her parents, and she promised us she would not go.

Suddenly however, one morning she sent for me and announced that she was going to travel with the visiting man of God. We did everything we could to prevent her from traveling, but when I looked straight into her eyes, I saw Samson's spirit in her eyes.

And it came to pass, when she pressed him daily with her words, and urged him, so that his soul was vexed unto death.
Judges 16:16

This was exactly what happened: as Delilah pressed Samson to succumb to her ploy, so also did the visiting man of God press her every night as they retired for the night since the man of God was lodged in her house. The visitor convinced her husband to accept to allow his wife travel with him by arguing that it would be wrong for her in-laws to die without their daughter seeing them. He also deceived her, saying that her parents might place a curse on her, and all of these things made her disobey the words of the Lord through the prophet and she agreed to travel.

The journey to her parent's village was uneventful. She spent a week with them and when her visit was over, she packed up and headed back to the city. Within a few miles to her final destination, the driver of the luxury bus she was traveling in lost control and the bus slammed into a ditch. Thirty-one passengers died. The woman of God did not die on the spot, but was taken along with the wounded to the hospital; there she gave her name and address of her house. She drifted in and out of consciousness, and managed to leave a short statement. She gave the names of two ministers who would be coming to claim her body and also confessed that it was because of her that the accident occurred, saying, "My parents are at my side to take me." And so in the night, her parents and the agents of darkness came in the spirit and demanded her life. They told her "Because of you, thirty-one souls lost their lives and perished, you must come with us as well." She was heard saying these words and screaming, "They have come to get me, my parents have come to get me, they are ..." Then she yielded up the ghost and the two people she mentioned went and claimed her body for burial.

Those people died because a woman, though a prayer warrior, who successfully interceded for others, failed to listen to God's numerous directives not to travel. Disobedience as seen here could sometimes take precedence over the fullness of one's prayer bank. (For further reading, read "witchcraft and manipulation" in chapter 8.) For the fullness of one's prayer bank gave rise to the grace and mercy to receive the warning in the first place. Disobedience of that warning then could not avert disaster. At the same time, thirty-one people who were without a prayer bank and spiritual strength to stop the accident died untimely deaths because of one person. If there was someone in that bus with a stronger spiritual standing having his bank saved up with prayer and the word, the accident may have been averted. Therefore a prayer bank is something that one has to take seriously.

SOMEONE WITH A PRAYER BANK

Let us assume you were planning a trip but did not have the necessary funds to embark on the trip, you may decide to call on your friends to borrow the funds. At this point you have already revealed your intentions to take a trip to several people. Now it is a well-known precaution that one should not reveal to everyone his travel itinerary or even that he intends to travel, after all, one does not know who harbors what intentions. But if you had enough funds saved up in your account, it would not be necessary to do so. Similarly, if there are stocked-up prayers in your prayer bank, you will spend less time worrying about what might happen on your trip. You might not need to call anyone to request for prayers. However due to the deficit in your prayer bank you automatically revealed your itinerary to many in the last minutes including both the well-wishers, and not so well wishers alike.

- ❖ A man that has a prayer bank is a man of vision: A concrete vision that does not attract division.
- ❖ He is a man with a clear dream: not one that dreams and forgets the dream.

- He is blessed with the gift of wisdom and knowledge, especially in spiritual matters.
- He is not easily taken unaware by circumstances.
- He is a man that looks before he leaps: not the other way round.
- The Lord orders his footsteps and also delights in his ways.
- He is always ahead of others in spiritual information.
- He is a go-getter because he is always prepared.

CHAPTER 4

MANAGING CRISIS – A SPIRITUAL APPROACH

There are three approaches in managing one's prayer bank. As a general in a war, there is always a need to attack the enemy on many fronts, or to have what is called, "Plan B" or "Plan C". He also must decide which weapon to unleash first. It would be foolhardy to send in the infantry when the enemy is docked hundreds of miles in the ocean and is raining missiles at your coastline. It may be more effective to send in your navy ships and air force to take out the gunship. Similarly, the decision to use one strategy or the other must first be carefully considered. When in doubt, begin with the spiritual approach as most problems take their origin there first.

1. Spiritual approach: This is dealing with various spirits that originate and control the problems. It is the most effective and requires a certain level of spiritual standing. It is termed, "tackling from the base or the source or the root or foundation." Depositing powerful prayers that destroy, bind, control and set the captive free require more than mere speaking in tongues, but maturity in spiritual matters and in the knowledge of how the Rhema (the Living Word) is arrived at through the meditation of the Logos (written Words), and the application of such Words as prompted by the Holy Spirit.

2. Topical approach: Topically selecting prayers that address your specific issue and problem and bringing these to the Lord's attention by frequently depositing them into your prayer bank by topic and subject.

3. A combination of both approaches. In many cases this will be the best course of action, applying a two-pronged attack that addresses the foundational problems and the effects that those problems have in your daily living. Attack, bind and dislodge the spirits and demons that are the source and reinforcement of a problem, and finish it off by pointedly asking the Lord to specifically remove the problem once and for all. We find that a combination of both approaches works all of the time.

THE PROBLEMS OF MAN ARE NOT MATERIAL BUT SPIRITUAL

We may be good at praying some powerful prayers but may still completely miss the mark. At such a time we may be mouthing prayers, which to listeners sound powerful but are wholly ineffective. As I have already stated before in chapter one, the problem of man is not material but spiritual. All of man's problems first take root in the spirit world before manifesting in the material world.

Therefore, in building a prayer bank one must take into consideration certain spirits that control and direct major events that befall man. Everything in life happens based on the operation and the direction of the spirits that control those events. This is regardless of whether one is dealing with a life-sustaining event, disaster, death, success or failure. Therefore, attacking these problems from the root goes a long way to pulling down the foundations which they are built on. Think of any sickness or affliction; cancer, high blood pressure, diabetes, madness, failure, etc., that befalls a man, there is a spirit that controls it. Before we construct our prayer banks, let us delve into the nature and characteristics of some of these spirits.

PROBLEMS, THEIR SPIRITUAL ROOTS AND SPIRITUAL SOLUTIONS

THE SPIRIT OF SETBACK

There are many ways that setback occurs. The spirit of setback works around the clock bringing people down, in sports, in politics, in health, in battles, in social life, in education, in ministry, etc. When it knocks on your door, the once famous person becomes a thing of laughter and mockery. It occurs when a small or weak nation without much military might and money defeats a well-fortified army of a super power status, or when an amateur boxer or wrestler defeats a professional with a knockout punch in the first, second or third round.

The children of Israel had barely conquered Jericho when Joshua sent men from there to spy on Ai. Ai was a much smaller country than Jericho that Israel defeated with nothing more than a shout, yet someone committed a sin against God and Israel suffered a major setback in their battle against Ai.

And Joshua sent men from Jericho to Ai, which is beside Beth-aven, on the east side of Bethel and spake unto them, saying, Go up and view the country. And the men went up and viewed Ai. And they returned to Joshua, and said unto him, Let not all the people go up; but let about two or three thousand men go up and smite Ai; and make not all the people to labor thither; for they are but few. So there went up thither of the people about three thousand men: and they fled before the men of Ai. And the men of Ai smote of them about thirty and six men: for they chased them from before the gate even unto Shebarim, and smote them in the going down: wherefore the hearts of the people melted, and became as water.
Joshua 7:2-5

It is not only in battles like the one above that one could suffer a setback. A setback occurs when you are far behind your colleagues in almost all aspects of life. Although you have shown concrete effort to measure up, you could still sink lower instead of improvement. This downward trend may continue to the end of your life unless you come in contact with Jesus. This contact could happen either directly or through a knowledgeable deliverance minister where deliverance based on the knowledge of what has taken place in the spirit world concerning this person could be exposed and dealt with.

Let us see how the spirit of setback operates using an example from the scripture. Let us study **Mark 5:21-43**, and allow the Spirit of God to talk to us about the situation of this woman commonly called, "The woman with the issue of blood." This story is written in a detailed form just to explain the concept of and the operation of the spirit of setback.

And when Jesus was passed over again by ship unto the other side, much people gathered unto Him: and He was nigh unto the sea. And, behold, there cometh one of the rulers of the synagogue, Jairus by name; and when he saw Him, he fell at His feet, And besought Him greatly, saying, My little daughter lieth at the point of death: I pray thee, come and lay thy hands on her, that she may be healed; and she shall live. And Jesus went with him; and much people followed Him, and thronged Him. And a certain woman, which had an issue of blood twelve years, And had suffered many things of many physicians, and had spent all that she had, and was nothing bettered but rather grew worse, When she had heard of Jesus, came in the pressed behind, and touched His garment. For she said, If I may touch but His clothes, I shall be whole. And straightway the fountain of her blood was dried up; and she felt in her body that she was healed of that plague. And Jesus, immediately knowing in Himself that virtue had gone out of Him, turned Himself about in the press, and said, Who touched my clothes? And His disciples said unto Him, Thou seest the multitude thronging Thee and sayest Thou, Who touch me? And He looked round about to see her that had done this thing. But the woman fearing and trembling, knowing what was done in her, came and fell down before Him, and told Him all the truth. And He said unto her, Daughter, thy faith had made thee whole; go in peace, and be whole of thy plague. While He yet spake, there came from the ruler of the synagogue's house certain

which said, Thy daughter is dead: why troublest thou the master any further? As soon as Jesus heard the word that was spoken, He saith unto the ruler of the synagogue, Be not afraid only believe. And He suffered no man to follow Him, saved Peter, and James, and John the brother of James. And He cometh to the house of the ruler of the synagogue, and seeth the tumult and them that wept and wailed greatly. And when He was come in, He saith unto them, Why make ye this ado, and weep? the damsel is not dead but sleepeth. And they laughed Him to scorn. But when He had put them all out, He taketh the father and the mother of the damsel, and they that were with Him, and entereth in where the damsel was lying. And He took the damsel by the hand, and said unto her, Talitha cumi; which is, being interpreted, Damsel, (I say unto thee,) arise. And straightway the damsel arose, and walked; ***for she was of the age of twelve years.*** *And they were astonished with a great astonishment.*
Mark 5:21-42

This Bible passage is copied in its entirety for me to explain fully the concept of the spirit of setback and how it operates. Let's assume that Jairus' wife and the woman that had the issue of blood were childhood friends. While Jairus' wife was married and became pregnant, her friend's bleeding developed. Now the child that Jairus's wife delivered was about twelve years old and as a twelve-year-old, she might have been able to help her mother with one thing or the other, but her friend had been hemorrhaging for the same number of years.

The woman with the issue of blood was being attacked or was oppressed by the spirit of setback. She had spent all she had to better the situation; instead it grew worse by the day. Except for her meeting with Jesus, there was no way this woman would have been able to measure up with her colleagues in life.

The spirit of setback pegs you and determines your growth level. It makes you waste a lot of resources and energy and ensures that you do not measure up. It is as if one was running on a treadmill, expending tons of energy and sweat but making no visible advance forward. When this spirit is on someone, he or she begins a downward movement financially, materially, politically, socially and spiritually and then stagnates. All past savings are usually spent up within months and before you know it, you are in a very terrible situation and in debt.

How do you know that you are attacked by a spirit of setback? Where does this spirit come from? You will know that you have been attacked by a spirit of setback when you start bleeding—financial hemorrhage, business hemorrhage, health hemorrhage, social hemorrhage and spiritual hemorrhage, and all other serious bleedings that might begin to set in. Like any other spirit, this could be contracted through some evil associates or relationships. The witches or the wicked ones could also cast it as a spell upon someone, which requires that we watch who we associate with and what we do.

Building a prayer bank that stops current or future bleeding is very important and necessary because this spirit, if allowed to take hold of someone, is always stubborn and may refuse to go. This spirit can attack organizational entities as well as individuals. It is often seen in certain churches. If the church is not prayerful enough and is not watchful, it can begin to hemorrhage suddenly and before the pastor notices it the whole church becomes empty; members leave daily, coffers empty out. Therefore, a prayer bank is strongly recommended to deal with the spirit of setback in its entirety.

Word Bank Sample

Matthew 9:20
Haggai 1:9-11
Joel 1:4
Exodus 14:15
Genesis 19:26

Prayer Bank Sample against Spirit of Setback

Father, in the name of Jesus, I stand here before You this day by faith declaring that I am the head and not the tail according to your words concerning me. Colleagues of mine shall not leave me behind. I reject that spirit that was in the woman with the issue of blood. I resist and refuse all kinds of bleeding, spiritual, financial, economic, social and political. I take my strong stand against the spirit of setback. I use every weapon at my disposal, the name of Jesus, the blood of Jesus, the Word of God and the fire of the Holy Spirit to neutralize and paralyze every spirit that tries to take me one step backward. One thing is sure, You made me in Your image and after Your likeness. You are not a failure, and therefore I am not and will not be a failure. You are blessed forever, I, too, am blessed forever. By the words of Your mouth all things were created, I believe also that the words of my mouth have creative power. I stand by Your Word concerning me, and whatever anyone says or thinks about me does not erase what You think or say about me. You say that You know the thoughts that You think towards me, the thoughts of peace, success and prosperity and not of evil, to give unto me a hope and a very successful future. You also assure me that You will give me the keys of the kingdom of heaven and the power to bind and loose on earth with a confirmation of binding and losing in heaven. Whatever therefore that I bind is bound and whatever I loose is loosed. It shall come to pass that when failure sees me it will flee. I stand strong in You today and deposit these prayers in my prayer bank before You and I am sure that I am free from the spirit of setback. I pray this prayer in the name of Jesus Christ who is the head of all powers and principalities. Amen.

***Benediction:** Whosoever shall by all seriousness read his or her bible and deposit prayers into their prayer bank shall never suffer any setback in their lives. Amen.*

SPIRIT OF LABORING IN VAIN (BLOCKING ALL MERCY OR SENSE OF CONSIDERATION, RECOGNITION OR APPRECIATION)

This is a terrible spirit that attacks marriages, but couples may not know about this mean spirit. It also causes joblessness, dismissals, terminations, demotions and even executions. It was Joab's spirit, the commander of the host of David's army, and he had to be executed by Solomon the son of David. It also attacked the chief baker, a servant of Pharaoh in Egypt.

JOAB

Joab the son of Zeruiah was the commander of David's army and also David's nephew. He had been with David from the beginning even unto the end of his life. He was very strong and faithful in protecting the king except for a few instances when he allowed self and personal concern to cloud his sense of judgment.

As a faithful captain, he had helped King David in many ways; he helped him kill Uriah the Hittite to allow David take his wife Bathsheba.

And it came to pass in the morning that David wrote a letter to Joab, and sent by the hand of Uriah. And he wrote in the letter, saying, Set ye Uriah in the forefront of the hottest battle, and retire ye from him that he may be smitten, and die. And it came to pass, when Joab observed the city that he assigned Uriah unto a place where he knew that valiant men were. And the men of the city went out, and fought with Joab: and there fell some of the people of the servants of David; and Uriah the Hittite died also.
2 Samuel 11:14-17

There was yet another example of Joab's faithfulness to King David. David at the time was struggling to overcome the devastating death of his son born by Bathsheba through adultery. David beseeched God to save his son alive but God would not grant his wish. David was also preoccupied with the birth of Solomon shortly afterwards. While preoccupied with domestic events in his household, he almost lost focus of God's assignment and the nations yet to be conquered. But Joab, his chief captain, was fully focused. He strengthened David's hand by assembling a strong and a well-coordinated army to continue his conquest of the surrounding nations.

And Joab fought against Rabbah of the children of Ammon, and took the royal city. And Joab sent messengers to David and said, I have fought against Rabbah, and have taken the city of waters. Now therefore gather the rest of the people together, and encamp against the city, and take it: lest I take the city and it be called after

my name. And David gathered all the people together and went to Rabbah and fought against it, and took it.
2 Samuel 12:26-29

As a commander of the host of Israel, he commanded David's mighty men. He also killed Sheba the son of Bichri who tried to form an insurrection against King David,**11 Samuel 20:16-22.** He ensured that the king was saved to the end of his life, even in his old age when the King could no longer fight in battles. At one time he acted as an adviser to King David against numbering Israel, the advice which the King rejected and which led to a great plague in Israel, **11 Samuel 24:3-4.**

Three major offences of Joab, plus one:

1. **The killing of Abner**
2. **The killing of Absalom**
3. **The killing of Amasa.**

ABNER

Abner was the son of Ner, Saul's uncle. He was the captain of the host of Saul's army. He killed Asahel, Joab's third brother in David's army. He also became the captain of host to Ish-bosheth, Saul's son. But when there was disagreement between Abner and Ish-bosheth the son of Saul, Abner came to reconcile with King David and to bring all Israel back to king David. But when Joab heard that Abner had visited the King and the King let him go in peace, he was not happy with the King but sent and brought Abner back and killed him because of his brother **Asahel** that he had killed, **2 Samuel 3:6-27.**

THE DEATH OF ABSALOM

The killing of Absalom by Joab was one thing that King David did not take lightly. Joab was instrumental to Absalom and King David's reconciliation and instrumental to Absalom's death:

And the king commanded Joab and Abishai and Ittai, saying, Deal gently for my sake with the young man, even with Absalom. And all the people heard when the king gave all the captains charge concerning Absalom.
2 Samuel 18:5

The news that came to King David of the death of his son did not go down well with him:

But the king covered his face, and the king cried with a loud voice, O my son Absalom, O Absalom, my son, my son! And Joab came into the house to the king, and said, Thou hast shamed this day the faces of all thy servants, which this day have saved thy life, and the lives of thy sons and of thy daughters, and the lives of thy wives, and the lives of thy concubines. In that thou loveth thy enemies, and hatest thy friends. For thou hast declared this day, that thou regardest neither princes nor servants: for this day I perceive, that if Absalom had lived, and all we had died this day, then it had pleased thee well. Now therefore arise, go forth, and speak comfortably unto thy servants: for I swear by the LORD, if thou go not forth, there will not tarry one with thee this night: and that will be worse unto thee than all the evil that befell thee from thy youth until now.
2 Samuel 19:4-7

Though Joab had just killed the king's son he spoke with great authority and command telling the king, "If you do not stop mourning the death of your son, I am ready to move all these people to another camp." Why was he exercising such authority? It became clear to King David that if not checked, then the young Solomon would be in trouble throughout his reign.

While Absalom died, his captain, Amasa was absorbed into the main Command with assurances from King David that he would take over the position of Joab as the commander of the host.

AMASA

Amasa was King David's nephew and a cousin to Joab. His mother's name was Abigail. But he supported Absalom, David's son against David and was made the captain of the host of Absalom's army.

And Absalom made Amasa captain of the host instead of Joab: which Amasa was a man's son, whose name was Ithra an Israelite, that went in to Abigail a daughter of Nahash, sister to Zeruiah, Joab's mother.
2 Samuel 17:25

Amasa had been promised to take over the position of Joab by King David. King David, for one reason or another was not very comfortable with Joab as the commander of the hosts of his army, even though Joab had saved the king's life very many times. Joab was becoming very tough for the king to handle as his influence in the kingdom was increasing and the king's confidence in him was eroding. King David had complained many times about Joab's attitude and viewed him with suspicion.

And say ye to Amasa, Art thou not of my bone, and of my flesh? God do so to me and more also, if thou be not captain of the host before me continually in the room of Joab.
2 Samuel 19:13

In King David's military system, there was so much leakage of information because there was a lot of cross-carpeting. Joab must have gotten wind that the king might replace him with Amasa and he sought for an opportunity to kill him. When he found one during the pursuit of Sheba, he did not waste it.

Of all the good things that Joab did to protect the life of King David throughout his reign as a king, both in Judah and in the entire house of Israel, the three crimes he committed wiped away the remembrance of his good deeds. He was actually suffering from the spirit of laboring in vain.

Before we bring in his fourth error, which was hinged upon his fear concerning Solomon, David had already instructed his son Solomon not to spare Joab when he took the throne:

Moreover thou knowest also what Joab the son of Zeruiah did to me, and what he did to the two captains of the hosts of Israel, unto Abner the son of Ner, and unto Amasa the son of Jether, whom he slew and shed the blood of war in peace, and put the blood that was upon his girdle that was about his loins, and in his shoes that were on his feet. Do therefore according to thy wisdom, and let not his hoary head go down to the grave in peace.
1 Kings 2:5-6

Towards the end of David's life, Joab had been alienated from the Army's major decisions and deliberations. This drove him to supporting Adonijah, Solomon's brother against Solomon. This was his fourth and final error, which eventually led to his death at the hand of King Solomon.

Even though Joab was overtaken by many other spirits like pride, usurpation of authority, murder, blood lust, covetousness, the one major spirit that threw him out of favor with the King and eventually led to his death was the spirit of laboring in vain.

This spirit, "laboring-in-vain" is a terrible spirit. It veils the people that it attacks and their efforts, and exposes their errors and mistakes.

As I had mentioned earlier, this spirit is particularly devastating to marriages. There are faithful women doing all that they can in their homes but their husbands would not see. But the day they commit offence which could be pardonable as co-owners of the home, divorce may follow. There are many workers in the offices doing their best for the growth of their companies or agencies, and none of their efforts are recognized. When evaluations are given at the end of the year and it is discovered that they had been late for work on two, three four or five times, they are written up and pay dearly for it, and may even be terminated.

In creating a bank for this type of prayer, one has to gather the types of words that will be sharp enough to penetrate the veils that this spirit has used to veil its captives. The attack must be many-pronged. It is a mass attack prayer or a "carpet-bombing" prayer as they say in the military: home, office, everywhere!

This type of prayer begins with the binding of the spirit of laboring-in-vain, veiling, un-recognition, un-appreciation; commanding the dark cloud to depart from blocking your star from shining. Your star must be repositioned where it will be more glorious and shine forth. A star that is under a dark cloud will not shine. Begin by selecting the words banks for your daily prayers.

Word Bank Sample

Psalm 78:46
Psalm 128:2
Proverbs 14:23
Eccl. 2:24
Eccl. 5:19
Isaiah 65:23-24
1 Cor. 15:58
Philippians 2:16

Prayer Bank Sample against Spirit of Laboring in Vain

Genesis 1:8, "And the Lord remembered Noah..." Father in the name of Jesus, There shall be a remembrance of all my labor and me. I shall not be abandoned nor forgotten neither will I labor in vain.

Isaiah 3:10, "...It shall be well with me; I will eat the fruit of my doing..."

Psalm 1:3, "And I shall be like a tree planted by the rivers of water, my fruit shall be brought forth in due season, my leaves will never wither, and all that I do shall prosper."

Esther 4:16 speaks of God's favor and recognition on married women. This also applies to office workers with their bosses.

Prayer:

Blessed Father, may the beauty of the Lord God be upon me, establish thou the works of my hands. Let me be a shining light. Let my labor be recognized and rewarded. Fruitfulness, recognition and promotion are all I claim. Lord, bring my star out of the dark cloud and position it where it will shine forth for the whole world to see. Every fault of mine shall be turned into a blessing; for such are the portions of those that wait on thee. My growth shall have no boundary and I shall excel in strength and favor. As I deposit this prayer into my bank with you daily, I know that the spirit of laboring in vain will neither see me nor come near me. I pray this prayer in the name of the only Son of God, Jesus Christ the righteous. Amen.

Benediction: *One who reads his/her bible and deposits these words of the Lord and observes the frequent deposition of these prayers in their prayer banks shall never labor in vain. Amen.*

SPIRIT OF ABANDONMENT, NEGLECT AND ISOLATION

Whenever we abandon our God-given responsibility or become negligent of our role in the family, we are giving the devil a chance to step in and steal our joy. The righteous God had found Adam to be lonely in carrying out the task that He assigned him; that of caring for all his creation and naming them. This was the first ministry that God gave man - ministry of care.

And the LORD God took the man, and put him into the Garden of Eden to dress it and to keep it.
Genesis 2:15

God needed to provide Adam a helper, someone who would help him meet the need of that ministry or calling. The work load for Adam was great and God decided to send a helper. He did not just think in terms of a help mate; someone who would live with Adam and wash his clothes and clean the house. But God was thinking in terms of someone who would help him meet his ministry and domestic needs, God's vision for Adam. Therefore, ministry of help was the next to be assigned by God.

And the LORD God said, It is not good that the man should be alone; I will make him a help meet for him... And Adam gave names to all cattle, and to all fowl of the air, and to every beast of the field; but for Adam, there was not found a help meet for him.
Genesis 2:18, 20

God therefore put Adam to sleep indicating that God deals with man better at the time of his rest and quietness. As he slept God came down and removed a rib from his side and with the rib God made a woman and brought her to him. The man Adam was created from a raw material (sand or dust) of the earth, but the woman was made from a finished product (rib) from the man.

By the time Adam woke up from his sleep he found out by divine revelation that the chief surgeon had removed a rib from him. And with the rib God made a woman and brought her to Adam. Adam, recognizing his incompleteness at the time he awoke from sleep, happily received his other part of the body and named her 'woman' meaning - now, I am complete and with a womb. Even though the use of a rib by God is always seen as a symbol of equality between the man and the woman, it has to do more with the fact that ribs are the only bones that protect the body's thoracic cavity. God in His wisdom protects all the delicate organs with the ribs. These are organs that are not commonly seen, but without them there is no life. Therefore Adam in receiving his woman declared:

...This is now bone of my bones, and flesh of my flesh: she shall be called Woman, because she was taken out of Man.
Genesis 2:23

Two things could be derived from what God did in Adam. The first one is, when God removed a rib from Adam there was an attachment of flesh to the rib bone. Therefore, the vision of a helpmeet also would enable the woman to tame the toughness of a man (bone), and also enable a woman to help strengthen the weakness (flesh) of a man. This explains why the great Samson could be brought to his knees by a woman, Delilah, **Judges 16:19**. It also helps us understand why Jezebel took charge in the killing of Naboth for his vineyard, a task her husband, King Ahab, could not perform. A woman brought down the strength of the most powerful man on earth, and the weakness of a feeble king was boosted by a woman. Bone of my bones and flesh of my flesh as a helper needs to be balanced in the context of helping to make the life of the man balance and also to remain in God's ministry and vision for the man.

he two last verses of **Genesis chapter 2** actually bring greater understanding of what God's purpose and plan for man was.

Therefore shall a man leave his father and his mother, and shall cleave unto his wife: and they shall be one flesh. And they were both naked, the man and his wife, and were not ashamed.
Genesis 2:24, 25

When God brought the woman to the man, the very first thing the man needed to do was to welcome her into a new home. He supposed to have introduced her to his God and God's given ministry, explain to her the commandments of God unto him and the way he would like his home to be patterned. He also would have enlightened her about the danger of disobeying God's commandments and the functions of the rib to the body. Some of the functions would have included the following: become a bone of bones and flesh of flesh for him, that is, help him become a balanced man in weakness and in strength, help him carry out his assigned ministry, and help him meet his domestic needs, sexual desires and his need for procreation. But Adam shirked his responsibility by not counseling his wife on his proper role in the relationship. This failure was perhaps the first impetus that allowed Eve to be tempted.

The woman in the other hand is not exempted by God from leaving her biological parents and cleaving unto her own husband.

Hearken O daughter, and consider, and incline thine ear; forget also thine own people, and thy father's house; So shall the king greatly desire thy beauty: for he is thy lord; and worship thou him.
Psalm 45:10-11

Here she is instructed to worship (submit to) him because she was made from him and for him. But the man on the other hand is instructed to love and cherish her. He is seen as a god to her. The earthly father and mother of the woman are just caretakers for her rightful man, while the earthly father and the mother of a man are his care takers for God. Therefore many look at the man "leaving" his father and mother and "cleaving" unto his wife only as the man detaching himself from the biological parents to focus on his wife. It is much more than that. The true father and mother of the man is God Himself, and now God is adding to the man's primary responsibility another complex responsibility; that of caring for the woman that God made for him. The man Adam has to sit down to rearrange his time to accommodate his care for his woman in addition to his primary ministry of caring for God's creation. If the man does not take care for God's creation, Jesus will see him as a man who loves his wife, children, mother and father more than God. If he does not care for his own household and provide for them, he will be seen as being worse than an infidel. Therefore a man leaving a father and a mother and cleaving unto his wife is an indication that a man has to share his time equally between his family and his ministry, God's assignment. To teach otherwise is to put asunder what God has joined together.

It was under the above circumstance that Adam failed. He was a good husband, a lover of his wife and a great provider, but he also had the spirit of abandonment, neglect, and isolation. This spirit makes you believe that as long as you are able to provide for your wife and children, you can abandon or isolate them as long as you choose. Today, no one can really answer the question where Adam was when the devil tempted his wife. The whole earth was occupied by the two of them, and since she was helping in the care ministry of her husband, she should have been with him if he was tending to flock or caring for the trees. And since she was also to help his everyday life, she should have been with him if he was sleeping. But the spirit of abandonment, neglect, and isolation set in and separated Adam and his wife for a moment long enough to accommodate the length of time that the devil needed to convince Eve to eat the forbidden fruit. By the time Adam got back to meet with his wife, something had been spoiled: the tempter had come, and the wife had been deceived.

Let us not confuse the concluding part of **Genesis 3:6** where the Bible says:

...she took of the fruit thereof, and did eat, and gave also unto her husband with her; and he did eat.

Does it mean that Adam was standing there watching his wife when the devil tempted her? No. What that portion is saying is that she had a husband that was living with her. The husband was not physically present at the time she was tempted.

This same spirit is still posing problems today in marriages and is always the beginning of all conflicts in any relationship.

Four pillars of existence: There are four ways that God has used to bring human life into existence. God gave birth to the man through the breath from His nostrils. The man gave birth to the woman through his rib. The coming together of the man and the woman becomes God's standard approval for reproduction and procreation. (Though it is clear that God commanded man to leave his parents and cleave to his wife, the general trend today is for same sex marriages. The society is increasingly allowing such anomalies to be the norm and this is contrary to God's purpose for man.) And finally, the woman through the Holy Spirit gave birth to the Savior of the world; Jesus Christ, the Son of God.

But I would have you know, that the head of every man is Christ; and the head of the woman is the man; and the head of Christ is God.
1 Corinthians 11:3

Out of these four pillars, three belong to God and have never been repeated. But one, God has given to man to profit therefrom. Once you have failed in the area of marital relations and intimacy with your spouse, you have made the Word of God of no effects and therefore have counted yourself out of the lineage of inheritance in Him, which is the end product of divorce and remarriage and same sex marriages.

But I say unto you, That whosoever shall put away his wife, saving for the cause of fornication, causeth her to commit adultery: and whosoever shall marry her that is divorced committeth adultery.
Matthew 5:32

Know ye not that the unrighteous shall not inherit the kingdom of God? Be not deceived: neither fornicators, nor idolaters, nor adulterers, nor effeminate, nor abusers of themselves with mankind, nor thieves, nor covetous, nor drunkards, nor revilers, nor extortioners, shall inherit the kingdom of God.
1 Cor. 6:9-10

This verse refers to all the deviant sexual behaviors today being legitimized in the society, lesbianism, homosexuality, bestiality and so on. Today, the spirit of abandonment, neglect and isolation has caused more divorce than the spirit of adultery and fornication. Although in the case of divorce through fornication, the Bible does not instruct to remarry still but to reconcile if possible. But ninety-nine percent of those I know to have divorced have other reasons. They either complain of neglect, communication breakdown, isolation, nagging, poor attitude toward one another and negligence in issues pertaining to each other's well-being. But all these excuses have no place in God's diary.

It is our stubbornness and failure to pay attention to the Biblical injunctions to not be equally yoked together with unbelievers, and our lust that drag us to an unbelieving spouse that puts on the believer's garments. A true believer will always be guided by God's Words: "husbands love your wives, wives submit to your own husbands." To qualify for the kingdom of God, we should be courageous to deal with the differences that we have in our marriages and solve our problems and remain married. "But if the unbelieving depart, let him depart. A brother or a sister is not under bondage in such cases..." **1 Corinthians 7:15**. However, **verse 27** of the same chapter clarifies the mind of God concerning marriage and divorce. "Art thou bound unto a wife? Seek not to be loose. Art thou loosed from a wife? Seek not a wife." It goes to confirm that if an unbelieving departs a believing brother or sister who is loosed from a wife or a husband should remain unmarried or be reconciled.

Therefore the three words that the man must take seriously are: leave, cleave and oneness. While the Bible says the man should leave and cleave, the woman must endeavor to make oneness possible through submission to his love. While the first two injunctions look mostly to the man, the last one is what makes them naked without being ashamed. When the Bible says that we are naked before God, it does not mean that we walk naked for Him to see us. But because we were in Him and He brought us out of Himself, He sees us and knows our inner part better than we know ourselves. Therefore the man and his wife were naked because one was in the other and they saw themselves and knew themselves even though they now have two heads and two faces. Being one and naked goes beyond physical nakedness in their room. It involves marital relationship and fellowship. It goes to show that one cannot do without the other: praying together and having devotional studies, joint bank account, signing contracts, sharing, eating, travelling, raising children, etc. It means complete openness and transparency.

DEATH OF A NURSING MOTHER

This story is not hearsay but an event that I witnessed; it is a life story. A woman who was nursing a two-week-old baby boy was using a water heater (an immersion heater or ring boiler) to boil water to give her baby a bath. She plugged one end of the boiler into an electric socket and put the ring boiler in a bucket of water. No sooner than the water was boiled than the lights went out because of power failure. This happens a lot in developing countries where there is irregular power supply. The lady forgot to remove the boiler from the socket (the power source) but removed it from the water, left it on the floor and went on to bath her son. As soon as she had finished bathing her son she put forth her hand and picked up the boiler not realizing that electric power supply had been restored. In her error she did not pick up the boiler by the handle but by naked iron. As she held on to the boiler she was being electrocuted. She shouted to her husband who was in the adjourning room watching a soccer match on television. "My husband, my husband I'm dying help! Help! Help me!" At that moment one of the teams had just scored a goal and he was too busy to run in and help his wife. By the time he went in to the bedroom, with words of blame on his lips and with an angry tone: "you like to disrupt my game when I'm watching soccer because you don't like…" he opened the bedroom door and found his wife's lifeless body on the floor, thoroughly burnt. The child was on the bed crying. But the woman died on the spot and her dead body was moved immediately to an unknown destination. This is what the spirit of abandonment, neglect and isolation can accomplish. Many people hear their children scream and call from another room and they respond with a question, "What is wrong, will you come here?" Why not run to them to find out what happened that made them scream? Do you know if there has been an accident? The spirit of abandonment, neglect, and isolation, makes you feel unconcerned, lazy and carefree.

Therefore, we approach this spirit with the concept of "the honeymoon never ends." This is the concept that motivates someone and moves him or her nearer and closer to loving his or her spouse much more than when they first met. In selecting the prayer point to use in fighting this spirit, one has to dwell on the doctrine of Christ:

Greater love hath no man than this, that a man lay down his life for his friends.
John 15:13

Word Bank Sample

2 Samuel 3:15-16
Proverbs 5:15-20

Proverbs 18: 22
Proverbs 19:14
Proverbs 31:10-31
Ecclesiastes 9:9
1 Corinthians 7: 3-5, 10-11
Ephesians 5:22-33

Prayer Bank Sample against Spirit of Abandonment, Neglect and Isolation

Most Holy Father, I thank You for giving me my spouse to live, to love and to cherish all the days of my life until death do us part. Lord, help me to be the best that You made me to be in this relationship. I resist, I refuse and I reject the spirit of isolation, neglect and abandonment in our family. We shall be there for one another; to care and to help, to comfort and to love, and to stand in faith, in winter and in summer, in prosperity and against adversity. Lord, make me conscious of the need of my spouse and children. Give me a quickening spirit at all times to be willing to answer the call of my spouse and children. As I deposit this prayer in my prayer bank, give me more burning love for my spouse especially when he or she is sick or calls for help under any circumstance. May we love and submit to each other as did Christ for the Church. Thank you Lord for answered prayer, in Jesus' precious name I pray. Amen.

THE SPIRIT OF DECEPTION

This spirit works with the spirit of stubbornness and disobedience. It was the same spirit that made Eve to sin against God, when she was drawn away on the basis of her own lust and enticed.

Now the serpent was more subtle than any beast of the field which the LORD God had made. And he said unto the woman, Yea, hath God said, Ye shall not eat of every tree of the garden? And the woman said unto the serpent, We may eat of the fruit of the trees of the garden: But of the fruit of the tree which is in the midst of the garden, God hath said, Ye shall not eat of it, neither shall ye touch

it, lest ye die. And the serpent said unto the woman, Ye shall not surely die. For God thus know that in the day ye eat thereof, then your eyes shall be opened, and ye shall be as gods, knowing good or evil. And when the woman saw that the tree was good for food, and that it was pleasant to the eyes, and a tree to be desired to make one wise, she took of the fruit thereof, and did eat, and gave also unto her husband with her; and he did eat.
Genesis 3:1-6

Yes, Eve was deceived by this spirit and made to disobey the Word of God. This spirit deceives, makes people to disobey and rebel against God and those in godly authority. It is the same spirit that made the prophet from Jerusalem commonly called, "The disobedient prophet" to fumble and was later killed by a lion. The old prophet at Bethel had deceived him, convincing him to come back with him against the Word of the LORD. But while they were together eating bread in the old prophet's house, the Word of the LORD came unto him through the man who deceived him:

And he cried unto the man of God that came from Judah, saying, Thus said the LORD, Forasmuch as thou hast disobeyed the mouth of the LORD, and hast not kept the commandment which the LORD thy God commanded thee, But camest back, and had eaten bread and drunk water in the place, of the which the LORD did say to thee, Eat no bread, and drink no water, thy carcass shall not come into the sepulcher of thy fathers.
1 Kings 13:21-22

And so it was that as soon as he left the old prophet's house on his way home, a lion, which was more obedient to God's Word than he, met him and killed him. The man whom the devil used to deceive him went and brought him, prepared him and buried him.

Once you know that God has given you the mantle of leadership, the best person to listen to should be the LORD Himself. If God has called you, let Him have a final say in your doing. This does not mean that God cannot give other people or prophets a message for you, but what it means is that every "Thus says the Lord" has to be weighed and measured in line with the initial message or vision that God had previously given you. Without that, one could be deceived and moved to go against the will of God for your life.

I remember a woman insisting that she saw me in her dream and God asked her to cook for me. I told her, "Thanks, but God did not tell me that He told you to cook for me. Until then, thanks." It was not long after that she led a rebellion against me and left the ministry. The enemy has used food and gifts as means of seducing God's ministers and has succeeded in bringing some of them down.

As a member of a strong prayer team, I remember being warned never to eat where we were sent to go and carry out deliverance, or any other spiritual assignments, nor accept a gift. There used to be announcements also that members of our congregation should not bring cooked food from home to any member of our prayer team or the ministers. It was good for me because there were series of reports where deliverance ministers were seduced and deceived to commit sin through indulgence in eating and drinking and becoming too familiar with the people they were sent to go and help. There was an alternative way to appreciate the warriors; turn your gift into cash and bring it to the group whenever and wherever we met. With that, it would be prayerfully received and used for the furtherance of God's work. At the same time, training and exposing various ways that the enemy could pass through to get us is very important. A well trained minister or warrior should be able to resist any temptation of being lured into feasting whenever they were on prayer assignment.

Word Bank Sample

Proverbs 1:10
John 8:44
Mark 16:18
Acts 5:2
Joshua 1:7
1 Samuel 15:15

Prayer Bank Sample against Spirit of Deception

Dear Heavenly Father, thank You this day for the opportunity You granted me to be Your child. Those that must remain as Your children are those that have believed and received Your only Son, Jesus Christ. I reject every lying word that the devil speaks to deceive me to compromise my faith, I resist him in every way and cause him to flee, I rebuke him and I stand against him and his deception. Lord, I shall be obedient to Your voice at all times and shall keep Your commandments. I bind every spirit of deception, lying tongues and enticing prophecy. I come against any spirit that seduces and manipulates people in order to deceive them and take them out of the will of God for them. The prayer that I deposit in my prayer bank shall stand for my defense and any day anybody will try to deceive me, let that person be exposed. May I also not be used as an agent to deceive others. I use the name of Jesus and come against every lying spirit that might seek opportunity to use me to tell lies to others. I know that to whom I yield my body, a servant of that person I am. I have decided to yield my body to the Holy Spirit; I am therefore a servant of the Holy Spirit. Lord Jesus, bless me with the gift of discernment of spirits to enable me know the spirits in those that work with me. Thank You Father for divinely enabling me to continue in Your Word as this will help me to know the truth that will also set me free. Thank You, Lord, because I am free from all deceptions, in the name of Jesus. Amen.

Benediction: *He who reads God's Word all the time and watch and pray and continually deposits his prayer into his prayer bank shall never be a victim of deception that will lead him to disobey the Words of the Lord, but forever shall be free, in Jesus' name. Amen.*

SPIRIT OF DELAY

This is yet another spirit that needs to be seriously watched and dealt with daily in our depository bank. It is a spirit that has caused many to make mistakes in their lives and live a life of regret forever. It breeds impatience, frustration, and disappointment.

KING SAUL

And he tarried seven days, according to the set time that Samuel had appointed: but Samuel came not to Gilgal; and the people were scattered from him. And Saul said, Bring hither a burnt offering to me, and peace offerings. And he offered the burnt offerings. And it came to pass, that as soon as he had made an end of offering the burnt offering, behold, Samuel came; and Saul went out to meet him, that he might salute him. And Samuel said, what hast thou done? And Saul said, because I saw that the people were scattered from me, and that thou camest not within the days appointed, and that the Philistines gathered themselves together at Michmash: Therefore said I, the Philistines will come down upon me to Gilgal, and I have not made supplication unto the Lord: I forced myself therefore, and offered a burnt offering.
1 Samuel 13:8-12

This spirit comes with trembling, confusion, intimidation and fear. King Saul lost his kingdom and was rejected by God. This is what the spirit of delay does. He had waited for Prophet Samuel for seven days, but he did not wait for him to the last minute of the seventh day. God is true to His Word and even in the very last second, He will do it. Whenever you have lost faith in the Lord, you can no longer represent Him, hence God's rejection of Saul.

But without faith it is impossible to please Him: for he that cometh to God must believe that He is, and that He is a rewarder of them that diligently seek Him.
Hebrews 11:6

EFFECT OF SPIRIT OF DELAY

There was a lady on our prayer team in the 1980s. A brother in the church approached her for marriage, and she objected to it. When asked, she simply said, "Well, I do not know if it is the will of God for me." That seemed to be fine except that she did not tell the whole truth. She was well trained and knew how to know the will of God for her life. God, on a few occasions, had used her to give words of encouragement to others and she was found qualified to be admitted onto the prayer team. The truth was that she had another suitor in mind that she preferred and did not even care to ask for the will of God concerning the brother that approached her for marriage.

Eventually, the person she had in mind disappointed her and the brother who approached her for marriage moved on as well. The spirit of delay set in; a year passed, two years passed and even five years passed and no one else approached her again to ask her hand in marriage. By this time my wife and I had moved on to our new ministry. We later learnt that she had fallen by getting pregnant out of "wedlock." One thing led to another and the cycle continued until her end.

The spirit of delay prompts you to make wrong decisions; decisions that you may live to regret all the days of your life. The spirit may sometimes deceive you by telling you that you are getting too old to be married and will force you into making hasty and drastic decisions. It will make you believe that once an opportunity has been missed, you may never get such an opportunity again. While it is keeping you delayed, it is also plotting your fall by hurrying you into making wrong, hastily considered decisions.

Many marriages today are entered into when the lady discovers that her time is far spent and her facial beauty has begun to fade. She will rush, out of fear that she may never find a husband, into a marriage that God has not ordained. It is a spirit to watch for and to guard against by depositing our prayers in our prayer bank against it daily, as well as diligently consulting God on our daily decisions.

ISRAELITES, MOSES AND THE SPIRIT OF DELAY

Another interesting story to note is that of Moses on the mountain of God. He had spent forty days on the mount with God because God had to show him the pattern of things to be done, both in the design of the tabernacle, the interior decorations, the measurements of every furniture in it, the nature of the anointing oil, the dresses of the priests and the high priest, and all that the Lord wanted Moses to do. But when the Israelites saw that Moses delayed coming down, they thought he must have died on the mountain and they came together unto Aaron and requested for a god.

And when the people saw that Moses delayed to come down out of the mount, the people gathered themselves together unto Aaron, and said unto him, Up, make us gods, which shall go before us; for as for this Moses, the man that brought us up out of the land of Egypt, we know not what is become of him. And Aaron said unto them, Break off the golden earrings, which are in the ears of your wives, of your sons, and of your daughters, and bring them unto me.
Exodus 32:1-2

As has been stated before, the spirit of delay throws the delayed person into confusion and causes him or her to lose valuables and precious gifts of God. The favor that God granted the children of Israel in Egypt, where they requested and received precious jewels and gold for their use, became a target of the spirit of delay. The spirit of delay caused them to surrender those items for use in making a molten calf, which was later destroyed. This spirit sent its fear into the hearts of the children of Israel and made them to conclude that Moses had died on the mountain.

HOW TO DEFEAT THE SPIRIT OF DELAY

How do you know this spirit and its operation, and how do you defeat it? Whenever you are waiting for something and there is a little delay, be careful what advice you receive. This is because the spirit of delay will certainly send the spirit of impatience to torment you, and the spirit of confusion will follow. Before you are aware of it, you will lose everything and at the same time make the wrong decision. Patience and seeking God's face are the only cure to the spirit of delay.

The spirit of delay not only attacks those seeking marriages as in the case of the lady above. It attacks and wrecks all aspects of human endeavor: employment, finances to meet your desired plans, housing, travel, studies, etc. Whenever it attacks, the person whom it attacks may likely make some costly mistakes that he or she will later regret. Delays do occur, but the way we handle delays explains what is going on inside of us. This spirit has made many impatient women going through delays in pregnancy to look for alternatives outside of God. Due to delay in growth caused by the spirit of delay, many pastors have gone out to seek other ways to make their churches grow.

Do we exercise enough faith or allow fear to reign during delays? Do we trust God enough or allow self-indulgence to dictate the pace? Therefore, it is time to get up and put up a spirited fight against the spirit of delay and shut your door against it before it comes in and makes a permanent habitation of your mind, psyche and consciousness.

Word Bank Sample

1 Samuel 13:8-12
Exodus 32:1-2
Mark 13:33-37
Psalm 40:17
Habakkuk 2:3
Genesis 45:9
Isaiah 46:13
Psalm 70:5

Prayer Bank Sample against Spirit of Delay

Father, in the name of Jesus, I bind every spirit of delay. It shall not stand in my way to hinder my progress. I confess and declare this word upon my life, "forward, ever and backward, never." I use the authority in the name of Jesus and attack the spirit of delay and cast it into the lake of fire. I release blindness against the spirit of delay so that it will be blinded and will not see me forever. Lord, as the clock ticks, the set time to favor me has come. My marriage shall be timely, children shall come timely, jobs shall come timely, house shall come timely; and everything pertaining to me shall come at a time You purposed in Your heart for me. Guide my spirit O Lord that I may not make decisions in haste. Every decision I make shall be according to your plan. The devil shall be late to come to me. It shall be that before he arrives my blessings have already been bestowed upon me. The spirit of delay shall not steal those precious things you have bestowed upon me. I will keep and maintain them for use to the glory of Your name, Amen. Lord, make me very watchful to be able to know what Your will for me is. I bind the spirit of distraction that follows the spirit of delay, help me Lord, to stay focused and continue to guide my spirit in every way, in Jesus' name I pray, Amen.

Benediction: *Anyone who trusts in the Lord and maintains his prayer as a daily reminder of the Lord shall never experience any delay. Timely observance of all of life's events shall be their portion in life. Amen.*

THE SPIRIT OF IGNORANCE

Many believers do not get blessed as they are supposed to because they do not understand God's plan for their lives. Not understanding a particular thing is quite different from having the spirit of ignorance. The spirit of ignorance makes you do the opposite of what God expects of you, it makes you perform with half your potential. This spirit has played a large part in our daily lives and relationship with God as well as in our dealings with one another. Some of these include, giving to God and to man, fellowship, friendship, relationship, traveling or relocating, marriages, choosing a career, pursuing a course of study, and a host of others.

My people are destroyed for lack of knowledge: because thou hast rejected knowledge, I will also reject thee, that thou shall be no priest to me: seeing thou hast forgotten the law of thy God, I will also forget thy children.
Hosea 4:6

The religious and political leaders in Israel became involved in idol worship and forsook the law of their God. The prophets never inquired from the Lord but spoke out of their own understanding. They prophesied lies and made the people to believe in falsehood.

The priests offered sacrifices to strange gods. They rejected the knowledge of the God of heaven. God did promise to stop them from taking the office of priesthood. God finally sent Jesus His Son to assume the office of High Priest and King. He, being from the house of Judah, fulfilled the prophecy that a scepter shall not depart from Judah. He also accomplished God's covenant unto David, saying that David will not lack a son to sit and judge God's people, Israel. Therefore taking the High Priesthood away from Aaron and the house of Levi, He combined both the Kingship and the Priesthood in one person, Jesus Christ His Son.

But the spirit of ignorance would not allow the elders of Israel to understand the plan of God for mankind through His Son Jesus Christ. They rebelled against His Words and finally crucified Him on the cross. This is what the spirit of ignorance can accomplish. It makes one fight against the will of God for one's life and opposes everything that God demands. Opposition to one's pastor, group leader, or anyone in the position of leadership is as opposing God. It is a most devious spirit with far reaching consequences for mankind. It is the destabilizer of civilizations, old and new. It is the interlocking nemesis and fulcrum that separates religions and the multiplicity of faiths. This Spirit must be fought head on and with tenacity.

KING JOASH

The next example that I am about to give shows how a spirit of ignorance works with other spirits to ensure that you do not succeed. The spirit of ignorance in conjunction with the spirits of weakness, discouragement, dullness and blindness, work to make sure you do not understand what you are supposed to do.

Now Elisha was fallen sick of his sickness whereof he died. And Joash the king of Israel came down unto him, and wept over his face, and said, O my father, my father, the chariot of Israel and the horsemen thereof. And Elisha said unto him, Take bows and arrow. And he took unto him bow and arrows. And he said to the king of Israel; Put thy hand upon the bow. And he put his hand upon it: and

Elisha put his hands upon the king's hands. And he said, Open the window eastward. And he opened it. Then Elisha said, Shoot. And he shot. And he said, the arrow of the Lord's deliverance, and the arrow of deliverance from Syria: for thou shall smite the Syrians in Aphek, till thou have consumed them. And he said, take the arrows. And he took them. And he said unto the king of Israel, Smite upon the ground. And he smote thrice, and stayed. And the man of God was wroth with him. And said, Thou shouldest have smitten five or six times; then hadst thou smitten Syria till thou hadst consumed it: whereas now thou shalt smite Syria but thrice.
2 Kings 13:14-19

King Joash did not know the purpose of smiting the arrow upon the ground. Even though God is a God of second chance, He wants us to make good use of the opportunity that we have today. Had King Joash been visionary enough to smite the ground five or six times, I do not think the country Syria would be in existence today.

IGNORANCE AND WEAKNESS DISGUISED AS COMPASSION

There were many other nations that the children of Israel failed to destroy and completely wipe off the surface of the earth, chiefly out of ignorance disguised as compassion. They compromised because of being ignorant of how dangerous the situation was. Today, many of those nations are the ones that trouble Israel and cause many of the leaders of the world much consternation. It is a crisis that occupies much of the attention of western civilization, this crisis born of ignorance will persist till the end when Jesus comes to establish His kingdom.

He was in the world, and the world was made by Him, and the world knew Him not.
John 1:10

IGNORANCE AND BLINDNESS

This is what ignorance does. It closes the eye of understanding of whoever has this spirit and darkens his mind so that he would not know what God's plans are for him. Nor would he know the identity of God Himself were He to come down and dine with him.

Satan has a well-coordinated network system and his agents are united in carrying out his commands. His goals are well spelled out, namely: deceive people, convert them, afflict them, retain them and ensure that they become part of satan's kingdom.

LEADERSHIP AND IGNORANCE

Throughout Jesus' ministry on earth, He tried His utmost best to convince the Pharisees, the Elders and all the religious leaders that He was the promised messiah. He was the messiah that Moses talked about in the law **Deuteronomy 18:15-19,** and all the prophets prophesied about. But the more He preached to them, the more they became offended by it. Why? It was because they were ignorant and blind toward God and His plan of redemption through His only Son, Jesus Christ. They read the scriptures every Sabbath day in their synagogues and interpreted what they thought was the truth to the blind followers that they led, but never really understood what the scripture said about the messiah. They had no real idea about His origin, nature, conception, birth place, life, ministry, death and resurrection. This spirit is very strong; it helps make the prophets tell lies for personal gains. It also causes divisions within the church and the family.

IGNORANCE AND COVETOUSNESS (BALAAM)

Balaam was one of the greatest prophets in his days. He used to see live visions without closing his eyes. But when Balak the king of Moab sent messengers, elders of Midian to go and fetch Balaam to come and curse the children of Israel, God strictly charged Balaam not to go.

Behold there is a people come out of Egypt, which covereth the face of the earth: come now, curse me them; peradventure I shall be able to overcome them, and drive them out. And God said unto Balaam, Thou shall not go with them; thou shall not curse the people: for they are blessed.
Numbers 22:11-12

What did God say unto Balaam? "Thou shall not go," period. Whether Balak had sent messengers two hundred times and promised him the treasure of the whole world, the charge remained, "Thou shall not go." But Balaam, whom everyone thought was very knowledgeable in spiritual matters, tried to force God into a compromise. He paid attention to the enticement of Balak's messengers and gave them more opportunities to visit him again and again. Then God forsook His perfect will and allowed His permissive will into play.

Balaam hypocritically concluded that even though he would now go, he would only speak of the things God put in his mouth to speak. But he failed to realize that he had offended God by going in the first place, because God had told him, "Thou shall not go."

Through the spirit of ignorance working with the spirit of covetousness, an angel of God almost killed him on his way to see Balak. For one who could see live visions with his eyes open, this time his Donkey actually had clearer visions than he did. Today, many donkeys, chickens and goats can prophesy better than the so-called prophets, bishops, pastors and church leaders. The spirit of ignorance has taken hold of our Church leaders resulting in lack of awareness of what God really expects of them. This lack of awareness due to the operation of the spirit of ignorance makes them to live in disobedience and to reject everyone God sends on their way to help them in the ministry. Which is why there is a paucity of deposited prayers to ward against the spirit of ignorance in their prayer banks, as this spirit now plays a major role in lying prophecies, deceptions, divisions and confusions in the church.

Word Bank Sample

John 20:24-25
Luke 24:30-32
John 21:3
Exodus 18:21
Luke 12:15
2 Peter 2:14

Prayer Bank Sample against Spirit of Ignorance

My Father, My Lord, and My God, I pray this day that the eyes of my understanding be enlightened to behold the things that are written in Your law. You have made it clear in Your Word that the memory of the just is blessed. I reject and bind the spirit of ignorance and cast it completely away from me. I decree, I declare, I announce and proclaim the wisdom of God, the knowledge of God, the understanding of God and the power of God. Since goat begets goat, cow begets cow, therefore the Spirit of the Living God, which is full of knowledge and wisdom, begets me. I cannot and will not be blind, I cannot and will not be deaf, and I cannot and will not be ignorant of God's plan for my life. This prayer that I deposit in my prayer bank before you shall keep me from the attack of the spirit of ignorance throughout my entire life. By your information I shall be transformed and not be destroyed for lack of knowledge. I shall be empowered not disenfranchised. I shall be enlightened not perplexed and entangled. I shall be the delight of the Lord not His desolation caused by ignorance. My donkey shall in no wise see, know or understand more than me. God's purpose and God's plan for my life shall not be obscured. I command the malevolent cloud of ignorance to dock far away from me. I put a seal upon this prayer and cover the express answer with the blood of Jesus, in Jesus' precious name I pray, Amen.

Benediction: *Anyone who regularly seeks the Lord's face and prays against ignorance and fills their prayer bank with it shall be free of* *the spirit of ignorance and become enlightened by the Spirit of God. Amen.*

SPIRIT OF INFIRMITY

And behold, there was a woman which had a spirit of infirmity eighteen years, and was bowed together, and could in no wise lift up herself.
Luke 13:11

Every sickness has a spirit in charge. It is assigned the responsibility to torment, afflict and even kill whomever they hold captive if there is no deliverance in sight. Some of these sicknesses like high blood pressure, diabetes, leprosy, cancer, madness, epilepsy, high fever, miscarriages that have the power to reoccur after being healed are basically controlled by a spirit called the spirit of infirmity. This spirit has a link, a connection and also roots like a tree that supply reinforcement if need be. If the person is treated on the surface, the sickness is sure to resurface. The only way to free the oppressed person of these spirits is to bind those spirits, overpower them, and cast them out and banish them from coming back to that body or person. The spirit of infirmity is very stubborn. It has the ability to call out the name of the person trying to cast him out and challenge him if he is not living a righteous life.

And they came over unto the other side of the sea, into a country of the Gadarenes. And when He was come out of the ship, immediately there met Him out of the tombs, a man with an unclean spirit, Who had his dwelling among the tombs; and no man could bind him, no, not with chains: Because that he had been often bound with fetters and chains, and the chains had been plucked asunder by him, and the fetters broken in pieces: neither could any man tame him. And always, night and day, he was in the mountains, and in the tombs, crying, and cutting himself with stones. But when he saw Jesus afar off, he ran and worshiped Him, And cried with a loud voice, and said, What have I to do with you, Jesus, Thou Son of the Most High God? I adjure thee by God that Thou torment me not. For He said unto

him, Come out of the man, thou unclean spirit. And He asked him, What is thy name? and he answered, saying, My name is Legion: for we are many. And he besought Him much that He would not send them away out of the country. Now there was there nigh unto the mountains a great herd of swine feeding. And all the devils besought Him, saying, 'Send us into the swine that we may enter into them. And forthwith Jesus gave them leave. And the unclean spirits went out, and entered into the swine: and the herd ran violently down a steep place into the sea, (they were about two thousand;) and were chocked in the sea.
Mark 5:1-13

The spirit of infirmity or the unclean spirit has the ability to demand where to be sent. He understands the scriptures and knows when his time of destruction would come. He communicates through the man that he possesses and has the ability to torment and even kill if the vessel that carries him fails to do his biddings.

A FRIEND'S DAUGHTER

One day a friend's daughter was walking by a garbage dump. An unclean spirit jumped into her and began to torment her. She almost became mentally impaired. She would tear off her clothes and run berserk spewing incomprehensible gibberish. She would be held down and tied with a cord, but the spirit in her was so strong that she would break free and attack the men that tried to bind her. In fact, anyone who came to assist would be surprised, as the evil spirit would call on the person by name and proceed to reveal to all within hearing distance all of this person's dirty activities the night before to their utter embarrassment.

The parents sent for me and it took the mighty hand of God for the demon to be cast out. I then realized that if one wanders about in a demon-infested area, one could contact an evil spirit. The easiest way to deliver people with this kind of spirit is for the minister to trace all the previous day's contacts and if possible the last dream that he or she had before the affliction began. If such a spirit is allowed to consolidate its position in the person he inhabits, it becomes a lengthy spiritual and medical battle.

A WOMAN WITH THE SPIRIT OF INFIRMITY

I can still remember vividly as a prayer warrior when we went to pray for a woman that was possessed by this spirit. We were seven in number and had fasted without food and water for three days staying together under one roof. When we arrived, as the Holy Spirit led us, we decided to surround the entire building and deal first with the spirit of reinforcement. Some of us took to the surrounding streets, in so doing we strategically sent all the evil spirits fleeing. We had already told the husband of the lady that was possessed how we were going to come into his home but not what we were going to do. He therefore left all doors unlocked. After taking authority over the territorial spirit, street spirit, neighborhood spirit and the spirit in the compound, our leader first went in through the entrance door and as soon as the woman saw her, she roared like a lion. She roared and roared and got up and walked toward her to challenge her. Then two warriors entered from the back door and before she was aware of it, the whole house was taken over by spiritual fire. She surrendered. Knelt down and begged: "leave me alone, what have I done that you come to send me away, please leave me alone!" She cried. While she was thus wailing, we held our hands and formed a circle with her in the center and began to pray powerfully.

Suddenly, something jumped out of her, which had the form of a lizard and went straight into one of the ladies in our prayer group. Her body was too spiritually charged for it to reside there, and it immediately leaped out, into one of the prayer warriors but could not stay there either. This activity continued as this spirit leaped from one prayer warrior to another seeking a sanctuary and finding each body too potent, it leaped onto the floor, wriggled and died right there in our sight. As it leaped into my body, I could feel it coursing from my hands to my head then to my legs before leaping out. Supposing there was any weak one amongst us, his or her body would have become the devil's new home.

Since it is common knowledge that the spirit or demon of infirmity can jump from one body to another to try to claim possession of that body if there is nothing to prevent him, or if a weaker spiritual person goes to deliver a person with a stubborn spirit, a prayer bank and a word bank has to be developed to prevent him from having any contact with you or any member of your family, especially if you are involved with praying for others. It is important for you to have a prayer bank stored up with prayers because you may be in a church where deliverance is being carried out, the devil could jump from the person that is being delivered into you. Or you may join another person to go and pray for someone possessed with the evil spirit without proper preparation and the spirit could leave the person and attack you. And since this seems to be a stubborn spirit, the prayer for this kind of spirit must be tough, powerful and forceful. See chapter 9 for the use of defensive armor.

Prayer Bank Sample against Spirit of Infirmity

1 Corinthians 6:19-20, Father in the name of Jesus, my body is the temple of the Holy Spirit and the Spirit of the Almighty God dwells in me; therefore I am not my own, I was bought with a price; my body therefore is to be used to glorify God.

1 John 4:4, I am making my stand known and clear that greater is Jesus Christ in me, than satan that is in the world.

Hebrews 1:7, Dear Lord as you make your angels spirit, make me your minister a flame of fire, I have become a flame of fire, Holy fire in my bones and marrows, fire in my mind, fire of God surrounding me. From the crown of my head to the sole of my feet, I am covered by divine fire and have become untouchable. I pray against bone sickness, heart disease or cardiac problems, against kidney failure, against bladder problems and all other form of infirmities. The fire of God in my eyes shall prevent blindness from coming upon me. The fire of God in my ears shall melt every wax or hearing impediment that the enemy will try to bring upon me. The fire of God in my body system shall fight and destroy every seed of cancer, diabetes, high blood pressure, heart disease and all kinds of skin disease. Once more, I declare that I have no fellowship with the unfruitful works of darkness but reprove them. In addition to the fire, Lord, I apply the blood of Jesus in all aspect of my life, and in the doorpost of my house. Thank You, Lord, for taking away the spirit of infirmity from my dwelling, in Jesus' name I pray. Amen.

Benediction: *Anyone who consistently reads his Bible and deposits his sanctified prayer into his or her prayer bank shall surely have victory over any spirit of infirmity he will encounter in life. Amen.*

SPIRIT OF REJECTION

The spirit of rejection makes people to look down on you. Everything you do is annoying to others. Your parents easily turn against you and before you know it, order you out of their home. When that spirit is upon someone, even one's parents may not want one as a roommate. And if married, your spouse might want to be considerate of you in some respect but the spirit might make it extremely difficult.

QUEEN VASHTI

As with any other spirit mentioned in this book, there is no spirit that operates alone; it must have a collection of other spirits to operate alongside it. Before the spirit of rejection strikes, it sends the spirit of stubbornness and disobedience ahead of him to begin the preparation of the way for him. These other spirits will make you disobey orders and fail to take instructions. It was the spirit of rejection that made Queen Vashti to lose her crown.

On the seventh day, when the heart of the king was merry with wine, he commanded Mehumen, Biztha, Harbona, Bigtha, and Abagtha, Zetha, and Careas, the seven chamberlains that serve in the presence of Ahasuerus the king. To bring Vashti the queen before the king with crown royal, to shew the people and the princess her beauty: for she was fair to look on. But the queen Vashti refused to

come at the king's commandment by his chamberlains: therefore was the king very wroth, and his anger burned in him.
Esther 1:10-12

Queen Vashti might never have intended to disobey the king's command for she knew as a queen to do so would mean her losing her crown. But the spirit of rejection working with/through her stubborn spirit hardened her heart to disobey her husband. God allowed it to be so in order to give Esther the palace because of the Jews. Queen Vashti did not know God, and as many that do not know Him are easily seduced and deceived. It is the same way that God allowed lying spirits to prophesy lies unto Ahab for him to go and die in the battle. God allowed the spirit of resistance, disobedience and confrontation to attack Queen Vashti who easily fell, by refusing the command of her husband to dance in the presence of all the people. This single act of hers led to her fall and eventual rejection and dethronement as the queen. This spirit also comes with loss of sympathy and consideration even as your best friends might not want to listen to your own side of the story. It is a spirit that one has to fight daily by depositing prayers in the prayer bank using the opposite words like favor to resist it from operating in one's life.

KING SAUL

King Saul was another person that the spirit of rejection brought down.

And the Lord said to Samuel, How long wilt thou mourn for Saul, seeing I have rejected him from reigning over Israel? Fill thy horn with oil, and go, I will send thee to Jesse, the Bethlehemite: for I have provided me a king among his sons.

But the Spirit of the LORD departed from Saul, and an evil spirit from the LORD troubled him.
1 Samuel 16:1, 16

First of all, the spirits of pride, self-indulgence, disobedience and confusion had taken hold of King Saul who saw no need to keep the commandments of the Lord. As all these spirits took hold of Saul, the spirit of sympathy, pity and sound mind from the LORD left him: this is what is called, "The Spirit of the LORD." As soon as the Spirit of the LORD moved out of Saul, the spirit of rejection came in with the spirit of depression and took charge of him. God was now telling Samuel not to mourn for Saul because His Spirit was no longer in him. The spirit of rejection then took over.

Let it be clear to everyone that God created the heavens and the earth. He created everything in them through His Son, Jesus Christ. He controls all spirits whether they are good or evil even as the Bible states it:

For by Him were all things created, that are in heaven, and that are in earth, visible and invisible, whether they be thrones, or dominions, or principalities or powers: all things were created by Him and for Him.
Colossians 1:16

God does not do evil, His Word guides Him and He does what He says and says what He does. His decisions and actions are righteously weighed in line with His Words. When the Bible says, 'evil spirit from the LORD troubled him,' it goes to confirm that wherever the Spirit of the LORD is, there is liberty. But where the Spirit of the LORD is rejected, evil spirits would occupy, and God permits it to be so. Therefore, God does not maintain a place where He accommodates evil spirits and sends them on errands. However whenever the Spirit of the Lord departs, evil spirits would seize the opportunity to occupy, for nature does not allow a vacuum even in the play of the occupation of spirits. If any man fails to follow strictly God's instructions that are clearly specified in His Word then that person has opened the door for the contrary spirits; evil spirits to come in and dwell in him. One has to use the spirit of acceptance, adoption or heir of God to fight against or counter the spirit of rejection.

Word Bank Sample

Judges 11:2
Romans 8:15, 23
Romans 9:4
Galatians 4:5
Romans 8:17
Galatians 3:29
Ephesians 1:6

Prayer Bank Sample against Spirit of Rejection

Father, in the name of Jesus, I declare today that my faith in Jesus has opened the door of acceptance for me in the sight of God and man. I am accepted by those who once rejected me. I declare that I am a child of God and wherever the Spirit of the Lord is, I am accepted. As a child of God, I am loved and beloved by all who love Him. I claim the spirit of adoption whereby I can proudly say, Abba, Father. I am an heir of God and a joint heir with my Lord and Savior Jesus Christ. I am accepted in the beloved to offer praises unto His name. In the home, I am accepted by my spouse and children. In the church, I am accepted by the brethren. When I am among friends, I am accepted and welcomed. Anywhere I go in the world that is good, I am accepted. But I shall be rejected in the camp of the witches, in the voodoo covens and in the kingdom of satan. I record this prayer in my prayer bank before You so that You will consider me as a precious ornament, as someone to be desired and sought for, and I shall bc called, a favored child. My parents will love me, my spouse will continually admire me. Friends will cherish me and I will be adorable before men and women of goodwill. I know that You were rejected for my acceptance. I pray this prayer in the name that is above all names, the precious name of Jesus Christ. Amen.

Benediction: *Unto those who take shelter in the Lord by praying against this spirit regularly, seeking to be filled by the Spirit of the Lord shall not face rejection in any sphere they operate in this material world. Amen*

SPIRIT OF FEAR

This is a spirit that says, "You cannot do it!" It makes every task that the Lord has given you to appear dangerous. "You cannot drive, you will have an accident. You cannot sing, your voice is not good enough and you will be laughed at if you try. You cannot enter into ministry because you do not have money. You are not good enough to preach, and you if you preach, nobody will accept your preaching. You are not sure God has called you and you do not know a lot of verses in the Bible. After quoting the few verses that you know, what are you going to say next? You cannot go back to school because you are too old to study. Remember how mathematics used to torture you? If you try and fail, you will be laughed at." This is the function of the spirit of fear, to bring suggestions that seem to suggest nothing is possible.

The disciples of Jesus had just celebrated their orientation after many hours with Jesus, their master on the mountain. Coming down from the mountain with their heads full with lectures, they wasted no time to accept the invitation of their master to cross over to the other side. Immediately they all entered into a ship, but while still a long way to the land, they encountered a storm.

And when he was entered into a ship, His disciples followed Him. And behold, there arose a great tempest in the sea, insomuch that the ship was covered with the wave: but he was asleep. And His disciples came to Him, and woke Him, saying, Lord, save us: we perish. And He said unto them, why are ye fearful, O ye of little faith? Then He arose, and rebuked the winds and the sea; and there was a great calm.
Matthew 8:23-26

Jesus saw how frightened they were and asked them why they were fearful. One thing should be made clear; if God has sent you on an errand you do not have to be afraid of a storm or tempest. If you are a carrier of God's covenant, you do not have to be afraid of a storm. If you are taking the gospel of peace to share with people on the other side, you do not have to be afraid of a storm. If you believe that He is right there with you, in the boat, ship, car, train, bus, plane or wherever you go, then you do not have to be afraid of a storm.

Jesus asked them why they substituted faith for fear. Faith goes ahead of you and brings the picture of where you are going and what you need to accomplish before you even begin the journey. Since you have already seen the other side and have seen what you have been able to accomplish before you arrive there, a storm on the way should not cause any panic or worry since it is already done.

The Bible says that fear brings torment, but perfect love casts away fear. The spirit of fear has denied many their livelihood. It has made many to crawl instead of soaring. But the spirit of power empowers and strengthens, the spirit of love is cheerful and harmless, and the spirit of a sound mind opens the doors of opportunity and leads to great exploit. What does God say to His children? "... *Fear not: for I have redeemed thee, I have called thee by thy names; thou art mine.*" **Isaiah 43:1.** Yes, you are His. He knows your going out and your coming in. He knows your name and also carries you on eagle's wings. Fear not for He is with you.

Word Bank Sample

Isaiah 43:1
John 14:1
Philippians 4:6
Psalm 23:4
Psalm 118:6
Roman 8:15
1 John 4:18

Prayer Bank Sample against Spirit of Fear

Great God of wonders, let it be known that You alone are God in heaven above and on earth beneath. There is no searching of Your wisdom and power. This day I kneel before you depositing this prayer into my prayer bank against the spirit of fear and torment. Many have been seduced and deceived to deny You. Many have lost faith in You and have committed suicide because of what the liar and the father of all liars told them about their future. But my foundation is on You. I am not afraid of tomorrow because it was not by my power that I went through yesterday. I am secure no matter what vial the wicked one might pour upon the earth. Give me the grace to resist him and cast him out of my sight. Will it be the fear of death, sickness, joblessness, or barrenness? I will fear no evil for You, O Lord, are with me. I shall travel to all parts of the globe and declare the works of the Lord, and shall not die because Your Spirit shall travel with me. I have your name to declare, I have your Words to preach and I have souls to win into Your kingdom. I will not allow the spirit of those who went back in Gideon's army to come upon me; I shall fight to the end and defeat all Your enemies and mine. Spirit of fear, I bind you in Jesus' name, we are not friends but adversaries. You spirit of fear, beware of me as I am a child of the Living God. I shall be a terror unto you and shall rule over you. You will encounter me and tremble, in the daytime and in the night. I shall finish my race and I will receive my crown. I will fulfill all that the Lord assigns me to do without further regard to you. Thank You, Lord for giving me the opportunity to prepare in advance against that day, for I have enough strength stored and ready to launch out by faith. I pray and live by faith, trusting that Jesus my Savior is alive and He has helped me overcome the spirit of fear. In Jesus' name I pray. Amen.

Benediction: *Fear is banished for one who takes shelter in His Word, who store up prayers in his bank and meditates daily and night. May this sample prayer be a blessing and help him in every way. Amen.*

SPIRIT OF LUST

The spirit of lust is yet another dirty spirit that attacks both men and women especially the ministers of God. It takes its roots from the spirit of immorality and acts as a husband to the flesh. When it has impregnated our flesh, then our flesh gives birth to sin:

Then when lust hath conceived, it bringeth forth sin: and sin, when it is finished, bringeth forth death.
James 1:15

The Bible has made it clear why most times our prayers are hindered. It is because we pray to enjoy the fruit of our lust.

From whence come wars and fighting among you? Come they not hence, even of your lusts that war in your members? Ye lust, ye have not: ye kill, ye desire to have, and cannot obtain: ye fight and war, yet ye have not, because ye ask not. Ye ask, and receive not, because ye ask amiss, that ye may consume it upon your lusts.
James 4:1-3

The above Bible reference is an indication that lust can prevent our prayers from being answered. The greatest enemy of man is the flesh; it is the flesh that invites the devil. When our flesh is weak, our entire body system is open to lusting and sin. The Bible sums up all that is in the world and divides it into three components: the lust of the flesh, the lust of the eyes, and the pride of life in **1 John 2:16.** If we can subdue the flesh by the Word of God, we can proceed to live a victorious Christian life.

Word Bank Sample

Galatians 5:24
2 Timothy 2:22
Titus 2:12
1 Corinthians 10:6
1 John 2:16-17
Proverbs 6:25

Prayer Bank Sample against Spirit of Lust

Dear heavenly Father, thank You this day for allowing Your Spirit to indwell in me. I know that there is nothing that You cannot do. As for me, I do not know how to take control of my body, because

I lust daily and this lust works against Your Spirit in me. I also know that if the lust in me conceives, it will bring forth sin which will lead to death. I therefore desire that my soul, my heart, my mind and my entire body be brought in subjection to the obedience of Your Son, Jesus Christ. I stand this day to deposit this prayer in my prayer bank requesting that Your Spirit in me will continually yield towards righteousness, love, peace, joy, good work, goodness, mercy, faith, hospitality and faithfulness. I stand this day in opposition of the spirit of lust and I attack the very foundation with which it stands. I attack all its pillars and cause them to crumble. I bind all its agents and command the spirit of holiness upon me. I believe that I will lust after Christ and not evil. I pray this prayer in the overcoming name of Jesus. Amen.

Benediction: *He who observes the Lord's ordinance and clothes himself daily with His Word shall be free of lust and shall attain the nature of our Lord Jesus Christ. Amen.*

SPIRIT OF SADNESS

Sadness is a state of unhappiness. When someone is oppressed with the spirit of sadness, he can eat all that he wants to eat, does the type of work he desires, drive the kind of car he wants to drive but his countenance will remain dull. There are two types of the spirit of sadness. There is a type of sadness that places a burden in your heart and moves you to act in a positive way to deal with an ugly situation. Such was the case with Nehemiah.

Wherefore the king said unto me, Why is thy countenance sad, seeing thou art not sick? This is nothing else but sorrow of heart. Then I was very sore afraid, And said unto the king, let the king live forever: why should not my countenance be sad, when the city, the place of my father's sepulchers, lieth waste, and the gates thereof are consumed with fire?
Nehemiah 2:2-3

Positive: The burden concerning Jerusalem was placed upon Nehemiah, and his countenance changed when he remembered his father's land that was consumed by fire. This kind of sadness motivates and encourages action. This is not a contrary spirit as it motivates us to act. It is called, "A holy anger or burden to act." The Spirit of God enables your spirit to see things differently and releases encouragement into your heart motivating you to take action that leads to achieving a desired goal.

Negative: The spirit of sadness hinders growth and most of the time is associated with the spirit of murder or suicide. It is a spirit that makes you believe that you are worse than everyone else, and your situation may never improve.

But Jezebel his wife came to him, and said unto him, Why is thy spirit so sad, that thou eatest no bread?
1 Kings 21:5

Yes, King Ahab ate no bread because a sad man has little or nothing to do with food. While believers are saying, "The joy of the Lord is our strength." Sad people say, "Eliminating those standing on our ways and removing them completely till they are no more, is our joy".

A lady with the spirit of sadness finds it difficult to get a husband. If she does then there is the likelihood of daily contention in the marriage. She does not smile, share jokes and chat with her husband. If she is forced to smile, her smile seems as if she is crying. Her marriage could be at the point of collapse because her husband might soon get fed up with her sour attitude at home and in public. This spirit is different from the spirit of contention and quarreling. The spirit of sadness most of the time does not quarrel but produces dullness, lethargy, slothfulness, ignorance, sleep and a sad countenance. One could use light or the spirit of joy to counter the spirit of sadness.

Word Bank Sample

1 Samuel 1:18
1 Kings 21:5
Mark 10:21-22
Isaiah 61:3

Prayer Bank Sample against Spirit of Sadness

Dear heavenly Father, I thank You for answering my prayers and restoring my joy. It is certain that I was created to praise the beauty of Your holiness. There are millions and millions of angels before Your throne singing daily to glorify Your name, in Your presence is fullness of joy, and at Your right hand are pleasures for ever more. Thank You for counting me worthy to be among the living, restore unto me this day, the joy of Thy salvation and cause me to rejoice and be glad in You. If there are things in life that try to steal Your joy from my heart and bring the spirit of heaviness and sadness upon me, Lord, turn my sadness into joy and put the song of praises on my lips. I stand this day before You to deposit this prayer in your prayer book and in my prayer bank. Let it come to pass that the veil of sadness is completely torn off my face as You clothe me now with the beauty of Your countenance. I pray this prayer in Jesus' name believing that the spirit of sadness and sorrow has no place in me. Amen.

Benediction: *One who believes in Him and His finished work of redemption at Calvary shall surely find peace and shall be blessed with the happy countenance of our Lord Jesus Christ and the spirit of enduring joy. Amen.*

SPIRIT OF JEALOUSY

The spirit of jealousy works hand-in-hand with the spirit of envy and carries a lot of sentiments with it. It makes you feel that you have been defeated or that someone somewhere is better than you are or has gone further than you have. Cain killed his brother Abel due to the spirit of jealousy.

And in process of time it came to pass, that Cain brought of the fruit of the ground an offering unto the LORD. And Abel, he also brought of the firstlings of his flock and of the fat thereof. And the LORD had respect unto Abel and unto his offering: But unto Cain and his offering He had no respect. And Cain was very wroth, and his countenance fell.
Genesis 4:3-5

There was no need for Cain to be envious of his brother; rather, he should have repented, improved upon his giving and the state of his mind. But he decided to allow the spirit of jealousy to control him even after God had called him to order.

And the LORD said unto Cain, Why art thou wroth? And why is thy countenance fallen? If thou doest well, shalt thou not be accepted? And if thou doest not well, sin lieth at the door. And unto thee shall be his desire, and thou shalt rule over him.
Genesis 4:6-7

To see the strength of the spirit of jealousy, this rebuke from the LORD did not deter Cain from carrying out the bidding of the spirit of jealousy: "Kill your brother!" the spirit implored him.

And Cain talked with Abel his brother: and it came to pass, when they were in the field, that Cain rose up against his brother, and slew him.
Genesis 4:8

Cain slew his brother, and that is the end product of jealousy. The spirit of jealousy works with the spirit of hate and it often ends with death. It is our place to deal with this spirit in our families, especially when we begin to see some petty squabbles between brothers or sisters in the family.

Joseph's story is worth mentioning here as well. Through the spirit of jealousy, envy and hatred, his brethren sold him as a slave into Egypt.

Now Israel loved Joseph more than all his brethren, because he was the son of his old age: and he made him a coat of many colors. And when his brethren saw that his father loved him more than all his brethren, they hated him and could not speak peaceably with him.
Genesis 37:3-4

To worsen the situation for Joseph, he began to tell them of his dreams. Dreams have always been a source of jealousy for dreamers. If you are a dreamer, you have to guide against telling people your dreams or else you pay with your life. After Joseph had told his parents and his brethren his two dreams, this is how they reacted:

And his brethren envied him; but his father observed the saying... And when they saw him afar off, even before he came near unto them, they conspired against him to slay him. And they said one to another, Behold, this dreamer cometh. Come now therefore, and let us slay him, and cast him into some pit, and we will say, Some evil beast hath devoured him: and we shall see what will become of his dreams.
Genesis 37:11-20

Dreaming here also indicates potential. Dreamers are always in danger. Even in our modern world we are aware of this danger. There was a great man who dared to dream of a time when men in America will be judged not by the color of their skin but by the content of their character. He paid dearly with his life for desiring this beautiful state of affairs. The key word here is, "And we shall see what becomes of his dreams." When the dreamer is dead, all his dreams and potentials die with him except there are people who fight to keep the dream alive. We must be careful therefore to whom we tell our dreams. Therefore, a dreamer must take time in selecting his or her word bank. Building such a prayer bank is always beneficial because with powerful dreams and vision comes envy, jealousy and enmity.

Word Bank Sample

Genesis 4:8
Genesis 37:1-20
Matthew 27:18
Proverbs 6:34
Song. 8:6

Prayer Bank Sample against Spirit of Jealousy

Most blessed Father, I thank You for maintaining me from my childhood until now in Your mighty hand. Your Word says that he that dwells in the secret place of the Most High shall abide under the shadow of the Almighty. If it has not been You, Lord, men would have swallowed me up. One thing is certain, You that had begun a good work in me will be faithful to complete it. I am not afraid of what man shall do unto me because You are always there for me. I pray that you also bless those that will become jealous of me so that they will take their minds off me. You did bless Esau for the sake of Jacob, and I believe that if Jacob had returned from Laban, his uncle a blessed man and met his brother, Esau, in wretchedness, his brother would have killed him. But to appease him You blessed him also. I am asking that You keep those that will be envious of me busy and give them the spirit of forgetfulness. May I also not envy someone in his or her success. Help me with strength to work hard and to compete with men and women of great status. Help me use the time I would have devoted to jealousy for things beneficial to me and the Body of Christ and to sing praises unto Your name. I deposit this prayer in my prayer bank with You and use it to neutralize the spirit of jealousy and envy, in Jesus' name I pray. Amen.

Benediction: *One who loves the Lord and give cheerfully and prays has already banished the spirit of jealousy and shall surely attain to* *his heavenly ordained height and become a symbol of attraction is the sights of God and man. Amen.*

SPIRIT OF ARROGANCE/PRIDE

This spirit is married to success. It lifts itself up and refuses to listen. It boasts a lot about achievement and/or beauty. It is the same spirit that sent lucifer out of heaven.

How art thou fallen from heaven, O Lucifer, son of the morning! How art thou cut down to the ground, which didst weaken the nations! For thou hast said in thine heart, I will ascend into heaven, I will exalt my throne above the stars of God: I will sit also upon the mount of congregation, in the side of the north. I will ascend above the heights of the clouds; I will be like the most high.
Isaiah 14:12-14

These Five “I wills” set the stage for the satan’s fall. When there are so many “I’s” it shows the nature of the person we are talking about, devil the liar. Added to that is the arrogance for being full of pride, then comes his acclaimed wisdom and beauty:

Son of man, take up a lamentation upon the king of Tyrus, and say unto him, Thus said the LORD God; Thou sealest up the sum, full of wisdom, and perfect in beauty.
Ezekiel 28:12

But what was God’s answer to the devil?

Yet thou shalt be brought down to hell, to the sides of the pit.
Isaiah 14:15

This is exactly what happens to those that are full of arrogance and pride. As I said before, this spirit is married to success. It makes you feel at the top of the world. You feel you have arrived. You may never listen to your parents again neither will you pay attention to your spiritual leaders.

Word Bank Sample

Luke 18:10-14
Proverbs 8:13
Proverb 16:18
Proverb 29:1, 23
James 4:6
Philippians 2:5-11

Prayer Bank Sample against Spirit of Arrogance/Pride

Most glorious Father in heaven, I submit myself to Your will and Your ordinances. I break the power of arrogance and pride in me. I welcome Your humble Spirit into my life. Sanctify me through Your word and make me a vessel of honor so that I will minister life and not death to my hearers. This day, I record all these prayers into my prayer bank trusting that You, O Lord, will use it to break the yoke of pride and arrogance in me. It shall watch over my life and bring me to order when I would have wondered astray. Let me learn to say, "It's all about you, and not me," all the time. Guide me particularly at the time of success, and may I learn to give You all the glory. Holy Father, remind me that a man can receive nothing except it is given him from above. And may I acknowledge the giver more than the gift. In whatever position I may find myself tomorrow, help me to esteem others more than myself. Keep reminding me why Lucifer fell and let me walk with You in fear and humility. Thank You, Lord for Your love for me, this I pray in Jesus' mighty name. Amen.

Benediction: *Anyone who surrenders to the Lordship or our Lord Jesus Christ and prays this or similar prayers regularly and deposits same into his prayer bank shall never fall into the temptation of arrogance and pride, in Jesus' name. Amen.*

SPIRIT OF LIMITATION

This spirit works to undermine the gift and the call of God upon our lives and therefore makes us to limit the omnipotent God. This is the same spirit that made the ten spies to bring an evil report back to Moses when they were sent to spy the land.

And Moses sent them to spy out the land of Canaan, and said unto them, Get you up this way southward, and go up into the mountain: And see the land, what it is; and the people that dwelleth therein, whether they be strong or weak, few or many; And what the land is that they dwell in, whether it be good or bad; and what cities they be that they dwell in, whether in tents or in strongholds; And what the land is, whether it be fat or lean… So they went up, and searched the land from the Wilderness of Zin unto Rehob, as men come to Hamath... And they went and came to Moses, and to Aaron, and to all the congregation of the children of Israel, unto the wilderness of Paran, to Kadesh; and brought back word unto them and unto all the congregation, and showed them the fruit of the land. And they told him, and said, We came unto the land wither thou sentest us, and surely it floweth with milk and honey; and this is the fruit of it. Nevertheless the people are strong that dwell in the land, and the cities are walled, and very great: and moreover we saw the children of Anak there. The Amalekites dwell in the land of the south: the Hittites, and the Jebusites and Amorites dwell in the mountains: and the Canaanites dwell by the sea, and by the coast of Jordan. And Caleb stilled the people before Moses, and said, Let us go up at once, and possess it for we are well able to overcome it. But the men that went up with him said, We be not able to go up against the people; for they are stronger than we. And they brought up an evil report of the land which they had searched unto the children of Israel, saying, The land, through which we have gone to search it, is a land that eateth up the inhabitants thereof; and all the people that we saw in it are men of a great stature. And there we saw the giants, the sons of Anak, which come of the giants: and we were in our own sight as grasshoppers, and so we were in their sight.
Numbers 13: 17-33

And all the congregation lifted up their voice and cried; and the people wept that night. And all the children of Israel murmured against Moses and against Aaron: and the whole congregation said

unto them, Would God that we had died in the land of Egypt! Or would God we had died in this wilderness! And wherefore had the LORD brought us unto this land, to fall by the sword, that our wives and our children should be a prey? were it not better for us to return into Egypt? And they said one to another, Let us make a captain, and let us return into Egypt. Then Moses and Aaron fell on their faces before all the assembly of the congregation of the children of Israel... And the LORD said unto Moses, How long will these people provoke me? And how long will it be ere they believe Me, for all the signs which I have showed among them?
Numbers 14:1-11

Other Scriptures echo God's frustration with the Israelites for limiting Him.

How oft did they provoke Him in the wilderness, and grieve Him in the desert! Yea, they turned back and tempted God, and limited the Holy One of Israel.
Psalm 78:40-41

If anyone will limit God, then the person has concluded that God has lost His power and therefore His value. God was rightly angry with them and vowed that none of them would make it to the Promised Land.

Doubtless ye shall not come into the land, concerning which I sware to make you dwell therein, save Caleb the son of Jephunneh, and Joshua the son of Nun.
Numbers 14:30

This is what happens when people limit the power of the Almighty God. God is Omnipotent God, He created all things, He can do anything, and all power is in His hand. Therefore, there is no searching of His understanding, and no one can question His wisdom. He owns the cattle upon a thousand hills, and He determines the fate of the nations of the earth, it is therefore an abomination for anyone to question the power of the Almighty God.

The second part of this is that we try to limit the power of God in us. Moses did it by questioning God and allowing personal limitations: poor self-esteem and self-image, his inability to speak well, and his fear of what answer he might receive when asked about who the God that sent him really was. Gideon had a similar problem, moving from a position of an intercessor for a deliverer to recognizing that his family was the poorest in Manasseh and he the least in his father's house. He was asked to take up the responsibility of a deliverer that he was praying for. We love to stand on the sideline and clap when someone that we know runs for the gold, but will not venture to step into the tract ourselves. In all those limitations that we place upon ourselves, we have to realize that God does not seek for experts, He is seeking for availability. Once you make yourself available to Him, He is able to turn foolish things into mighty pillars.

Word Bank Sample

Psalm 46:1-5
Psalm 121:1-8
Revelations 12:13-16
Joshua 1:5-9
Isaiah 40:28-31

Prayer Bank Sample against Spirit of Limitation

Mighty Deliverer, King of kings and Lord of lords, let it be known this day that You are God that holds the whole universe with the Words of Your mouth. Arise and show Yourself strong because of Your name. You are the God of all flesh, is there anything too hard for You to do? Out of nothing You spoke and it was created, You commanded, and it was established. I know that I can do nothing of myself, but I can do all things through Christ who strengthens me. I therefore deposit this prayer into my prayer bank that I am strong through Him. I am not weak, I am a winner, and I am not a loser. You are everything to me, and I cannot limit or question Your power. Spirit of limitation, you have no hold on me, my God is all in all and I am fearfully and wonderfully created. I am a marvelous creature of God. It shall come to pass that whenever the fear of limitation and faithlessness comes near me, this prayer from my prayer bank shall rise up, fight and defeat it. And because I know my God, I am strong and can do exploit. I further make the following declaration that I am rich, I am healed, I am blessed beyond the curse, I am successful and I can stand in time of trial. I confess that I was made in His image and after His likeness, and therefore, I am who He is. I pray this prayer in the name that is above all names, Jesus Christ of Nazareth, Amen.

Benediction: One depositing prayer against limitation in his or her prayer bank shall never be weak nor see limitations in all his dealings in this world, Amen and Amen.

SPIRIT OF ANGER

The spirit of anger is associated with violence, confusion and murder. Anger is like an epidemic, when it gets hold of a man, it tears him apart and puts an end to his future progress. No sooner than Jacob settled in Shalem the city of Shechem in the land of Canaan that Shechem the son of Hamor forcefully slept with his only daughter, Dinah. Two of Jacob's children, Simeon and Levi displayed a serious spirit of anger by killing a whole city of Shechem after deceiving them to circumcise before marrying their sister.

And it came to pass on the third day, when they were sore, that two of the sons of Jacob, Simeon and Levi, Dinah's brethren, took each man his sword, and came upon the city boldly, and slew all the males.
Genesis 34:25

Jacob later disassociated himself from his children's anger and cursed their action.

Simeon and Levi are brethren; instruments of cruelty are in their habitations…for in their anger they slew a man, and in their self-will they digged down a wall. Cursed be their anger, for it was fierce…
Genesis 49:5-7

Strictly speaking, an angry man is a murderer. When the spirit of anger is on him, fifty years' investment could go up in flames in a second. Apostle Paul had this to say to the Ephesian church:

BE YE ANGRY, AND SIN NOT: let not the sun go down upon your wrath: Neither give place to the devil.
Ephesians 4:26-27

What this means is that there is no real man that has never been angry at one time or the other. But when you stretch anger beyond a certain time: allowing the sun to go down upon your anger, and allowing the devil the opportunity to use your anger and achieve his purpose, then your anger has turned to sin in the sight of God.

As a young boy, I used to know an elderly woman who lived near my father's house. She did not have any children and was angry at anything and everything children from other mothers did in the compound. Whenever an airplane passed in the sky, she would come out of her hut and pronounce curses. All the children were always making fun of her as she would curse at everything and everyone that dare cross her path.

DEATH OF A PREGNANT WOMAN

There was this man who told his wife that he was going to buy a big machete (a long sharp knife used in clearing bush for farming mostly in African countries). The wife answered: "My dear, when you buy it I will use it to cut meat." He turned to the wife and said, "Can you say that again?" The wife repeated what she said before, "I said when you buy the machete I will use it to cut some meat, especially the bones." To her greatest surprise, the last word, bones, that she said ended simultaneously with two blows that her husband directed at her mouth. Instantly she lost four teeth. The loss of teeth was repairable; he added a kick with his right leg that went straight to her lower abdomen. The woman, who was at the time a few months pregnant slumped, rolled over and began to bleed. It was not long before she was pronounced dead in a local hospital. The husband later died in prison awaiting trial. He had not bought the machete yet but he had already killed someone on account of it.

An angry man does not have real life pleasure; his spirit terrorizes him all the time. He is angry with everything and even with himself.

Today, many people who have been jailed for murder later realized in prison that what led them there was a simple thing and would have been resolved differently had they acted differently.

One has to pray fervently, depositing his prayers in his prayer bank against the spirit of anger.

Word bank Sample

Nehemiah 9:17
Psalm 4:4
Psalm 37:8
Proverb 15:1
Proverbs 16:32
Proverbs 22:24
Matthew 5:22
Ephesians 4:26
Titus 1:7

Prayer Bank Sample against Anger Spirit

Father, in the name of Jesus, thank You for sparing my life and giving me another opportunity to seek Your face. I confess all my sins before You and ask that You forgive them all. I resist, refuse and reject every invitation by the devil to live a life of violence and abomination. I am asking God through this prayer to control my temperament even when I am wronged or provoked. Your word is clear concerning anger; it says I can be angry without committing sin by not allowing the sun to go down on my anger. I also recognize that a prolonged anger can lead to murder, arson and all kind of evil. Help me Lord because I am blood and flesh and can easily be tempted to live in it. In the place of anger give me love, for love shall cover the multitude of sins. I declare that I shall not be angry with my wife, I shall not be angry with my children, and I shall not be angry with the government and with the authorities, and I shall not be angry with brothers and sisters in the church and with people around me. I deposit this prayer in my prayer bank before You and use it to fight against every spirit of anger that might attack me at any time. Thank You, Lord, for my answered prayer, in Jesus' name I pray. Amen.

***Benedictions**: Lord, fill your children's hearts with joy and drive away anger and let the prayer that is prayed in this book transform the hearts of the readers in Jesus' name, Amen.*

MONITORING SPIRIT

A monitoring spirit is a spirit sent by the enemy to track your movements and to entice and seduce you so as to ensure that you sin and fall. This spirit is particularly after God's ministers especially those involved in clubs and other social gatherings apart from the church. The bible says:

Abstain from all appearance of evil.
1 Thessalonians 5:22

One of the ways that Peter denied Jesus was when he had to warm himself by the devil's fire.

And Simon Peter stood and warmed himself. They said therefore unto him, Art not thou also one of His disciples? He denied it, and said, I am not.
John 18:25

Yes, whenever it is cold the devil has to make fire for you to go and warm yourself. This fire of affection and pleasure has made many to deny Him even in this day of civilization. This warmth may come in the form of a seductress, a warm soft body for your cold nights, a substance taken to keep you warm or a place where such comforts are paraded! One who takes shelter of them is liable to deny Jesus and fall! Better to take shelter of Jesus' ever warm and comforting Words.

A monitoring spirit is sent when the person monitored is projected and brought into the view of the person monitoring him through an object like a crystal ball or spiritual mirror, videoing or photographing process in order to ensure that the person being monitored falls from grace.

A monitoring spirit works with spell or charms or enchantment. Its major function is to trace you until you are in a wrong place; a place you suppose not to be, and he will seduce you to fall into a terrible sin - especially immorality. It is also the spirit that makes ministers fall by raping young girls and children.

The Bible uses the term, observe as in the case of David and Saul or spy as in the case of Elisha and the Syrians or Joshua and Jericho. When these people sent to monitor their opponents, they wanted to know the source of their strength, their military might, equipment and their supporters.

Spending 40 nights sleeping on the altar in our church while fasting, one night the Lord opened my eyes and I beheld a man making a video of me. He would move to different directions to try to get my face, but my face was down while I was kneeling in prayer. Again I saw a second man taking pictures of me. Then I began to cover myself with the blood of Jesus, sending bullets to destroy their equipment, and immediately I saw the video camera shatter in pieces. I did not stop there, I directed fire at their kingdom and their store houses in case there were other videos or photographs of me made which I did not know about.

These prayers are necessary. Those who do not understand what you do will question why you pray certain prayers. That is why you do not allow skeptics to come into your prayer closet.

Word Bank Sample

Numbers 13:1-2
Joshua 2:1
Joshua 7:2
Judges 1:24
Judges 18:2
2 Samuel 15:10
2 Kings 6:13
2 Kings 2:7

Prayer Bank Sample against Monitoring Spirit

Most merciful Father in heaven, thank You for Your security and protection over me. It is by Your grace that I am alive today. You, through Your wisdom and power, have defeated the devil and all his agents and have used the blood of Your dear Son as a shield upon my life. As I stand to deposit this prayer in my prayer bank before You, I bind satan and all his agents and also destroy all the monitoring equipment used to monitor my movements or lure me to fall. If those monitoring agents are human, I curse them to be blinded, if they are crystal balls, I command the thunder of God to strike and destroy them, if they be magical mirrors, I direct the bullets of God at them and pray that they be shattered. Whoever and whatever being used to monitor my life and movements, Lord, disfigure and completely dismantle them and wreak havoc severely anywhere they get their power from. Thank You, Lord for the victory I have today through Jesus Christ my Lord and Savior. Amen.

Benedictions: *Anyone who reads his Bible and takes the idea in this book and watches where he goes or what he does shall not be trapped, threatened or forced to deny Him. Amen.*

SPIRIT OF DRUGS, DRUNKENNESS, PROSTITUTION, LIES, STUBBORNNESS AND STEALING

This is one spirit that is involved in various activities operating through agents called demons. These demons are assigned roles to inflict and police their captives, making their hearts hardened through the stubbornness of their will power, so that they cannot be released. These captives are therefore thrown into various acts like stealing. They steal every valuable item in their path: gold, diamonds, rings, clothing, footwear, etc., and all the stolen items are sold at a price not commensurable with the worth of the items. This spirit hates loneliness but loves to operate through people with similar spirits, knitting them together and forming a gang mentality. Therefore people with this type of spirit need to be isolated; completely taken out of the operating areas to neutral areas where none of his or her friends or colleagues are available.

In selecting the word bank for prayers in relation to this difficult and stubborn spirit, one has to look at the lives of children or people who had a difficult beginning or time with things around them but stood up for themselves (or their parents stood up on their behalf) and God honored them, and they succeeded at the end. They include: Jabez, Jacob, Gideon, Joseph, David, Paul, Mary Magdalene, etc.

Word Bank Sample

1 Chronicles 4:9-10
Genesis 27:41
Genesis 37:4
Judges 6:15
1 Samuel 19:9-11
Luke 8:2

Prayer Bank Sample Against Spirit Of Drugs Drunkenness, Prostitution, Lies, Stubbornness And Stealing

Holy Father, thank You for loving me with an everlasting love and also drawing me unto You with Your loving kindness. If You, O Lord, were to count iniquity, no man would be saved, no, not one, but so that You may be justified when You speak that there is forgiveness in You, You have thoroughly washed me with the blood of Your Son, Jesus Christ and have cleansed me and made me whiter than snow. Now I can say with rejoicing in my heart, the Lord is for me, what can any man do unto me? Thank You for putting Your Spirit in me, which has helped drive away all the evil spirits that once held me captive. As I deposit my prayer in my prayer bank, I stand against the spirit of drugs, drunkenness, prostitution, lies, stubbornness and stealing. I also stand against all the spirit of oppression, self-pity, inferiority complex and the spirit of the past from haunting me. I declare myself more than a conqueror through our Lord and Savior Jesus Christ. Thank You Father for helping me and making me an overcomer, in Jesus' name I pray. Amen.

Benedictions: *Lord, may Your hands spread over and cover every soul particularly children of your chosen ones who labor in the Vineyard and save them unto Yourself. Amen.*

THE UNITED SPIRITS: (CONFEDERACY)

It is very important to talk about this spirit because it is one of those spirits that has weakened the church of Jesus Christ. Satan and his followers are more united than the keepers of the church of Jesus Christ. Let's take a few examples from the Bible:

And the whole earth was of one language, and of one speech. And it came to pass as they journeyed from the east, that they found a plain in the land of Shinar; and they dwelled there. And they said one to another, Go to, let us make brick, and burn them thoroughly. And they had brick for stone, and slime had they for mortar. And they said, Go to, let us build us a city and a tower whose top may

reach unto heaven; and let us make us a name, lest we be scattered abroad upon the face of the whole earth. And the LORD came down to see the city and the tower, which the children of men built. And the LORD said, Behold, the people are one, and they have all one language; and this they began to do: and now nothing will be restrained from them, which they have imagined to do.
Genesis 11:1-6

This clearly shows the power of evil union. God Himself acknowledged that nothing would be restrained from the power of evil people when they unite to fight God's people. It is this evil unity that satan and his disciples use to cause disunity in the church. And when there is disunity amongst churches, the power of Pentecost is threatened, it is almost irretrievably gone: the power of Pentecost came through unity in worship, but now the demonic spirits are more united in their attempt to stop the church's influence. Let us see what one demon said to Jesus:

And He asked him, What is thy name? And he answered, saying, My name is Legion: for we are many.
Mark 5:9

He is saying we carry a lot of power because we are united as one; and that is the reason one person possessed by many demons could beat up seven sons of Sceva, casting them down and wounding them, **Acts 19:14-16.**

And any attempt to evict them, if it is not backed up by strong follow-up spiritual warfare, fasting and dedicated prayer, it may open the door for demonic reinforcement which eventually could make the later end of the possessed person worse than the beginning, **Matthew 12:43-45.**

Therefore while the demons unite to cause disunity in the church, the church should take a stand and pray a prayer of unity for the Body of Christ and also send shelling to scatter the unity of the demons.

Word Bank Sample

Matthew 12:25
Acts 2:1
Acts 4:24-32
Ecclesiastes 4:9-12
Matthew 18:19

Prayer Bank Sample against United Spirits and Demons' Confederacy

Dear Father, dear Son, dear Holy Spirit, let it be known this day that the church of Jesus Christ has agreed to come together in one accord, one Spirit, one baptism, and one fellowship and communion to take a stand against the spirit of disunity in our midst. We drop the bomb of disunity into the kingdom of darkness; they have to be judged with thunder, with earthquake with great noise, with storm and tempest, and the flames of devouring fire. Lord, send Your lightning to strike and discomfit the gathering of all the demonic forces. As I deposit this prayer in my prayer bank, it shall come to pass that every day the ground will pull from under wherever the agents of satan shall plan to gather to fight against Your church. In the air, let the air be too hot for them to congregate. In the water, let the sea get to its boiling point and send them drowning. On land, let the earth begin to quake until they bow and worship the Living God in heaven. I also take a stand against demonic confederacy against me and my family. I resist them, I rebuke them and I bind and destroy all their activities; in the air, on the land and in the sea. I pray this prayer in the one and only name of Jesus Christ, my Lord and Savior. Amen.

Benediction*: Whosoever shall deposit his prayer in his prayer bank and believes the Word of the Lord and pray shall not be defeated by the united forces of his enemies, Amen.*

SPIRIT OF WASTE

The spirit of waste is a typical spirit that specializes in making you forget precious belongings and other valuable things. It is the same spirit that made the woman with the issue of blood, that we discussed earlier in the book, to waste all her resources but without solution.

How does it operate? One may purchase a new gadget, car, accessory, tool or implement and may not have used it for more than a couple of days when one loses it. You may try to comprehend how it happened and never come up with an answer. The spirit of waste will partner with the spirit of forgetfulness to hide it from you and will suggest wasteful alternatives. It may have been stolen by a thief! One might have carelessly dropped it somewhere and forgotten it there. One might have given it away without much thought as in making a bad loan or a bad trade. Without use of the original tool or accessory, one is forced to go back to the shop and again lay out funds for another one of exact or higher value. This is obviously wasting of God's resources. Money has been provided by the Lord for our upkeep and these funds must be managed properly. To the extent that we manage money and financial resources properly for the greatest good, to that extent does the Lord bless us to do the greatest good in our families, communities and the world.

At other times, it is God's natural resources that we waste. We perceive the earth's natural resources as abundant and limitless. These resources include water, land, and other resources such as wood, coal, and plants. If we happen to be in control of these resources we must use them judiciously and despite the appearance of their unlimited availability, we must use them understanding that they are given as resources for our well-being and not for our abuse and waste. The earth itself suffers if we collectively abuse its natural resources. Future generations would also suffer from our insensitivity to the limitations of our natural resources. The world and especially advanced countries are gradually waking up to this understanding. Hence the various green movements such as "Save the Rain Forest," "The Sierra Club," and others. But all of these movements can only be effective if in our private lives and individual homes we remember to turn off the water faucet when not in use, turn off the electricity when not at home. Turn down the thermostat when going away for the weekend.

I know of a pious man who used to brush his teeth every morning by plucking a twig from a local tree that stood in his yard. This is a practice common in most African countries. One morning he asked his son to go and break off a twig for his morning brush. His son went and actually cut down a whole branch of this tree and brought it to his father. The pious man sat his son down and asked him "Why did you unnecessarily *bother* this tree by removing the whole branch when I only have essential use for just a tiny twig? Son, we must be respectful of all of God's creation and we must only remove or take from nature the exact quantity we need and leave all else in God's creation to Him. Do not unnecessarily *bother* other living entities even if they are stationary unfeeling trees as they are all part of God's creation and are important in the larger scheme of things"

His son was very surprised at this lecture. The old man removed a twig from the branch and asked his son to go back and plant the rest of the branch in the yard so it may grow into another tree!

God does not waste resources. He does not even waste anointing. As a leader of a group or as a minister of God, if you know you will not be able to cater for one hundred souls, why ask Him for a thousand? Or if you know that you cannot manage ten thousand dollars responsibly, why ask Him to make you a millionaire? Jesus in the parable of the talent, speaking about the kingdom of God had this to say:

For the kingdom of God is as a man traveling into a far country, who called his own servants, and delivered unto them his goods. And unto one he gave five talents, to another one and another one; ***to every man according to his several ability;*** *and straightway took his journey.*
Matthew 25: 14-15

If God does not waste, then why do you waste? Today your umbrella is gone, you forgot it in the taxi, and tomorrow your phone is lost. Another day it is your car or house keys, and the next day it is your wallet. By the time you are through replacing them you will understand that you have wasted God's resources to do so. The spirit of waste keeps on attacking and taking things from us. Now is the time to corral him.

But we have to also understand that the spirit of unfaithfulness through our inability to pay our tithes and give the right offering can produce waste. In **Malachi 3:11,** the LORD promises to rebuke the spirit of waste or the devourer from devouring the fruits of our ground, our vines, our labor, money, material and spiritual resources and even stop miscarriages if we will bring all our tithes into the store house of the LORD to make food available in the house of the LORD. When we do not tithe at all, or tithe in the inappropriate amounts, the spirit of waste takes over. The devourer enters our life and takes over. Usually we find out that the amount we would have voluntarily given to God as a joyful tithe is much less than the amount we lose to the devouring spirit of waste. Sometimes we lose even more than we can imagine. We either give it to God lawfully and joyfully or the devourer will take it from us forcefully, shamefully and when we least expect it, and therefore painfully.

Word Bank Sample

Isaiah 49:17-19
Isaiah 58:12
Isaiah 61:4
1 Peter 4:11
1 Kings 17:14
2 Kings 4:6

Prayer Bank Sample against Spirit of Waste

Father God, thank You this day in the name of Jesus. Thank You for providing for me and my family all necessities of life. All glory to You also for the privilege for me to use Your blessings to thank You. I know that as my Father, You love me and it is Your desire for me to use Your blessing upon me and prosper there from. I bind the spirit of waste, I resist it and I rebuke it and I cast it out of my life and my household. As I record this prayer in my prayer bank, I stand against the loss of time, gold, diamond, jewels, property, money and anything You, Lord, have given me to use for Your glorification. I close every loophole and any indirect way the enemy would like to pass through to make me wasteful. I stop the waste from dependent relations: my spouse, children or any relatives. Thank You, Lord for helping me to stop this spirit from operating any further in my household, and thank You for the victory that I have today, this I pray in the name of Jesus Christ. Amen.

Benediction: *One who reads the scripture daily and believes it and practices its tenets shall be very efficient, never losing any valuables to the devourer. The whole import of tithing shall be theirs to understand. The benefit of tithing shall be theirs to claim. They shall be able to recover all material and spiritual things that the spirit of waste has caused them to lose in this lifetime in Jesus' name. Amen.*

SPIRIT OF SLEEP AND SLUMBER

This spirit causes weariness, slothfulness and weakness. When it attacks one becomes very heavy and lazy. It has contributed to a lot of people being fired from their jobs when caught sleeping on duty. It comes with the spirit of worries and anxiety, and attacks nerves and weakens them, then sends a message to the mind and makes one to conclude that all hope is lost through discouragement and dullness. It is called "the system wrecker." God at certain times had used the spirit of sleep and slumber to defeat mighty armies that fought against His people Israel. The spirit of sleep and slumber was brought upon those prophets who failed to wholly commit themselves to the truth of the Word of God. It contributes immensely to one's misery and poverty in life. One has to recognize it and deal with it directly.

Word Bank Sample

Isaiah 56:10
Exodus 14:24-25

Romans 11:8; 13:11
Ephesians 5:14
Matthew 13:25

Prayer Bank Sample against Spirit of Sleep and Slumber

Dear Father in heaven, thank You for Your love and kindness toward me. As I kneel before You, help me to pray like the Psalmist prayed: "Why art thou cast down, O my soul? And why art thou disquieted in me? Hope thou in God: for I shall yet praise Him for the help of His countenance," **Psalm 42:5.** I am rejoicing today because You have taken the spirit of sleep and slumber away from me and caused me to awake to my responsibilities. When my enemy will be cast down, Thou, O Lord will raise me up and I shall triumph over them all. I bind the spirit of sleep and slumber; I rebuke it and resist it. As I deposit this prayer in my prayer bank, I understand that you will use it to protect me against wreckage of nerves, worries and intimidation. Every spirit of heaviness, dullness, and weariness is rebuked, resisted and cast out. I shall be up and doing, no spirit of slothfulness, tiredness and laziness shall weigh me down. Thank You, Lord for my answered prayer, in Jesus' name I pray, Amen.

Benediction: *As many as will take prayer seriously and deposit same into his or her prayer bank regularly shall neither be slothful nor slumber in Jesus' name, Amen.*

SPIRIT OF COMPLACENCY

It is one thing to have dreams it is another thing to know what to make out of your dreams. Many people have at one time or another been talked to by God through dreams or visions or revelations. They categorize their dreams into two groups: good and bad dreams. The good dreams are when they dream someone blesses them with a bag containing a large amount of money, or they pass their exams, or move into a bigger home than the one they occupy. As soon as they wake up, they will congratulate themselves and quickly call on their friends and enemies alike to report the big blessing that is about to fall from heaven. But whenever they dream the so called "bad dreams" about accidents, death, fire, etc. they wake up and feel sad. Some dismiss it with a wave of their hands saying, 'God forbid, not me,' while many others do not do anything about it. Here is what the Bible says about dreams:

A dream cometh through the multitude of business…
Ecclesiastes 5:3

This means that most of the dreams that we term good are the results of the transactions, meditations, and the thoughts that have been going on in our hearts and minds. This does not mean that all good dreams are as a result of thinking, but the majority of them are. After all, I am where I am today because of the dreams that God gave me at various times.

But those dreams that are termed "bad" are actually good because we never thought about those events before we dreamed about them, therefore they are pure revelations. As soon as we wake up we have to begin to analyze every segment of those dreams, and deal with every aspect of them through prayer.

We are indifferent and cavalier towards our dreams and revelations from the Lord, but when those same dreams manifest themselves negatively we tend to complain and lay the blame on God for allowing them to happen. He had faithfully revealed the future to us and we failed to ask Him to help us deal with them or take them away, or we were just too spiritually insensitive to be able to acknowledge the dreams.

THE CHIEF BAKER

This was the same spirit that led to the execution of the Chief Baker, Joseph's prison roommate. Though it was revealed to him three days before his execution what might happen to him, his weakness and failure to deal with it led to the fulfillment of the dream.

When the chief baker saw that the interpretation was good, he said unto Joseph, I also was in my dream, and behold, I had three white

baskets on my head. And in the uppermost basket there was of all manner of baked meat for Pharaoh; and the birds did eat them out of the basket upon my head. And Joseph answered and said, this is the interpretation thereof: the three baskets are three days: Yet within three days shall Pharaoh lift up thy head from off thee, and shall hang thee on a tree; and the birds shall eat thy flesh from off thee. And it came to pass the third day, which was Pharaoh's birthday that he made a feast unto all his servants: and he lifted up the head of the chief butler and of the chief baker among his servants. And he restored the chief butler unto his butlership again; and he gave the cup into Pharaoh's hand: But he hanged the chief baker: as Joseph had interpreted to them.
Genesis 40:16-22

Before I proceed to talk about the spirit that was behind this man's execution and the mistakes that he made, I have to first of all talk about the activities of birds in the Bible.

Birds as a sign of the Holy Spirit: The dove has been used as a symbol of the Holy Spirit that descended upon Jesus after His baptism.

And Jesus, when He was baptized, went up straightway out of the water: and lo, the heavens were opened unto Him, and He saw the Spirit of God descending like a dove, and lighting upon him.
Matthew 3:16

Birds as messengers: The raven and the dove also acted as messengers to Noah during the flood.

And he sent forth a raven, which went forth to and fro, until the waters were dried up from off the earth. Also he sent forth a dove from him, to see if the waters were abated from off the face of the ground.
Genesis 8:7-8

Birds as providers: As soon as Elijah prophesied the shutting of heaven in the days of Ahab, King of Israel, God used the raven to provide food for him by the brook Cherith.

Get thee hence, and turn thee eastward, and hide thyself by the brook Cherith that is before Jordan. And it shall be, that thou shalt drink of the brook; and I have commanded the ravens to feed thee there.
1 Kings 17:3-4

Moreover, eagles have been depicted as symbols of strength, and turtle doves have also been used for making sacrifices unto the Lord. Birds shall also play a part in the last day judgment of God in the eating of the carcasses of those slain through wars upon the earth.

In the contrary, there are also evil birds used by the devil to eat up our seeds, or monitor our movements and words or eat up our sacrifices unto God or devour our lives. Whenever we dream about these evil birds carrying out these activities, we should not give the least chance for these dreams to materialize.

And when he sowed, some seeds fell by the way side, and the fowls came and devoured them up. When any one heareth the word of the kingdom, and understandeth it not, then cometh the wicked one, and catcheth away that which was sown in his heart. This is he which received seed by the way side.
Matthew 13:4, 19

These seed-eating birds are sent by our enemies to eat up the words of God sown in our hearts so that we do not have the opportunity of understanding them at all so as to be converted and healed. These seed eaters have to be resisted, rejected and driven away through the depository of our prayers in our prayer bank.

Abraham and the Sacrifice-eaten Birds:

And he took unto him all these, and divided them in the midst, and laid each piece one against another: but the birds divided him not.

And when the fowls came down upon the carcasses, Abram drove them away.
Genesis 15:10-11

Abram was making a sacrifice unto the LORD, but the birds (fowls) came down to eat up the sacrifice which was to be set on fire, Abram drove them away. When we allow evil birds to eat up our sacrifices, it shows that God has not received such sacrifices.

Curse not the king, no not in thy thought; and curse not the rich in thy bedchamber: for a bird of the air shall carry the voice, and that which had wings, shall tell the matter.
Ecclesiastes 10:20

The birds being talked about in the above passage are what I will call, "monitoring birds." They build their spiritual nest right there on the roof of our house and we allow them even in our bed chambers. As long as we allow them by not evicting them daily with our prayers, they record all our private discussions and even those that we think are too private to be shared with friends. But as soon as we have uttered a word inside our inner chamber, it gets out and is leaked to the public. These monitoring birds should not be allowed to nest around us.

I will now demonstrate how the spirit of complacency played a major part in the death of the Chief Baker, Joseph's prison roommate. Whatever he did that prompted his being thrown into prison is not important here. But his attitude towards his recovery poses a great concern as there are many people in our generation who do not care about the door of opportunity or freedom that God opens for them. This man made three major mistakes:

1. His number one error was that, out of the three baskets that he carried on his head in the dream, the third one-the uppermost basket that contained all manner of bake meats for Pharaoh was uncovered. In the natural, it is unfathomable to see food meant for a king uncovered. And that gave room for the flesh-eating birds to eat it out of his head. Looking much deeper into this man, he never had a spiritual

covering; someone over his life for nurturing and counseling or for intercession.

2. His second error was that he never made any effort to drive away those birds that ate out of the baskets on his head. One cannot imagine how weak or sluggish this man was that the king's food in a basket on his head was eaten by birds and he never made any effort to send the birds away. Abram refused to allow those covenant-destroying birds to eat his "covenant sacrifice" unto the Lord; he took charge and drove them away.

3. Finally, the Chief Baker did not plead with Joseph to help pray to see if God would spare his life, nor did he make any attempt to seek help for himself though he had three days before his dream would materialize. Silence is a mark of acceptance. As long as we take the revelations that God gives us for granted, we will always pay dearly for it. He became complacent and careless. It is a lesson for us today to wake up and take control of events in the spirit world before they manifest in the natural. Every negative dream that we have should be canceled as soon as we wake up, and every positive dream should be confirmed and claimed. No dream, negative or positive should be left untouched.

Word Bank Sample

Joel 3:10
Isaiah 60:1
1Timothy 6:12
11 Corinthians 10:3-6
Romans 8:37
Isaiah 54:17
Galatians 2:20

Prayer Bank Sample against Spirit of Complacency

Father, in the name of Jesus, I stand this day to deposit my prayer into my prayer bank against evil birds that my enemies might send after me. I bind and destroy the power of all the seed- devouring birds. I bind and blind the eyes of all the monitoring birds sent after me. I bind and resist the power of all the birds sent to eat up the sacrifices that I offer unto the Lord. I put my selected stones in my catapult and use them against all the birds that eat up my anointing and my calling off my head; all the flesh-eating birds are destroyed. I begin to rise and shine because my light has come and the glory of the Lord is risen upon me. This prayer in my prayer bank shall expose every hidden nest built by monitoring birds in my roof and the equipment used by evil birds to record my conversations. I use every spiritual trap available to me to catch evil birds and destroy them as I also pray the favor of God upon my soul. I decree that no weapon formed against me shall prosper. I pray that in the place of ignorance, knowledge shall be found, in the place of weakness, strength shall be found. Lord, help me understand the dreams You show me and whatever I bind shall remain bound, those that I allow shall be allowed, this I pray in Jesus' name. Amen.

Benedictions: *Anyone who reads his Bible and is awake in his spirit shall never lose sight of God's vision and shall not die prematurely. Amen.*

SPIRIT THAT HELPS OUR INFIRMITIES

Just as satan has a collection of spirits working together to help each other accomplish his mission, God by His Spirit assigns various ministry gifts to His elect. The Spirit of the Lord God is one and operates as one and not a multiplicity of spirits like those of satan. The Spirit mentioned above is usually sent by God to help His elect or His anointed in their prayer lives and also to overcome stress, pressure, temptation, trial and discouragement. When we stand to pray, we do not know exactly how to pray and what to pray for, but this Spirit of God helps us by making intercession for us with groaning. He searches the hearts and intentions of our associates and also supports our battle against sin. He helps us go through the test that we need to go through without compromising and quitting. This is the Spirit that helped Abraham become the father of faith when he was tested to sacrifice his son, Isaac. He has also helped me too.

And it came to pass after this thing, that God did tempt Abraham, and said unto him, Abraham: and he said, behold, here I am. And He said, Take now thy son, thine only son Isaac whom thou lovest, and get thee into the land of Moriah; and offer him there for a burn offering upon one of the mountains which I will tell thee of. Then Isaac spake unto Abraham his father, and said, My father: and he said, Here am I, my son. And he said, Behold the fire and the wood: but where is the lamb for a burnt offering? And Abraham said, My son, God will provide Himself a lamb for a burnt offering: so they went both of them together.
Genesis 22:1-2, 7-8

This was a serious and great test by all means. Despite the fact that Abraham loved God, and was willing to do everything God asked him to do, let us not forget that he was also human. Such a test could sink any man devoid of the spirit of courage, firmness and faith. God did not surreptitiously whisper in Abraham's ear, "I'm just joking with you, I don't really mean what I'm saying." Yet Abraham, having known that this might be the end of his beloved son, Isaac, allowed the spirit of faith to play out. By answering Isaac that God would provide Himself a lamb for a burnt offering, he spoke the faith that was in him into existence and it happened as he had spoken. He later came to be known as: the father of faith, because there was a spirit that stood up for him during his time of trial.

THE SPIRIT OF THE LORD HELPED ME

In the late 1980s, I brought my mother to the city to help my wife and I care for our newborn baby. She came and spent a year with us and was of great help to us. I was a member of a very strong, faithful and dedicated prayer team that was willing to sacrifice everything to liberate those sold into witchcraft and held captive by the powers of darkness. Our leader had announced a seven day fast to wait upon the Lord for a crusade that was to take place and other things that we had planned to do. As usual, she charged everyone to examine him or herself before embarking on the fast, as no one would be allowed to visit his or her home and come back to rejoin the group until seven days were completed.

I was very excited about the fast. I did the necessary preparations and was set to depart to the prayer center. Suddenly two hours before my departure, a voice spoke to me and questioned me in this manner: "Should anything happen to your mother after your departure would you come back home before the completion of the fast?" I knew the rule and was prepared to follow it to the end. A struggle ensued within me trying to know from whence the voice came, and then I began to pray. But the more I prayed the stronger the message registered in my heart. I openly exclaimed: "Lord, I am only obedient to Your word, I am going to do Your will. If my mother is called home by You when I depart, I will finish this program, then come back and bury her. As soon as I finished speaking there was quietness; peace returned and I was again bent on going. Then came 5.00 p.m. that Sunday evening, a time to say goodbye to everyone: my mother, my wife, and my one-year old. We held our hands and I prayed for them and my wife escorted me a little further while my mother held the baby.

The prayer team members all arrived at the prayer camp and at 6.00 p. m. the door was shut. No one was allowed to leave except if the leader of the group sent one out on an errand.

Not quite two hours after we started to worship, we heard a knock on the door. Our leader went to see who was knocking, behold it was a family member of mine who had received the address of where we were camping from my wife and took a taxi to come and inform me that my mother was dying and that I was badly needed at home. I stood still and recollected what I told the Lord before I left my home. I told my guest to go and help my wife any way he could, but that if it pleased God to take her home, he should make arrangements to take the corpse to the mortuary until I had completed my prayer program. Our leader held her peace; looked straight to my face as I called people back to prayer and exclaimed, "Mmh!"

She saw in me faith, firmness, courage and determination. The Spirit of the Lord was heavy upon me and I was neither shaken nor doubtful. She stopped the prayer, sent two ladies- members of our team to go with my visitor and bring my mother. "Dead or alive, bring her," she said. By the time these ladies arrived at my house, the compound was swarming with people. My mother already smelled like a corpse. She was down with cholera: throwing up from the mouth and excreting all at the same time. They chartered a minivan, removed the seats and brought her straight to the prayer camp on her death bed.

By the time she was carried into our prayer room, she appeared to be gone. The warriors quickly surrounded her as we began to bombard heaven. I spoke into her ears but she could not hear me, as she could move neither legs nor hands. Our leader commanded that we stop praying and begin to praise. As we praised and clapped continuously for thirty minutes, we began to feel a movement in her body, her feet and arms became warm again. We continued to praise, clap and sing for another fifteen minutes, she opened her eyes and saw me and closed them back again. We continued to praise and sing for another fifteen minutes, then she opened her mouth and called my name and held my hand and requested for water. Then we loosened the grip of the spirit of death and called down the spirit of life upon her. We now mixed the praise songs with prayer, beginning to bind and to loose: bind the spirit of death and loose the spirit of life.

Not very long from then, her countenance began to emerge from the grasp of death to the embrace of life, hallelujah! One hour later, she was talking, singing with us and telling us what she had seen in her short trip beyond: she saw heaven and angels singing, she saw beautiful gardens, she also saw a man who told her to go back and showed her the way out. My mother actually lived ten more years after this episode described in this book before she finally went to be with the Lord.

The Spirit of faith, firmness, power and courage is seriously desired by anyone who wants to succeed in ministry. Our spiritual leader asked all the warriors to surround me and pray for me for such faith, courage, firmness and power. But I confessed that His Spirit helped my infirmities because I cannot even imagine how I did it. If we do not deposit prayers in our prayer banks asking the Spirit of God to help our infirmities, we should also be prepared to fall as soon as temptation comes and spoil the testimony of Jesus Christ in our mouth.

This is what God said to Abraham through His angel at the end of the test:

And the angel of the LORD called unto Abraham a second time, And said, By myself have sworn, said the LORD, for because thou hast done this thing, and hast not withheld thy son, thy only son: That in blessing, I will bless thee, and in multiplying I will multiply thy seed as the stars of the heaven, and as the sand which is upon the sea shore; and thy seed shall possess the gates of their enemies.
Genesis 22:15-17

It takes the Spirit of God that helps our infirmities for us to be secured in faith, boldness, firmness, understanding, wisdom, power, and courage; for a child of God to attain his goal in ministry. In addition, when we are obedient to this Spirit as He leads us through the process of forgiveness, God can take His rightful place in our hearts. The spirit of power, the spirit of love and the spirit of a sound mind will manifest with the fruit thereof. Then our true ministry would have just begun. I have not seen anyone operating a ministry involving deliverance and compassion without the spirit that helps our infirmity being fully involved.

Word Bank Sample

Roman 8:26
Hebrews 11:6
2 Timothy 1:7
Joshua 1:6-7
Psalm 37:3-7
1 Corinthians 4:20

Prayer Bank Sample for Spirit that Helps our Infirmities

My Almighty Father in heaven, I give You praise and honor for who You are. You have shown me the way of life; in Your presence is fullness of joy, and at Your right hand are pleasures forever more. Lord it is always a good thing when I proclaim that I love You, but whenever my love for You is tested, I tend to fumble and compromise. Lord, since our father Abraham's love and faith were tested and he did not waiver, that is the reason I deposit my prayer in my prayer bank today against that day that my love for You and faith in You will be tested. Lord, on that day may Your Spirit also help my infirmities, so that even if I do not know what to pray as I ought to pray, let Your Spirit make intercession for me with groaning which cannot be uttered. Let this Spirit search all hearts and reveal every plan of the enemy concerning my family and me. I use this prayer point to fight against all contrary spirits that satan might release against us. Such spirits as: discouragement, fear, feebleness, intimidation, death, sickness and many other spirits as may be unleashed against me by my adversaries shall be defeated. I declare victory through my Lord and Savior Jesus Christ, Amen.

Benediction: *Whoever willingly releases themselves to this Spirit shall receive help for their infirmities and shall be strong, bold, courageous, powerful and full of faith. Amen.*

A SPIRITUAL APPROACH PRODUCES A QUICKER AND A BETTER SOLUTION

Certain spirits such as the spirit of confusion can affect so much of the peace of a family or organization. When a gossiping spirit is upon a person or group it does not spare anything, but makes the family or organization's secrets and plans known to its enemies. Mary Magdalene had seven demons (evil spirits) in her before meeting with Jesus, **Luke 8:2.** But Mary Magdalene's contact with Jesus produced an everlasting transformation and brought her into the fold of recognized personalities in the Bible.

Paul the Apostle writing to his son Timothy, said, "For God hath not given us the spirit of fear; but (the spirit) of power, and (the spirit) of love, and (the spirit) of a sound mind," **2 Timothy 1:7.** Even though some people might think that these are emotional spirits, they are also controlled by higher spirits. Every emotion is controlled by a spirit.

"Now the Spirit (of God) speaketh expressly, that in the later times some shall depart from the faith, giving heed to *seducing spirits*, and doctrines of devils," **1 Timothy 4:1**. Seducing spirits are a combination of lying spirits and the spirit of hypocrisy. The devil uses these spirits to deceive their captives. These are the "do as I say, and not as I do" type of spirits. They deceive people to sow or give into things that are unrelated with the work of God. Many pastors use what is known as "charismatic witchcraft spirit" to deceive and retain their captives. These captors do not waste time to pronounce curses upon members of their congregations if they think they have offended them.

Some children are possessed with the spirit of waywardness which turns them into prodigal children. Closely associated with this spirit is the spirit of stubbornness and pride. Many are afflicted by the spirit of confusion which makes one not to arrive at any major decision timely. The spirit of indecency makes one to appear dirty and dress like a mad man or woman in the street. It is closely linked to criminality and waywardness. The spirit of worries makes one to lose faith in God. It sends anxiety and trembling to the hearts and minds of its captives and makes them overlook what God's Word says in every situation.

Spiritual problems, no matter how you perceive them, require spiritual solutions. If a man is possessed with the spirit of laziness, it is by casting out that spirit and encouraging or helping him to return to active life that will stamp out the sloth in him. To be effective at this, pastors must accomplish this with a great deal of compassion and love. Most of these spirits are contracted through evil associations and relationships. While we plan to dump our loved ones in psychiatric wards and surrender them to evil spirits to claim their lives forever and make perpetual habitation of their minds, let us first give the Lord, the creator of heaven and earth, the opportunity to deal with the spirits that afflict them. Let us render love to them by bringing them to their Creator for deliverance while we help to rehabilitate them. In due time, their lives shall be completely restored. It is even better to guard our young ones and bring them under the umbrella of God and the Holy Spirit than leave them to the wimps and caprices of the devil; bringing them to the Lord only after they have been afflicted.

In conclusion, anyone that is sick, oppressed or in a difficult situation should first identify what spirit is in charge of that situation or sickness or oppression and bind it or evict it by casting it out. One should resist all possessions using the Holy Spirit and its revealed solutions. It is very necessary to prayerfully seek counsel and help from men and women of God who are knowledgeable in spiritual matters. Do not settle with the belief that poverty is a sign from God to test your faith. Fight against the spirit of poverty, defeat it and send it away from you. Never accept any notion that a particular sickness or condition is from God as a test of your faith; you are being deceived by the devil. Fight against the spirit that brings the sickness and the sickness itself (spiritual and topical approaches), and defeat it and get healing in the name of Jesus and through the blood of Jesus. Remember, you were created in the image and the likeness of God. Do not accept to be what He is not. There is power in what you believe and confess. Do not believe lies and confess negative things as these will bring you into perpetual bondage. But knowing the truth and confessing same shall surely make you free.

CHAPTER 5

MANAGING CRISIS – TOPICAL APPROACH

Now that we have taken a look at managing the spirits that are responsible for most of our everyday problems, let us look at the topical approach. For without containing the spirits, no earthly solution shall ever be effective. And without handling topical issues in our lives, they will linger on, persist and take us unawares.

As soon as you begin to tackle those spirits that give birth to crisis and empower them, you can also organize your prayer bank topically to deal with issues that are close to heart. Those topics that you are going to work on still have spirits that control them; some of them fall under those spirits we have already discussed. But dealing with a crisis spiritually and topically helps you leave no stone unturned. It helps you uproot the foundation of a crisis and also to destroy the structure.

What are some of the future life events that you think might happen that you do not have complete control over? Try as much as possible to identify and connect with a life event listed in this book. Utilize the essential verses provided and regularly deposit your devotion through the sample prayers and you will see the power of our God in action. After regularly depositing these inspired prayers in your prayer bank you will come to agree that God is not a man, that He should lie, neither will He go back on His promises.

MARRIAGE

A young believer just beginning his or her journey in the Lord should bear in mind that one day he or she is going to want to settle down with a wife or husband. One has to start to fertilize the ground by selecting one's essential marriage words to be used in opening one's prayer bank to ensure that the account comes in handy in times of marital crises.

Word Bank Sample

Genesis 2:18
Proverbs 18:22
Psalm 128:3
Proverbs 31:12-23
Matthew 19:5-6
James 1:17

Prayer Bank Sample for a Right Partner

Lord, may I not be married and still remain lonely. Give me a spouse that will quench my taste of loneliness. Let the partner You, O Lord, give me help me to meet the needs of my ministry and comfort at home. My partner should be a good thing that brings favor from the Lord. A witch or wizard must not cross my path as a potential partner. Even if I am being manipulated or hoodwinked, may I never marry a witch. My spouse should be like a fruitful vine planted by the side of the house. My partner will do me good and not evil all the days that we are together. My voice shall be heard in the street because of my partner and as You, Lord, will be the one who joins us together, nobody shall put us asunder, in Jesus' name I pray. Amen. Use this prayer that I deposit into my prayer bank daily and the overflowing devotion to help us in our marriage. If the enemy shows up to test our relationship and faith in You, if any of us starts acting contrary to Your word or expectations, let our account be visited and grant us victory through Jesus Christ our Lord and Savior. Lord, I am putting Your Word back to You, and because You hate "putting away". We shall live together and prosper. I pray and ask in the name of Jesus. Amen.

This is not only for a young unmarried believer, but also for married couples with children. There may be some elements of rebellion in your spouse or children's lives. You have to continue to seek the Lord and deposit prayers in your marriage bank until there is peace, unity, cooperation, and support for each other in your marriage. Why are there so many divorces today in the church? It is because there are no prayers in the bank concerning one's spouse. Children may be on drugs through questionable associations in their schools, work and place of business. Word bank and prayer bank are some of the effective solutions we can employ to solve these problems. Credit your prayer bank and call God to remembrance.

CHILD DELIVERY

Word Bank Sample

Genesis 35:16-18
Exodus 1:19
Psalm 127:3
Psalm 127:5

Prayer Bank Sample for Child Delivery

Dear Lord the covenant keeper, it is written in Your holy Word that children arc an heritage of the Lord. I therefore share in Your inheritance with abundance of children and claim them as a reward for my marriage. Lord, let my quiver be full with God-fearing children. Lord, in the day that my child will be born, there shall not be any complications or difficulty because of Your covenant with me. It shall even be like Hebrews' women in Egypt since we are children of Abraham by faith. There shall not be any hemorrhage after delivery. The placenta shall not be delayed after the birth but will be delivered as soon as the baby is born. There shall be great joy at our child delivery. As I open this bank to record this prayer, let it also be recorded in Your book that such an account is kept before You, Lord. The Bible says that the expectation of the righteous shall be granted him. Since through Christ Jesus I am counted righteous, this prayer is my expectation concerning my child delivery. I am certain that my petition has been granted through Jesus Christ my Lord and Savior. Amen.

FAVOR

Word Bank Sample

Genesis 39:21
1 Samuel 2:26
Psalm 30:5
Proverbs 14:9
Daniel 1:9
Luke 1:30
Luke 2:52
Isaiah 60:10

Prayer Bank Sample for Favor

Lord God my Maker, I am asking You to grant me favor in life. Your Word says that by strength shall no man prevail, it therefore takes favor for doors of opportunity to open for man. I recognize that nothing is accidental in Your sight, but that which You have determined in Your heart before the world began. You gave Joseph favor in Egypt, Daniel favor in Babylon, Ruth favor with Boaz, may Your favor not depart from me. May I find favor with God and with man all my entire life. Mary, the mother of my Lord Jesus Christ may not have been the only virgin in her time, but she found favor in Your sight and was elected to be the mother of the Son of God. I know that through Jesus Christ my Lord and Savior, I am elected and granted special favor to succeed and do exploit in life. May I find favor in education, sports, marriage, children, business and other aspects of human endeavor. This I ask knowing that I have the answer, in Jesus' name. Amen.

BLESSING

Word Bank Sample

Genesis 1:28,
Genesis 22:17
Deuteronomy 28:1-6
2 Samuel 6:11
Numbers 23:20
Job 42:10

Prayer Bank Sample for Blessing

Father, I do know that You created me in Your image and after Your likeness and You blessed me from the beginning to be fruitful, multiply, replenish the earth, subdue it and to have dominion over all other creature of Yours. Dear Father, that is who I am; I am blessed beyond the curse, with long life and prosperity will You satisfy me and bless all that belongs to me. It shall come to pass that after You have blessed me that the devil will come to try me so that I will not remember to thank You. He may also try to make me not to respond to You with my tithes and offering and may blind me to forget the poor in the society. I am asking that with the blessing You bless me, You will also take control of my heart, my soul and my mind so that I will love You with all my heart, soul and mind, and my neighbors as I love myself. Since You are a covenant keeper and there is no unrighteousness in You, I have assurance that Your blessing will make me rich and You will add no sorrows with it. Thank You in advance for answering this prayer, in Jesus' mighty name I pray. Amen.

CHILDREN IN SCHOOL, SPORTS AND THE MILITARY

Word Bank Sample

1 Samuel 10:23
Job 42:15
1 Samuel 14:1
Isaiah 8:18

Prayer Bank Sample for Children in School, Sports and the Military

Father, in the name of Jesus, the children that You give me shall be outstanding in every field of human endeavor. You blessed Abraham with Isaac and he grew up to continue in the covenant that You made with his father. You blessed Isaac and chose Jacob his son to further the covenant You made with his grandfather and his father. I therefore desire that my children are chosen to further the covenant You made with me. You blessed Jacob (Israel) with twelve sons who have become a force to reckon with world without end. Since I have become the seed of Abraham by faith, I claim all the promises of God that the generation of the righteous shall not have an end. I also claim all spiritual blessings in heavenly places to be mine and my children's and children's children for ever and ever. In sports they will be outstanding. In the military they will fight mighty wars and return home alive. And since my children are for signs and for wonders, they represent God's purpose in life and their names represent God's plans for my household. None of them shall be cut off in the midst of their years. They shall be free to choose any profession of their choice, but all shall minister before the Lord. The pilots among them shall retire at old age and lecture other pilots. The soldiers shall retire at old age and train other soldiers, and so shall it be with those in other professions. Thank You, Lord because none of my children shall be wayward. I record this special request in my prayer bank before You trusting that You will honor me according to Your words for me, in the name of Jesus I pray. Amen.

JOBS/WORK

Word Bank Sample

Genesis 26:2-3
Matthew 20:1-2
Matthew 21:28
John 5:17
1 Thess. 4:11
2 Thess. 3:10

Prayer Bank Sample for Jobs/Work

Dear heavenly Father, Your Word says that anyone who does not want to work should not eat. I am willing to work to be able to support my family and the works of Your house. In the name of Jesus, I reject the spirit of joblessness. There may be a time when there would be scarcity of jobs in the land, the ground may likely be dry, but when I step out, may jobs readily find me. May I step my feet on fertile ground and may I reap a hundred fold in the midst of famine. I shall not at any time suffer unemployment. Employers may not hire, but I shall be hired in a well-paying job. This prayer is stored up in my prayer bank against the season of economic depression in our land. My vow therefore is that as long as the Lord will provide me with a job, I will not fail to pay my tithes with thanksgiving unto the Lord. Thank You, Father, for honoring my prayer concerning this matter, in Jesus' name I pray. Amen.

COURAGE

Word Bank Sample

Numbers 13:20
Deuteronomy 31:6-7
Joshua 1:6-9
1 Samuel 30:6
1 Samuel 14:6

Ezra 10:4
Psalm 27:14

Prayer Bank Sample for Courage

LORD God Almighty, mighty in battle, the Rock of my salvation, thank You for all Your protection. I am asking You specifically for courage in the time of trial and temptation. I need courage, wisdom and power to take the gospel of our Lord Jesus Christ to the unreached. I need courage to fight and defeat all my enemies and remain steadfast in the midst of adversity. I need courage when I am faced with hostility even among Christians who will try to pervert the gospel of Jesus Christ for their selfish gain. Thank You for helping me to continue to deposit this prayer in my bank before You. Use it, Lord, at the appointed time to grant me the courage I need for daily victories. I need courage to be able to rebuke, reproof, instruct, encourage and correct with long suffering and perseverance. I need courage to lead God's people to the "Promised Land" which is Your eternal dwelling place. Let Your Spirit drive away fear out of my sight. Cover me with Your dread as with Your people Israel in the wilderness, so that no man with evil intent will be able to stand before me. I end this prayer by thanking You, Lord, for answering my prayer and giving me courage and boldness to take the race to an end in Jesus' name. Amen.

PROMOTION

Word Bank Sample

Genesis 45:8
Deuteronomy 28:13
Psalm 75:6
Proverbs 4:8
Proverbs 14:34
Proverbs 18:16
Proverbs 22:29

Daniel 3:30
Matthew 23:12

Prayer Bank Sample for Promotion

My Lord and my God, thank You for letting me know You. I did not choose You, Lord, but You chose me that I should go and bring forth fruits, and not just fruits, but fruits that will remain. I also recognize that promotion does not come from north, south east or west, but from You. I believe Your Word that I will be the head and not the tail. I know that You have the power to catapult me to a height of honored men in Your sight. I recognize that there are also pride and other devices that come with promotion, but I trust that while You move me from glory to glory You will also take control of my spirit so that pride and arrogance will not creep in. Let Your gifts in me make a way for me and also bring me before great men. I desire that You promote me to be able to defend the gospel openly. I know that a man of low status cannot speak in the open, but with the promotion that You will promote me I also shall speak openly concerning things that pertain to Your kingdom. My financial promotion will help sponsor missionaries and open doors of ministries in all the countries of the world. My spiritual promotion shall set the captives free and bring the doubters on their knees before Your throne. Thank You because with Your Word in my mouth, I shall be diligent to bring sinners to repentance. Thank You, Lord, for your preservation in elevation, in Jesus' name I pray. Amen.

RECOGNITION

Word Bank Sample

Ruth 2:5-6
Esther 6:1-10
Proverbs 18:16
Proverbs 22:29
Acts 10:4

Prayer Bank Sample for Recognition

Faithful Father, may all my labor for You not be in vain. Let a day come that You will look into Your record and remember me and also cause men to recognize me. As You search in Your record, let it be discovered one good thing that I have done in Your sight and use it, Lord, to open the doors of blessings for me. I know that we are not saved by works, but let my faith in You produce good works which will further bring more people into Your kingdom. My Father, my Lord and my God, I am asking You to reject the accusation of the accuser who will try to accuse my wrong doing before You. Before he tries to accuse me before You, let me first remind You why he lost his position and left Your throne. He was made perfect and covered with all precious stones. He had a better position than I have now but lost it because of pride. He instigated rebellion against You, Lord, and also plotted to overthrow You. He boasted much about himself and was full of pride. He therefore lost his heavenly abode for me and was cast into this dark pit. Daddy, You know that he is a liar and the father of all liars, therefore whatever accusations he brings before You against me is a lie. I present the blood of Jesus as my defense, and I overcome him by the blood of the Lamb and by the word of my testimony. I pray that You reject his accusations and recognize my labor of love in Your vineyard. Thank You Lord because at the end I will be with You to inherit the position that he lost while he and his angels will forever have their place in hell. Again, since we are not justified by works but by faith in Your only Son, Jesus Christ, let my faith in Him bring me to the position of recognition before You and man. Thank You, Lord, for lifting me above all my equals, in Jesus' mighty name I pray. Amen.

PEACE

Word Bank Sample

Numbers 25:12
Psalm 29:11
2 Peter 3:14

John 14:27
John 16:33
Hebrews 12:14

Prayer Bank Sample for Peace

My Lord and my God, I have often asked, if there could be peace in a troubled world. But Your answer to me has always been in the affirmative. Daddy, Your Word has shown me that I first need to have peace with God before I can have the peace of God. Now, O Lord, help me to have peace with You through Jesus Christ my Lord and Savior. May I receive Him into my heart, may I daily seek His face, may I receive assurance of forgiveness through the confession of my sins. May I worship the Father daily in the name of the Son and in the power of the Holy Spirit, Amen. And now, O Lord, may the peace of God that passes all understanding be with my spirit, soul and body. May I not be afraid of sudden fear. Let Your peace live within me, go with me and stay with me. Thank You, Lord, because You know that there can never be any progress without peace. I am confident that there shall be peace in my marriage, with my children, with my neighbors and at work and in my ministry. My prayer bank concerning peace shall never be empty and I will never lack peace in my lifetime. When there shall be news of impending earthquakes, tornado, tsunami or any form of danger, may Your Word whisper a word of peace into my heart, "son, it is well with your soul." Thank You for answering my prayer and giving me sustainable peace, in Jesus' name I pray, Amen.

GIFT OF FAITH

Word bank sample

Genesis 15:6
Genesis 22:8
Joshua 14:12
1 Samuel 17:37
Job 19:25

Daniel 3:17
Mark 11:24
Romans 10:17
Hebrews 11:6-11, 33

Prayer Bank sample for Gift of Faith

Most merciful Father in heaven, I thank You for Your grace and encouragement. I believe that You can do all things and that all power belongs to You. Help me therefore to live a life of faith. Your word says that without faith it is impossible to please You and that those that come to You must believe that You are everything unto them and a rewarder of those that diligently seek You. Father, please, help my unbelief and cause me to take every word that proceeds out of Your mouth as the apple of my eyes. Since You have mentioned faith as one of the gifts of the Spirit, bestow upon me this gift and help me to develop the little faith in me to the point whereby I can move the mountain with it, and can also receive all the promises that You have for me. At any time that my faith in You is tested, help me to stand firm and also come out victorious. I therefore request the gift of faith to move all mountains, to trust You to the end, to lay down my life for the kingdom's sake and to always say "yes Lord" at all times. Thank You, Lord, for strengthening my faith in You through Jesus Christ my Lord and Savior, Amen.

HELP/SUPPORT

Word Bank Sample

Psalm 124:8
Psalm 118:13
Matthew 15:25
1 Chronicles 12:20-22
Joshua 1:15
1 Kings 5:18

Prayer Bank Sample for Help/Support

Daddy, I recognize and declare that my help is in the name of the Lord. Help me out of all the problems that might come my way tomorrow. Send the necessary support, ministry, spiritual, financial and personal so that nothing shall be lacking in time of need. Daddy I know that there are people who are very intelligent but have no support to further their education. There are many who are good in sports but are suppressed for lack of helpers. There are those with beautiful voices who have even written their own songs but cannot go further for lack of finance and support. I declare that my heaven shall not be iron, or my earth brass. I prophesy to the mountains, to the hills, to the rivers, to the valleys and to the dry land to release my blessings that are in them. I declare open heaven and open door which no man can shut. I deposit this prayer in my prayer bank against the day I will need help or support, I confess that such help will readily be available. My case shall be different because You are on the throne working for me, and because You are on the throne, I can rightly say, "it is well." Thank You Lord for sending Your Spirit to make intercession for me when I do not know what to pray for, and how to pray in times of weakness. Thank You for sending Your angel to fight my battle even when I am fast asleep. Thank You, Lord, because I know You are always there for me. In Jesus' name I pray, Amen.

STRENGTH IN TIME OF WEAKNESS/DISCOURAGEMENT

Word Bank Sample

Nehemiah 8:10
Psalm 46:1
Isaiah 26:4
Revelations 3:8
1 Samuel 2:9

Prayer Bank Sample for Strength in Weakness/Discouragement

Dear heavenly Father, I desire to begin this prayer with a song that says: "guide me through, Lord Jesus, guide me through. Guide me through, Lord Jesus, guide me through. There is a race to be run, there is victory to be won, give me power every hour, to be through." Since no man can prevail by his physical strength, let Your spiritual strength which was released from heaven unto us in the day of Pentecost rest upon me and set me upon my feet for the task that You set before me. I need physical strength to be able to sleep and wake up. I need spiritual strength for global evangelization and to overcome the devices of my enemies. I know that a day will come when the wicked one will bring discouragement to try to weaken me by attacking my mind and my health, let this prayer in my prayer bank appeal to You and cause You to remember me according to Your faithfulness unto David in the days of his weakness. And as Caleb at eighty-five requested and claimed the mountain which You promised him when he was young and full of life, so also shall I claim all my mountains even at a hundred because I am also a carrier of good news. As You encouraged Joshua not to faint but to be strong and courageous through the meditation of Your word, I receive encouragement today through the meditation of Your word and will forever remain strong and courageous to finish the task that You committed into my hand. Thank You for answered prayer, in Jesus' name I pray, Amen.

PRAYER FOR UNDERSTANDING

Word Bank Sample

Deuteronomy 4:6
1 Chronicles 12:32
Psalm 119:104
Proverbs 2:6
Proverbs 4:7
Matthew 2:2
2 Timothy 2:7

Prayer Bank Sample for Understanding

Lord God Almighty, as I kneel before You this hour, I am asking You to fill me with understanding. By Your wisdom, Lord, You founded the earth and by understanding You established the heavens. I know through Your word that without understanding of Your purpose and plan for me, I shall never be established. Lord, it was You that blessed the children of Issachar with the understanding to know the times and what Israel ought to do. I also believe that with understanding I shall be able to know the times and what I'm supposed to do and when in Your ministry. I therefore ask You to fill me with understanding of the dreams that You give me, their interpretations and applications. I also ask You to enable me know the sign that You give concerning what might happen next, to know the people that come around me, and Your plan for me. I reject the spirit of confusion and blindness. I store up this request in my prayer bank before You so that in all my ways I will acknowledge You and will not lean on my own understanding. As I make my daily declarations, fill me with wisdom, knowledge and understanding every day to be able to know and lead the people that You commit into my care. I pray this prayer in the name of Jesus because He alone is the wisdom of God. Amen.

PRAYER FOR PATIENCE

Word Bank Sample

Numbers 9:18, 19, 22
Isaiah 40:31
Matthew 24:13
Luke 8:15
Romans 15:4-5
James 1:3-4
James 5:10-11

Prayer Bank Sample for Patience

My Father, my Lord and my God, thank You for Your leadership. My prayer is that You sustain me and grant me patience to walk with You as I work for You. The road is long, the distance is far but with patience, following You will be satisfying. Do not allow evil to entice me out of Your way and do not let me go ahead of the cloud. Help me to move with the cloud as the children of Israel in the wilderness. Give me the divine enablement to understand things as You put them in Your order in case I am tempted to go ahead of You. Use this prayer that I store up in my prayer bank to speak to my spirit and tame my spirit to succumb to Your will. Give me patience in tribulation, patience with my spouse and children, patience with my neighbors, and patience with one another in the ministry. Grant me patience when things do not go my way, when expectations are not met and when I am disappointed by a fellow man. Cause me to know that with the disappointment by man, You have a better plan for me. Uphold me to be patient to the end in order to receive my crown, in Jesus' name I pray, Amen.

PRAYER FOR HEALING

Word Bank Sample

Exodus 15:26
2 Kings 20:5
Psalm 23:3
Psalm 103:3
Jeremiah 17:14
Hosea 6:1
Mark 7:27

Prayer Bank Sample for Healing

Thank You Father, for I know that healing is bread for Your children. I have the assurance that when sickness comes the Lord will heal me. I claim mental healing, spiritual healing, emotional healing, financial healing and physical healing. May I not retain any bitterness in my relationship with others. Lord, grant me a sound mind to be able to do Your will. I shall declare without any doubt whenever I sense sickness around me: "I am healed, I am healed and I am healed", and I shall receive healing immediately. Your word says that if I will hearken unto Your words and keep Your precepts that none of the diseases that the world will suffer shall cleave to me. I truly believe this truth and have made Your holy Son, Jesus Christ, my Lord and Savior and also believe in Him, therefore none of the sicknesses of this world shall cleave to me. I apply the blood of Jesus upon my door posts and the lintel of my house for healing and protection. I apply it upon my forehead, upon my business, finances and upon my spouse and children. Use this prayer as recorded in my prayer bank and prevent sickness, whether spiritual or physical and command healing upon my body, soul and spirit. I thank You, Lord, for healing me, in Jesus' name I pray, Amen.

PRAYER FOR BREAKTHROUGH

Word Bank Sample

Deuteronomy 28:8
Deuteronomy 30:5
Joshua 1:8
Psalm 1:3
Ezekiel 36:30
Daniel 11:32

Prayer Bank Sample for Breakthrough

Dear Father, my source and my provider, thank You for providing me with the key to success, Your word. You have made it abundantly clear that if I will hearken unto Your voice and observe to do Your will and meditate daily on Your word, Your blessings will come upon me and overtake me. Therefore my Father, help me to hearken diligently unto Your word. I truly need this breakthrough, this overtaking blessing in every aspect of my life. I shall have breakthrough in my Marriage, in my business, in my ministry and in every field of human endeavor. I thank You Father for keeping my heart in Jesus, and not allowing me to depart from His ways. In addition, You have assured me that if I will meditate on Your word, I shall be like the trees planted by the rivers of water that will bring forth their fruits in due season and their leaves will never wither and that I also shall have good success. Help me set Your word before me in order to claim these promises. I bind the spirit of setback that usually attack at the time of breakthrough. As I deposit this prayer in my prayer bank, I have confidence that my breakthrough is at hand. I give You thanks, Lord, for answering my prayer, in Jesus' name I pray, Amen.

PRAYER FOR GOD'S POWER

Word Bank Sample

Job 42:3-5
Psalm 110:1-3
Isaiah 40:28-31
Jeremiah 32:17-19
Jeremiah 51:20-24
Luke 5:17
Luke 10:19
Acts 1:8

Prayer Bank Sample for God's Power

Most glorious Father and Lord of the universe, thank You for entrusting me with Your power. Once You speak, I am assured that power belongs to You. You have declared me to be Your battle axe and weapons of war: for with me You will destroy nations and kingdoms, break in pieces the horse and his rider, the chariot and his rider, the captains and the rulers. You have also transformed me into a "defenced" city, and an iron pillar, and brazen walls. I have authority over the whole universe, to pull down and to build up, to plant and to uproot. I shall thread upon serpents and upon scorpions and none shall hurt me. I claim the power to set the captives free and to preach the Word of God with boldness and without fear. This power of the Almighty God shall be available to me wherever and whenever I stand to minister the Word of God; miracles, signs and wonders shall be my portion and souls shall be won into the kingdom of God. As I deposit this prayer into my prayer bank, I have confidence that witches that are sent to disrupt activities in churches and afflict families shall be brought down and disgraced. They shall not go free but shall confess their activities and repent. I pray this prayer in Jesus' name, Amen.

PRAYER FOR THE GIFT OF DISCERNMENT

Word Bank Sample

2 Kings 5:26
Acts 16:16-18
Romans 8:27
1 Corinthians 2:14
1 Corinthian 12:10
Hebrews 4:12
1 John 4:1-2

Prayer Bank Sample for Discernment

Most blessed Father, the author of wisdom and knowledge, I pray for the gift of discernment to enable me to know those with deceptive spirits around me. No man can discern between good and evil except by Your Spirit. Fill me with Your sound spirit: spirit of wisdom, knowledge, understanding and of revelation. I bind veiling spirits that are used by the wicked one to block the spirit of discernment. As I prepare this prayer for my bank, I am asking that discernment takes a center stage in exposing the various intents in people's hearts, as they come close for fellowship, for ministry, for worship and for friendship. I pray that all wolves in sheep's clothing, all false prophets and prophecy, and all seducing spirits be exposed. May I not be deceived, seduced and made to compromise my faith due to lack of the spirit of discernment. Thank You Lord for giving me the understanding that I need anytime through this prayer bank as I climb the ladder of promotion in Your ministry. I pray this prayer in the name of Jesus Christ. Amen.

PRAYER FOR SPIRITUAL GIFTS

Word Bank Sample

Isaiah 56:5
Jeremiah 24:7
Ezekiel 11:19
Matthew 25:15
Romans 12:6
1 Corinthians 4:7
1 Corinthians 12:8-11
Ephesians 4:8, 11

Prayer Bank Sample for Spiritual Gift

My Lord and my God, thank You for the gift of Your only Son, Jesus Christ who came from heaven to die and redeem me from my sins. I am praying for spiritual endowment and outpouring of Your gift to enable me to operate my ministry gifts effectively. I recognize that these are gifts that You promised Your Church before You went back to heaven and generously poured upon Your disciples on the day of Pentecost. I come in agreement with Apostle Peter that these gifts are for us, our children and children's children and for those afar off who will later believe in Your name. I am a believer in Your name and therefore desire these gifts for the benefit of the Body of Christ. I now open a spiritual gift prayer bank and deposit every anointing that comes with every gift into the bank. Whether it be words of wisdom or knowledge or faith or gift of healings or of working of miracles or prophecy or discernment of spirits or of tongues or interpretation of tongues. Or whether it has to do with ministry gifts and offices such as: apostolic, prophetic, evangelistic, pastoral and teaching, give me the understanding and the grace to make it a worthy ambassadorial representation of Your glory before people, this I pray and ask in the name of Jesus Christ, Amen.

PRAYER TO STRENGTHEN MY PRAYER LIFE

Word Bank Sample

1 Chronicles 16:11
2 Chronicles 7:14-15
1 Thessalonians 5:17
Matthew 7:7-11
Matthew 26:41
Luke 18:1-8
John 16:24
Ephesian 6:18
James 5:13

Prayer Bank Sample to Strengthen My Prayer Life

Dear covenant keeping God, there is none like You in heaven above and on earth beneath. I submit my life into Your able hands and ask You to wake my spirit to pray without ceasing. You made it clear that if I will humble myself and pray and turn from my wicked ways and seek Your face, then You will hear from heaven and You will heal my land. Lord, I ask that You humble me and steer up my spirit to pray. I acknowledge my sins before You because I know that there are times I ought to be praying but I am sleeping or doing things that are contrary to Your will. One thing is sure, You O' Lord love me with everlasting love and with Your loving kindness have You drawn me. I know that whenever I am weak, You are strong and my weakness cannot prevent Your strength. When I am in doubt, You are faithful and my doubting cannot stop Your faithfulness. Neither can my disobedience hinder Your Word from being active, nor my laziness and complacency prevent the move of Your power. Blessed Father, help me overcome my weakness and keep my prayer life active. May I pray without ceasing. Even when I know not what to pray, may Your Spirit make intercession for me with groaning. Thank You, Lord, for waking my spirit to pray daily, and for reminding and strengthening my heart, through this prayer bank, to do the right thing, especially when I am weak and seem to forget to pray. Thank You and thank You again for Your love, mercy and help, this I pray through Jesus Christ my Lord and Savior, Amen.

PRAYER TO REMEMBER TO PAY MY VOWS

Word Bank Sample

Genesis 28:20
Jonah 1:16
1 Samuel 1:11, 27-28
Ecclesiastes 5:4-6
Psalm 116:14

Prayer Bank Sample to Remember to Pay My Vows

Dear faithful and covenant keeping Father, I am asking You to help me to keep my own covenant and vows that I made to You. Many a time the enemy tries to confuse me and to bring the spirit of forgetfulness upon me so as to prevent me from fulfilling my obligations and redeeming my vows unto You. But You are stronger than my heart and more powerful than the devil. Clothe me with Your fear and trouble my heart daily to keep my vows. Father, in the name of Jesus, I refuse to compromise and I reject any invitation by satan to sin against You with my tongue. Let Your Spirit that helped Abraham to pay his vow, and also Israel as a nation to keep the word of their vow and also helped Jephthah not to rescind the words of his vow, keep me and continue to remind me to be faithful in all things big or small, toward You. I know that You are able to do all things. Please, Daddy, help my heart to accept the fulfillment of its obligations towards You, and through this I shall be abundantly blessed through Jesus Christ our Lord and Savior. Amen. As I deposit this prayer in my prayer bank before You, I ask that it will stand as a reminder every time to direct my heart to do what is good and right by fulfilling my vows, in Jesus' name I pray. Amen.

PRAYER FOR WISDOM

Word Bank Sample

1 Kings 3:9
2 Chronicles 1:10
Psalm 104:24
Proverbs 9:1
Isaiah 11:2
James 1:5
Matthew 25:2

Prayer Bank Sample for Wisdom

Dear Lord, the author of all wisdom, knowledge and understanding, I stand before you today to deposit this prayer into my prayer bank concerning wisdom for living. Your Word makes it clear that wisdom is the principal thing, therefore I request that You bless me with wisdom; wisdom in communication, wisdom on how to handle disputes, wisdom in investment and how to manage my finances, wisdom in all things. It is clear that out of the ten virgins that came to await the arrival of the bridegroom, only the five wise ones made it in, but the other five failed for lack of wisdom even though they were all virgins. You have instructed me to ask for wisdom if I lack it, Lord, I ask that You envelop me at all times with wisdom and help me to conduct Your business with discretion. I give You thanks because I know that You are faithful to keep Your promises. I know that if I will ask anything in the name of Jesus You will give it to me so that my joy may be full. Thank You, Lord, for answered prayer, for in Jesus' name I ask, Amen.

PRAYER FOR A CLEARER VISION

Word Bank Sample

Genesis 15:1
Amos 3:7
Habakkuk 2:3
Acts 16:9
1 Corinthians 2:10
Proverbs 29:18

Prayer Bank Sample for Vision

Abba Father, Your Word declares that where there is no vision, the people perish. I pray this day that You make me a visionary leader in the execution of Your calling. I pray that You open my eyes of understanding to behold the things that are written in Your law. I request that in due season, my vision be made clearer in every aspect of my life. Cause me to see events as they build up in the spirit realm before they manifest in the physical so as to stop those events that need to be stopped and to allow those that should be allowed. I bind every spirit that veils and blinds spiritual sights so that I do not see what danger is ahead of me. As I deposit my prayer concerning vision into my prayer bank, I declare that I shall never be a blind leader so that those You give me to lead and I will not fall into a pit, together. I also pray and ask that You make those You have chosen to follow me to understand the reason You chose me to lead them. Lord, expose every witch who shall disguise and camouflage herself to be another person. Reveal her true personality and identity and let her not have any hiding place in our midst. Thank You, Lord, for my answered prayer, this I pray in Jesus' name. Amen.

PRAYER FOR STRENGTH FOR SPIRITUAL WARFARE

Word Bank Sample

2 Corinthians 10:3-4
2 Timothy 2:3-4
Ephesians 6:10-18
Jeremiah 51:20-24
Exodus 14:25
1Timothy 6:12

Prayer Bank Sample for Strength for my Warfare Life

Father, in the name of Jesus, I stand before You today to deposit my prayer in my prayer bank against that day; the day that is determined that I will enter into battle against enemies of progress. I pray that when such a day comes, the devices of the enemies be defeated and let all their equipment malfunction. You, O Lord, will clothe me with knowledge, wisdom, understanding and power to defeat them. Their weapons shall be rendered unworkable and their chariots' wheels shall fall off from under them. I shall be clothed with offensive, defensive and protective armors. I will rise and stand therefore with my loin girded about with truth and my heart protected with the breastplate of righteousness. May my feet be shod with the preparation of the Gospel of peace and clothe me with the shield of faith to be able to quench all the fiery darts of the wicked ones. I cover my head with the helmet of salvation and let the sword of the spirit be in my hand to cut asunder every witchcraft spell cast upon me. Help my mouth to release all prayers and supplications which the Spirit of God shall motivate me to pray and let me watch with all perseverance and supplication for all saints and to see how the devil's kingdom scatter. I know that I am an overcomer and have overcome the enemies by the blood of the Lamb and by the word of my testimony. Thank You in advance for my already answered prayer, in Jesus' name I pray. Amen.

PRAYER FOR SPIRITUAL HUNGER

Word Bank Sample

Matthew 5:6
Acts 17:11
Psalm 42:1
Jeremiah 33:3
Philippians 3:10

Prayer Bank Sample for Spiritual Hunger

Dear Lord who satisfies my hungry soul with fatness, let it be recorded this day in Your record that I have made a determination to seek after You all the days of my life. As the deer pants and longs for the water brooks, so pants my soul after You. Lord, cause me to hunger daily for You as I would hunger for natural food. Take away laziness and sleep from me and cause me to have no rest until I have read, meditated, and received a Rhema from You. Help me to study in order to show myself approved unto You and to be a workman/ workwoman that does not need to be ashamed, but rightly dividing the word of truth. I stand against the spirit of weakness, discouragement, entanglement, busybody and diversion. I resist the devil and all his agents and refuse to bow to unnecessary pressure of life and wicked devices of the enemy. According to Your promise, anyone who hungers and thirsts after righteousness shall be filled. I ask that You, in Your mercy, fill me with true spiritual hunger and cause me to be filled and satisfied. Make me to know Your perfect will for my life through the study of Your word. Thank You Lord for granting me my request, in Jesus' name I pray. Amen.

PRAYER FOR GOD'S CONTROL

Word Bank Sample

Exodus 14:13
2 Chronicles 20:15
2 Chronicles 32:8
Psalm 24:1
Psalm 46:10
Isaiah 43:1-5
Matthew 28:18

Prayer Bank Sample for God's Control

King of all kings and Lord of all lords, take all the glory, honor, adoration, dominion, majesty and power, in Jesus' name, Amen. I stand in faith and believe and also claim all Your promises. I bind the spirit of fear, intimidation and worry. Lord, take control of my life, the life of my spouse and of my children. If there will arise any occasion, which would have brought trembling into my life, let these words readily be available in my record to defend me, "God is in control" and "I will fear no evil for You are with me." When it seems that all hope is lost and there is a concern over a situation, help me Lord to remember that You are on the throne and are watching over me. When there is a rumor of an impending danger let me rest in Your promises, and if the enemies are pursuing me as did the Egyptians at the red sea, let my desperate situation turn to confusion in the camp of my enemies and let me remember what Your mighty hand did in delivering Your people. In all, let Your peace settle in my heart and help me always to remember that You are in control. I pray this prayer in Jesus' name because I know that he that dwells in the secret place of the Most High shall abide in the shadow of the Almighty. Thank You for taking control of my life. In Jesus' name I pray. Amen.

PRAYER TO POSSESS MY POSSESSION

Word Bank Sample

1 Kings 21:3
Psalm 119:111
Isaiah 61:7
Obadiah 1:17
Ezekiel 44:28
Matthew 6:33
Acts 20:32

Prayer Bank Sample to Possess My Possession

Dear heavenly Father, thank You because You are my possession in the land of the living. Help me to hold onto You. May I not miss the Kingdom for I know that if I possess the kingdom all other things in this life are mine. As I deposit this prayer daily, You will be my defense when I need one, You will be my healer when I need a doctor, You will be my provider whenever I need provision. From coast to coast my blessings shall flow. Your covenant with me is that You will shake the heavens, the earth, the sea and the dry land, and the treasures of all nations shall flow in my direction. Your Word says that Your cities shall be spread abroad through prosperity. Therefore the covenant of possessing the gates of my enemies is established and sealed forever. As I deposit this prayer in my prayer bank, I believe that my possession is mine. I bind every familiar spirit that will seduce me to let me miss my possession in God, which is Christ Jesus. I refuse to yield to lies and falsehood but stand by Your word that in Mount Zion there shall be deliverance and there shall be holiness and my house shall possess our possessions. My house shall be a fire and a flame and the houses of my enemies shall be stubble and they all shall be consumed. Thank You, Lord, for reminding me that my labor of love will not be forgotten but that I shall be rewarded in due season. I pray this prayer in Jesus' name. Amen.

PRAYER FOR SPIRITUAL GROWTH

Word Bank Sample

2 Peter 1:5
2 Peter 3:18
2 Timothy 2:15
1 Thessalonians 3:12
1 Thessalonians 5:21
Ephesians 4:13
Hebrews 6:1

Prayer Bank Sample for Spiritual Growth

Dear Father, help me to grow in grace and in the knowledge of Your Son, Jesus Christ. I reject any spirit of stagnation. I ask You, O Lord, to fill me with all understanding whenever I study Your Word. I recognize that without spiritual growth there can never be other growth in all aspects of my life; ministry, finance, social and political. Help me O' Lord and bestow upon me all the necessary ingredients that will help me grow spiritually. May I also grow in love and understanding with my spouse, children and other people that come around me. This prayer bank shall stand as a reminder every time I seem to have spiritual stagnation through lack of fervent prayer and study of Your word, may I be fired up from within and in my mind. Thank You, Lord as You renew my visions, dreams, sense of humor, spiritual understanding and revelation knowledge, especially when I study Your Holy Book. Let me find joy in reading Your words and educate me more on what it takes to be a champion of faith and of works. I pray this prayer in Jesus' name knowing that if I grow, the harvest is Yours. Amen.

PRAYER FOR HUMILITY

Word Bank Sample

Daniel 4:29-34
Proverbs 15:33
Proverbs 22:4
Matthew 23:12
Isaiah 14:12-15
Philippians 2:5-11
1 Peter 5:5

Prayer Bank Sample For Humility

My Father, my Lord and my God, send the spirit that You gave to Your Son, my Lord and Savior Jesus Christ upon my heart. Remove arrogance and pride far from me. I know You will surely bless me but in the midst of that blessing, may I remain humble. May I not esteem myself better than others, but always consider others better than myself. May I humble myself to search the scriptures and may I not claim that I already know. May I humble myself to pray and seek Your face and not rely on my own understanding. May I humble myself and listen to others when they preach or teach and may I not conclude that I know better than them. Help me to listen to my spouse and my children alike and not to term them inferior or without knowledge. I bind the spirit of pride and arrogance and cast it out of my life. I resist the temptation to look down on someone You created in Your image. Use this prayer in my prayer bank to keep reminding me to remain humble in the midst of promotion and success. Thank You Lord for answering my prayer, in Jesus' mighty name I pray. Amen.

PRAYER TO MAINTAIN HONESTY

Word Bank Sample

Leviticus 19:35
Proverbs 11:1
Joshua 7:21
1 Samuel 12:4
2 Kings 5:16
Acts 5:1-2
Romans 13:13
1 Timothy 2:1-2

Prayer Bank Sample for Honesty

Dear Lord, keep me from the pollutions that come as a result of dishonesty. The sin of Achan shall not find its way into my dwelling neither shall the sin of Ananias and Sapphira his wife be my portion and my family's. I shall worship the Lord with all my substance and I shall pay all my vows in the presence of all His people. Lord, keep this prayer open before You so that any time I go astray You quickly bring me back by reminding me of the effects of dishonesty. Take far from me deliberate sins and help me to speak the truth even in the smallest matter. As I deposit this prayer in my prayer bank, let it keep reminding me that I am Your ambassador in this world. I bind, reject, refuse and resist every spirit of dishonesty. Help me have an honest conversation with my spouse, children and other members of my family. Help me present Your word with honesty and truth. I refuse to bear false witness against anyone, even against my enemy. Let accountability and integrity be my standard and may I not forget that I will one day stand before You to render the account of my stewardship unto You. Let Your sound Spirit of honesty take control of my heart. Thank You, Lord, for answering my prayer. In Jesus' name I pray, Amen.

PRAYER FOR FAITHFULNESS

Word Bank Sample

Genesis 4:4
Genesis 18:19
2 Kings 12:15
Matthew 25:21
Mark 14:6
Acts 4:36-37
Acts 10:1-2
Numbers 12:7

Prayer Bank Sample for Faithfulness

Faithful Father, give me a sound spirit to remain faithful in all my dealings not only with You, Lord, but also with my fellow brothers and sisters. Help me now to be faithful in a little thing and when You have blessed me, stir up my heart to remember to be faithful in much. As I stand today to record this prayer in my prayer bank before You, help me prevent the spirit of madness from coming after me in the days of my success. In the days of heavy rain and snow, let me be reminded that they are Your messengers. They are faithful to Your words and honor You by coming to wet the earth to make it bring forth and bud so as to give seed to the sower and bread to the eater. And in the day of sunshine, keep my heart at peace to know that the sun also is faithful and obedient to Your words by coming to warm the earth. I therefore through this prayer request that neither rain nor sun will make me to be unfaithful to Your words by refusing to step out and accomplish what You assigned me to do. I shall not only be faithful in tithes and offering, but also in evangelism, visitation, helping the poor and the needy, answering Your call to travel and doing whatever You ask me to do to the glory of Your name. May I be faithful to my spouse in our marriage relationship and to my children in our family. Let Your spirit of faithfulness envelope me round about and thank You Lord for this shall be my portion in the land of the living through Jesus Christ my Lord and Savior. Amen.

PRAYER FOR FRUIT BEARING

Word Bank Sample

Proverbs 11:30
John 15:4, 16
Mark 11:13
Luke 3:10-14
Galatians 5:22-23
Philippians 1:11
Colossians 1:10

Prayer Bank Sample for Fruit Bearing

Dear Father, I thank You for Your love for me. My request to You is that I abide in the vine so as to produce more fruit. Lord, help me not to get detached from You. It is Your command that every tree that does not bear fruit should be cut down and thrown into the fire, I therefore ask that You have power over my heart to keep me attached to You, the Vine so that I can continually bear fruit. Father in the name of Jesus, I begin to take care of those things that could make me detached from the Vine: sin of all kind, faithlessness, unproductiveness, taking the grace of God in vain, being complacent in my duty to God and compromising my faith to buy the favor from man. My Lord, let not my season pass without me bearing fruit; physical and spiritual fruit alike. As I record this prayer in my prayer bank before You, I bind the spirit of dryness and decree that everything that I do shall be fruitful. Thank You Lord for answering my prayer, in Jesus' name I pray. Amen.

PRAYER FOR ANOINTING

Word Bank Sample

Isaiah 10:27
1 Samuel 10:1-7
Acts 10:38
2 Corinthians 1:21
James 5:14
1 John 2:27

Prayer Bank Sample for Anointing

Dear Lord, I am praying that You anoint me with Your oil of gladness. I understand that anointing is the mark of recognition, approval, acceptance, and empowerment. I stand upon Your promises that when I am anointed with fresh oil my horn shall be exalted above all my equals. I deposit my anointing prayer into my prayer bank with You, that the word of my mouth be anointed, the meditation of my heart be anointed, the ministration and the move of the spirit in me be with anointing. All the favors that follow anointing shall be my portion, and every yoke upon me shall be destroyed because of the anointing. Anoint my feet that you may order them where You want them to go. Anoint my head for sound memory. Anoint my tongue to speak the mysteries of God, words coated with salt and honey in season and out of season, to satisfy the needs of the hungry souls. Anoint my hands for miracles and anoint my eyes for divine vision and direction. With the anointing that You anoint me, give me also self-control so that pride does not take hold of me. I know that when You anointed Saul to be a king over Israel, the prophecy upon him was that men would meet him and he would be favored with salutation and gifts. He was also told that when he met prophets prophesying, he would prophesy with them and he would be turned into another man. I sincerely believe this is what anointing can do, and, by Your anointing upon me, let me be transformed and used. Please Daddy let me receive favor that come with salutations and gifts and also be turned to Your image when I am in the midst of people, whether they be friends or enemies alike. Thank You, Lord, for answered prayer, this I ask and pray in Jesus' name. Amen.

PRAYER FOR DIVINE DIRECTION

Word Bank Sample

Psalm 32:8
Proverbs 14:12
Isaiah 26:2
John 10:9
John 14:5-6
Romans 5:2
Revelation 3:8

Prayer Bank Sample for Divine Direction

Holy Father, I pray and ask that You divinely direct me to where You have determined for me. It is written that the steps of the righteous man are ordered by You, and that You also delight in all his ways. I therefore request that You order my steps and also delight in all my ways. Dear Lord, I reject the leadership of my senses and flesh, I have acknowledged You as my Shepherd, and also request that You go before me while I follow closely behind. May I not go ahead of You, Lord, so that I do not make a wrong turn, and may my sins not stand against me and prevent me from being focused, paying attention to Your divine direction and command. I request that You store this prayer up against that day that the deceiver will try to make me veer off from the path that You have me walk, and Lord, lead me to the Rock that is higher than I. I pray that You build me upon that solid rock where no storm can shake. You know me more than I know myself and can also keep my heart from pollution and evil work. I bind the spirit of contamination, wandering thoughts and diversions and I clothe myself with Your beauty and ask Your Spirit to permanently indwell in me, so that it shall be said of me, "Christ in me, the hope of glory." I pray that this prayer that is recorded in my prayer bank before You guide me to success in ministry and all other undertakings through Jesus Christ my Lord. Amen and Amen.

PRAYER FOR LEADERSHIP

Word Bank Sample

Exodus 13:21
Psalm 23:2
Psalm 25:9
Isaiah 30:21
Isaiah 42:16
John 10:27

Prayer Bank Sample for Leadership

Shepherd of Israel, thank You for providing a clear and purposeful leadership unto me from my birth until now. Your faithfulness is from generation to generation. As You did swear unto Abraham Your friend, You led him and guided him through the desert and provided water and food in the wilderness for him and all his substance, blessed be Your name for ever and ever more, Amen. Thank You dear Daddy because I have confidence that You will also lead me all the days of my life, Amen. As a person clothed with flesh, I am not immune to distractions and diversions. I therefore deposit this prayer in my bank before You that You, O Lord, allow Your rod and staff to comfort me. Lead me to the green pastures and to the waters that run slowly. Restore my soul and also lead me in the path of righteousness for Your name's sake. Let me not fear any evil even when I walk through the valley of the shadow of death, let my spirit always see Your presence with me and be strengthened. When the enemies of progress seem to block my way and stand against me, may You open a new high way which no man can shut. Lead me and give me patience in following You. Lead me and impart Your spirit of leadership upon me so as to be able to lead Your people.

You made it clear to Your disciples that a student is not greater than his teacher, therefore Lord, give me a leader's mindset, a leader's knowledge, a leader's mentality and leadership spirit so that my followers will learn from me and become great leaders of tomorrow. Thank You, Lord, for being a good Shepherd to me and an example that I must follow all my life. I pray this prayer in Jesus' name I pray. Amen.

PRAYER FOR SOUL WINNING

Word Bank Sample

Proverbs 11:30
Daniel 12:3
Matthew 28:19-20
Mark 16:20
1 Corinthians 9:19
James 5:20

Prayer Bank Sample for Soul Winning

Most blessed Father, make me a practical instrument for Your use. Use me O Lord to win souls into Your kingdom. No matter my other daily activity, help me make soul winning a priority. I know that anything that any man does is dependent upon his vision, interest and his desire in it. Give me a burning desire for soul winning so as to empty hell and make Your kingdom full. Keep the spirit of soul winning burning in me and give me no rest if I slack and get overwhelmed with other events or activities as I grow. Keep kicking my heart and reminding me that the heart-cry of God is for souls. It is because of the redemption of souls that Jesus had to come and die and not for mere activities and administration works. Count me as one of the wise men before You because he that wins souls is wise. And let me be a shining star before You forever because as many that turn others to righteousness shall shine as stars forever. Thank You Lord as You continually use this prayer in my prayer bank as a mark to keeping me in remembrance of soul winning all the days of my life. I pray this prayer in the name of Jesus my Lord and Savior. Amen.

PRAYER AGAINST PERSECUTION

Word Bank Sample

1 Kings 19:2-3
Isaiah 53:7-8
Daniel 3:20
Nahum 1:9
Matthew 5:10-12
Acts 7:60
Luke 23:34

Prayer Bank Sample in Persecution

Dear Lord, I commit my life into Your able hand. I am asking You to protect me and shield me from my persecutors. You have already made it clear to me that in the world we shall have persecution, but that I should rejoice because You have overcome the world for me. As You have made me an overcomer according to Your word, I am asking You, O Lord, to be there for me when that trying time comes. You said that if a man's way pleases You, You will make his enemies to be at peace with him. I acknowledge all my sins before You, confess them and turn away from them unto You. And because I am made righteous through Jesus Christ my Lord and Savior, all my persecutors shall acknowledge You as Lord and King and shall bow and worship You. I also pray that You give me the spirit of endurance to go through persecution as a good soldier of Jesus Christ. A persecutor Saul was converted to Apostle Paul, therefore arrest my persecutors and cause them to repent and surrender to the Lordship of Jesus Christ. Let the blessedness of enduring persecution be my portion in the name of Jesus Christ. Let this prayer wake up in the day it is needed most and dismantle the weapons of my persecutors.

Thank You Lord for I have already seen victory ahead of me, in Jesus' name I pray. Amen.

PRAYER AGAINST BARRENNESS

Word Bank Sample

Luke 1:36
Exodus 23:26
Deuteronomy 7:14
Genesis 24:60
Genesis 15:4
Genesis 17:2

Prayer Bank Sample against Barrenness

Most blessed father in heaven, I take my stand today against the spirit of barrenness. I reject all forms of barrenness; financial barrenness, spiritual barrenness, mental barrenness and barrenness in the fruits of my body. My plants shall not cast off their fruits before time, as there shall be no barrenness in my house. I bind the spirit of miscarriages in my family and among my children, male and female. My sons and daughters shall be fruitful in their marriages as Eliezer of Damascus shall not be the heir in my house. If I choose to adopt a child, it shall be out of love to help but not out of lack of children of my own. I sincerely believe that those Word collections are Your words concerning this issue and You will honor Your words on this subject matter. Since You are not a man that You should lie, and You have never lied and will never lie, I believe You sincerely that since I have hearkened unto Your words to observe and to do all Your commandments, the blessedness of obedience shall be my portion now and forevermore. In Jesus' name I pray, Amen.

PRAYER AGAINST SICKNESS

Word Bank Sample

2 Kings 20:1-6
Isaiah 38:1-5
Matthew 8:16-17
Mark 16:18
John 11:3
James 5:14-15

Prayer Bank Sample against Sickness

Dear Father, I stand on Your authority upon my life as a child of the Most High God and lock my door against the spirit of sickness from coming into my dwelling. You are the greatest physician, and you know and own every organ in my body. You know how to preserve them from the attacks of the enemy. I bind all the Egyptian plagues from entering into my body and my dwelling place. Such sicknesses as cancer, leprosy, issue of blood, internal bleeding, blindness, ulcers, heart attacks, etc. are perpetually bound and kept out of my life and home. You, O Lord, have promised not to put any of the Egyptian diseases upon me, in the name of Jesus, I reject them and take my stand against them from coming into my body. I sprinkle the blood of Jesus at my door posts and at the lintel of my house. I also sprinkle the blood of Jesus in the air, water and the land as this will prevent air pollution and disease, water pollution and disease and sand contamination. I bind food poisoning and all forms of eating in the dream. Any sickness that attacks as a result of sin shall not see me as I confess my sins daily before You. Any sickness sent by the witches or enemies to afflict me shall not come because I am a worshiper of You. I also bind and resist all spiritual sicknesses, weakness, prayerlessness, spirit of sleep and slumber, eating and merry making in my dreams. This prayer in my prayer bank through the Word of God shall block sickness from getting into me and my household, in the name of Jesus. Amen.

PRAYER AGAINST DEPRESSION

Word Bank Sample

Psalm 34:19
Psalm 119:28
1 Samuel 16:14
1 Kings 21:4
Judges 16:16
Matthew 11:28
James 4:9-10
1 Peter 1:6-7

Prayer Bank Sample against Depression

Holy Father, thank You for the sound spirit that You have sent into my heart. There shall not come near me the spirit of stress, heaviness or depression as I will not open my heart to evil thought and worries. Lord, keep me focused on what You have me do and my mind active in all that concerns You. Let not the pressure of life overwhelm me and set my mind into much thinking. But let me be satisfied with the fullness of Your joy. Let the blood of Jesus wash me from all filthiness and contamination and let my soul sing Your praise every day of my life. Give me the spirit of satisfaction and appreciation in all that You have done and remove worries and filthy communication from my life. Let me be content with what You give to me for godliness with contentment is great gain. Remind me to live by faith for if You can take care of the birds of the air that sow not neither reap, how much more me Your child. Thank You, Lord, for the comforting of my spirit, thank You for the assurances through Your word. This prayer stored in my prayer bank shall awake for my defense and deal a heavy blow to the spirit of depression. I seal this prayer with the name of Jesus Christ of Nazareth, to Him be glory for ever and ever more. Amen.

PRAYER AGAINST WITCHCRAFT ACTIVITIES

Word Bank Sample

Exodus 22:18
Isaiah 54:15-17
Matthew 18:18
Mark 3:27
James 5:5
1 John 4:4

Prayer Bank Sample against Witchcraft Operation

Lord, God Almighty, thank You for sending Your Son Jesus Christ to come and shed His blood to redeem man from all the powers of darkness. Lord, I pray against all the powers of witchcraft in my family, in Your church and near my dwelling. Wherever I shall live, let there be spiritual traps all around my house. Those traps shall be all over the roof of my house, all around the building itself and even the very foundation which it stands on. Those traps shall capture and expose all witches and their agents. There shall not arise any spirit of rebellion in my family influenced by the spirit of witchcraft. I destroy every spell cast to subject me and my family to the influence of witchcraft. I sprinkle the blood of Jesus in the air, sea and the land and make those places uncomfortable for witches to operate. Let the wings of all the flying witches be cut off, and let their transportation system be dismantled. I release the blood of Jesus to flow in camps and all their meeting places. I deny them a place to congregate. Any witch that will rise up to challenge me, privately and publicly, let them meet an open disgrace and repent so that they will know that heaven and earth belong to You, Lord. Any witch that refuses to repent let the word of God that says that we should not allow a witch to live go after them and annihilate them. May the blood of Jesus, the name of Jesus, the Word of God and the fire of the Holy Spirit destroy and devour the power of witchcraft in the church and in the world and set their captives free. I pray this prayer in the name that is above all names, in Jesus' name I pray. Amen.

PRAYER AGAINST CURSES

Word Bank Sample

Genesis 8:21
Numbers 22:12
Galatians 3:13
Proverbs 26:2
Genesis 12:3
Numbers 23:23
James 3:9
Revelation 22:3

Prayer Bank Sample against Curses

Father, in the name of Jesus, I reject any curse that anyone might bring upon my family and me. You have said that causeless curses shall not stand, therefore Jesus died to set me free from the curse of the law. All curses, whether they be from the witches, generational, through any property that I will purchase, curses by association, curses through marriage or curses through and from my parents, or from friendship, shall never cleave to me in the name of Jesus, Amen. Every action of mine that would have brought a curse upon me is covered by the blood of Jesus. I am redeemed, I am purchased, I am justified, I am cleansed and washed and I am forgiven through the blood of Jesus, Amen. I confess all wrong doings and move on because I have assurance that the blood cleanses me from all sins. This prayer bank stand as a reminder before God that through the blood of His Son, Jesus Christ, that was shed at Calvary, the curse of satan and his agents shall not come upon me nor all that pertains to me. I cover myself with the blood of Jesus, everyone in my family is covered with the blood of Jesus and the church of Jesus Christ is covered with the blood of Jesus. Thank You Father for Your divine hand upon my life, in Jesus' name I pray. Amen.

PRAYER AGAINST EPIDEMIC/PLAGUE

Word Bank Sample

Exodus 9:10
Exodus 9:23-25
Numbers 12:10
Exodus 15:26
Psalm 91:10
Mark 5:34

Prayer Bank Sample against Epidemic/Plague

Lord, I come before You this day in the name that is above all names. I recognize that the wicked one might cast his epidemic virus into the air to bring affliction upon the sons and daughters of men. My spouse and the entire members of my household shall not be touched by such a plague. You, O Lord, will envelope us and cover us with Your wings. Every available weapon that You have given to us to use to fight against our enemies such as the blood of Jesus, the name of Jesus, the Word of God and the fire of the Holy Spirit shall readily rise up in battle against all epidemic and plagues assigned to afflict us by our enemies. We will stoutly resist the devil and he and his agents shall flee from us. Whether it is going to be air-borne or water-borne disease or contamination or pollution of the land or any form of food poisoning, it will not affect us in any way in Jesus' mighty name. We dip ourselves in the pool of the blood of Jesus, we are also baptized unto Him in that pool of His blood as we are partakers with Him in His death, burial and resurrection. And since the creator of the heavens and the earth is our God, the plague sent to afflict the world shall never hurt me and my household. I pray this prayer in the name of Jesus Christ. Amen.

PRAYER OF ESCAPE DURING EARTHQUAKES

Word Bank Sample

Numbers 16:30-32
Matthew 7:26
Matthew 27:54
Matthew 28:2

Prayer Bank Sample about Earthquakes

I thank You Father for Your word. The Bible says there shall be earthquakes in diverse places. But I will only *hear* about them and they will not affect me and what is mine. In as much as I am not involved in the sins of Korah, Dathan and Abiram, the earth will not open its mouth to swallow me, it will swallow neither my belongings nor any from my family. This prayer is stored up in my prayer bank against all such occurrences and the devastations and shocks that may follow. Your Word is true that if I pray according to Your will, You will hear me. It is written, "How beautiful upon the mountains are the feet of he who brings goods tidings, who publishes peace..." You have chosen me to carry good tidings and to publish peace, I and mine therefore shall not be the victims of earthquakes. You have said that I will hear of the rumor of earthquakes and of wars but they will not come near my dwelling. I use this prayer in my prayer bank and close all avenues for earthquakes around my area of residence. I tie down the spirit that causes rumblings and eruptions of the earth, I bind it and cast it into the abyss. My presence in my area of residence shall prevent any earthquake from happening in that area. And souls shall know that a child of God is in their midst and bow and worship his God. I pray this prayer in Jesus' name. Amen.

PRAYER OF PROTECTION IN TIMES OF WAR

Word Bank Sample

Joshua 23:3
Matthew 24:6
Ecclesiastes 3:8
Psalm 27:3
1 Corinthians 15:32
2 Timothy 4:7

Prayer Bank Sample about War Times

Father, in the name of Jesus, it is certain that there will be war one day either in my life time or my children's as Your word has affirmed. It is even certain that one of my children might fight in a war to defend his or her country, my prayer and my request is that no member of my family shall die through war; either through friendly fire or the bullets of the enemy. Lord, I have seen You use wars to downgrade people and You have also used wars to upgrade people. Let every war that might come be a source of promotion for me and members of my family. I bring all members of my family into this prayer bank deposit and I degree that violent death shall not be our portion. Many have fought in battles and come back to tell their war stories and many have come back to rule. The dead cannot praise You, only the living can sing praises unto Your name. I therefore declare that my family members shall fight and live to testify and be decorated. Like King David, they shall come back to rule and even rule over their defeated enemies. In the times of war may we find peace, happiness and joy. I also recognize that there are other wars that we must fight; war against hunger, against drug usage, against prostitution, against sickness and against all manner of ills that the wicked one might unleash upon the earth. Yet we still have to fight against all kinds of sin. But in all these, I say, we are more than conquerors through Jesus Christ our Lord and Savior. Amen and Amen.

PRAYER AGAINST INVESTMENT LOSSES

Word Bank Sample

Genesis 26:12
Deuteronomy 28:11
2 Chronicles 31:10
Haggai 1:6, 11
Malachi 3:11
Hebrews 11:1

Prayer Bank Sample against Investment Losses

Father, in the name of Jesus, I know that You know the beginning from the end. You know what might happen to my investments tomorrow, and as you helped Isaac to get a hundredfold in the midst of a famine that consumed the land, help me to overcome losses in the days of investment downturn. As I have made a covenant to pay my tithes and give my offerings according to Your command, I believe that the devourer will not devour my investments. I open this account in my prayer bank solely to make deposit against losses, and I know that Your word is abiding. So then, it is not me that will, nor me that run but You, God, that show mercy. Thank You in advance for protecting my investments in the days of famine ahead. Help me to continue to reap a hundredfold as long as I have not forsaken Your word nor denied Your name and let me be like the tree planted by the rivers of waters. May I continue to bring forth my fruits in due season and my leaves never wither and may all my endeavor prosper. Thank You for my answered prayer, in Jesus' name I pray. Amen.

PRAYER CONCERNING RELOCATION

Word Bank Sample

Matthew 10:23
Genesis 12:1
Genesis 13:10-11
Genesis 26:1-3
Genesis 45:5

Prayer Bank Sample concerning Relocation

Dear Father, thank You because You know all things. You know that a day will come when I will need to relocate to a new place. Lord, let that move be according to Your plan. The devil will not manipulate me to move so as to destroy me. Neither will I move without direction from You, Lord. I begin to cover the new place with the blood of Jesus; the road, the means of transportation and other things that will help me to relocate. I will not relocate my spouse, children and family only to lose them or bring harm to them in a new place. I will not relocate and later regret it. All relocations shall be according to Your plan, vision and purpose. May the vision, reason and the purpose for the relocation be made plain by Your Spirit, and may I not relocate and forget You. I block every spirit of deception, lies and manipulation that will make me to relocate to where I will encounter problems. I use the authority in the name of Jesus to block any dream concerning relocation which is not from You. May Your Words in this prayer bank arise to my defense, and may I live to continually praise the beauty of Your holy name, in Jesus Christ name I pray. Amen.

PRAYER AGAINST DIVORCE

Word Bank Sample

Genesis 2:24-25
Proverbs 5:15-20
Ecclesiastes 4:9-12
Malachi 2:16
Matthew 19:6
Ephesians 5:21-31

Prayer Bank Sample against Divorce

Most glorious Father, thank You for the good spouse that I have found and married and will live with, all the days of my life. She/he is the spouse of my youth and shall be the spouse of my old age. She/he will not only be a wife/husband but a mother/father, a friend, a companion and a lover. If at any time our marriage goes through a test, Lord, give us the wisdom to get through it together, and may the grace to cope and bear with one another be sufficient unto us. I reject the spirit of separation and divorce in our marriage. I resist all outside influences that might cause confusion in our marriage. Mothers and fathers in-law, brothers and sisters-in-law, friends, relatives shall have no power to destroy our marriage relationship. This word of God prayed and deposited in my prayer bank shall fight for us and unite us together to the end of time. I shall love my wife as Christ loved the church and gave Himself for her, (I shall submit unto my husband as unto the Lord). We shall team up together and fight against the spirit of neglect, abandonment and unfaithfulness. I bind the agents of home invasion, lust, communication breakdown, dislike for each other and gossip. We shall be sincere to each other in everything and not give the enemy room to destroy our peace. We shall jointly raise our children in the way of the Lord, and not divide them between mother and father. We shall rebuke them jointly and also praise them jointly whenever they do anything bad or good. May we not cheat on each other and may we be an example to other couples to emulate. We stand against all other unforeseen activities of the devil that may arise in the midst of our marriage. May we overcome them all and remain united unto the end. I pray this prayer in the name of Jesus Christ. Amen.

PRAYER FOR VICTORY OVER TEMPTATION

Word Bank Sample

Genesis 3:4-5
Genesis 39:7
Matthew 4:1-11
1 Corinthians 10:13
Hebrews 2:18
Hebrews 3:13
James 1:2-3, 12

Prayer Bank Sample for Victory over Temptation

Dear Father in heaven, thank You for assigning Your angels to keep and protect me, particularly in times of temptation. I am registering this prayer against any form of temptation that might come my way as I continue my life journey. Daddy, I know that temptation itself is not a sin but falling into its trap is terrible and also leads to death. Father, I know that Your Son, Jesus, was tempted yet without sin. This was so because He knew the purpose why He came and stayed focus on it. I pray that You reveal to me in advance before it knocks and also show me the way out of it. The Bible has revealed many kings who lost their kingdoms through the power of temptation and sin. But You have made it abundantly clear that with each temptation You will also make a way of escape. Let Your words, Lord, in the Bible and my prayer bank before You empower me to resist every temptation that comes my way. For I know, Lord, You do not tempt with evil, neither tempt You any man. But I am tempted when I am drawn away of my own lust and enticed. I therefore bind the spirit of lust that drags man into temptation and entices him to sin. I pronounce the spirit of lust, barren so as not to conceive and bear sin that will eventually lead to death. May I overcome temptation so as to receive the crown of life which the Lord has promised to those who love Him and keep His words. I thank You Lord for my answered prayer, in Jesus' name I pray. Amen.

PRAYER FOR VICTORY OVER SIN

Word Bank Sample

11 Samuel 11:1-4
Hosea 10:13
Matthew 7:17
Acts 5:1-5
Romans 1:29-32
Galatians 5:19
James 1:15
1 John 3:9

Prayer Bank Sample For Victory Over Sin

Lord, keep me away from every presumptuous sin. Your Word has taught us a lot about sin and the effects of it. The Israelites did not move for seven days because of Miriam's leprosy, which was as a result of sin. This means that sin slows progress, kills vision and also throws the sinner out of Your kingdom. The Israelites also suffered defeat in battles because of one man, Achan. So many things happen as a result of sin, I therefore ask You Lord to keep me from deliberate sin. Lead me not into temptation but deliver me from all evil. Lord, I refuse to compromise my faith, because I know that a day is coming when my faith shall be put to test. Keep me away from strange men/women, from lust, from fornication and adultery and from lies, and from all manner of things that are contrary to Your words. Expose them and give me the strong will to overcome them all. I bind sin by association, sin through marriage, sin through business undertaking, and sin through deception of satan. May I not regard some sins to be minor and some to be great, but help me see sin for what it is, whether big or small, sin is sin. Thank You, Lord, for giving me victory over sin, in Jesus' precious name I pray. Amen.

PRAYER CONCERNING SUDDEN TRIP

Word Bank Sample

Genesis 19:22
1 Samuel 21:8
2 Kings 4:29
Zechariah 8:21
Luke 1:39
Luke 14:21
Exodus 12:31-33
1 Samuel 16:1

Prayer Bank Sample concerning Sudden Trip

Lord, I pray that if it happens that I make a sudden trip, an unprepared journey which I did not prepare for, You O Lord, will lead, guide me and provide help on my way. May You not allow me to fall into the hands of the wicked ones; thieves, robbers, con-artists and those that pickpocket, neither will You allow me to lose any of my belongings. But You, O Lord will send Your angels to keep the way for me and bring me safely to my destination. You will also grant me favor in all that I might desire on my way as I go. Let it come to pass that this prayer in my prayer bank takes care of every danger that would have happened to me on my trip. If anyone marked for destruction is in the vehicle, train, plane, ship or any other means of transportation that I shall use, may my presence in that vehicle prevent evil from coming to all. I bind all demons that cause accidents, all territorial spirits and assigned agents and declare a hitch-free trip all the time. I pray this prayer in the name of Jesus because I know that He will always go with me. Amen.

PRAYER AGAINST MISFORTUNE

Word Bank Sample

Exodus 14:25
Judges 21:2-3
1 Samuel 30:3-8
Jonah 1:5
Luke 13:4
John 11:33-36

Prayer Bank Sample against Misfortune

Father in the name of Jesus, I thank You for keeping me and preserving all that I have committed into Your able hand against danger, mishap or misfortune. A wall will not fall on me or my spouse or children. The ship that transports my wares shall not be destroyed by storm or fire. The plane that I enter shall not crash. My house shall not be engulfed by fire, nor shall my children be involved in any kind of accident. As I deposit this prayer in my prayer bank, let it also be recorded in Your book of remembrance that You did promise to show me kindness and not evil. You did say that those who gather against me shall fall for my sake, and that no weapon formed against me shall prosper. My enemies will not laugh at me and ask "where is your God that you trust?" Let not those who trust in You be put to shame. Let Your angels always surround me, drive with me when I am driving, dine with me when I am eating and sleep with me when I lay down to sleep. Let my words stored up in this prayer bank wake for my defense and cast every misfortune out of my life and house, in the most excellent name of Jesus. Amen and Amen.

PRAYER AGAINST FAILURE

Word Bank Sample

Deuteronomy 28:1-2
Deuteronomy 31:6
Joshua 1:8
Joel 2:23-26
John 31:6
1 Samuel 2:35

Prayer Bank Sample against Failure

Father, I ask that I be the head and not the tail. I also declare that I be not a failure but a very successful person in the world. In as much as I have hearkened unto Your voice to be the doer of Your Word, all the blessings written in Your Word shall come upon me and overtake me. Colleagues of mine, friends and loved ones shall not leave me behind. It shall be forward ever and backward never. I refuse to fail and also reject failure in its entirety. It shall be when I climb any hill, I shall ascend to its top very easily. It shall be success at home, success in the public service, success in education, and success in all endeavors of life. I claim success over all my dreams, those that have manifested and those that have not. One thing is sure, You made me in Your image and after Your likeness. Since You are not a failure I also cannot be a failure. The words from Your lips created all things, similarly the words from the breath You gave me has creative power. I stand by Your Word and it shall come to pass that when failure encounters me it will flee far away from me. It shall be that when failure hears of me, it shall drink a cup of trembling and take a different and separate route! This I ask in the sweet name of Jesus. Amen.

PRAYER AGAINST UNTIMELY DEATH

- **Through child bearing,**
- **Through car accidents**
- **Through plane crashes,**
- **Through boat mishaps,**
- **Through motorcycle or bicycle accidents,**
- **Through sports**
- **Through bullets of war,**
- **Through collapsed buildings;**
- **And other spirits of violent death.**

Word Bank Sample

John 11:26
Psalm 91:16
Psalm 118:17
Job 1:18-19
Isaiah 65:20

Prayer Bank Sample against Untimely Death

Lord, You did promise to satisfy me with long life and prosperity. You said there shall be no death of infants in my household. You did promise that my children shall surround my table and that I shall see my children's children. Therefore untimely death has no power over me and members of my household. I reject untimely death by any form of accident. This prayer is stored up against that day the enemy will raise his ugly head to try to cause havoc in my life and that of my family. At such a time let the air be too hot and peppery and become uncomfortable for the prince of powers of darkness to operate. The water shall be at a boiling point and will not permit the spirit in it to use it as a base to operate. All channels that the wicked ones operate to cause accidents and cut people's lives short will be closed. The sun by day shall be as a scorching, eviscerating, blinding laser beam to shoot the devourer down. I sprinkle the blood of Jesus in the air, land and sea. As I pray daily depositing my prayers in my prayer bank, let a wall of protection be built around me, and as long as I live, let me continue to worship in Your presence. Thank You, Father for the victory that overcomes the world, as I keep our faith in the one and only name of Jesus Christ, Amen.

PRAYER FOR OLD AGE

Word Bank Sample

Genesis 15:15
Psalm 71:9
Psalm 92:13-14
Isaiah 46:4
Joel 2:28
Titus 2:2-3

Prayer Bank Sample about Old Age

Father, in the name of Jesus, thank You because my old age shall be a blessing and not a curse. I shall still be fruitful in my old age according to Your word. My children, children's children and the third, fourth and fifth generations shall bring gifts to celebrate with me. I know that You are the same yesterday, today and forever, therefore as You blessed Abraham with good age without blindness, I claim that favor that at my old age I will still have my eyes to see my great-great-grandchildren. You have said that the glory of old men is their gray hair; therefore I shall fulfill my days and be steadfast to the end. Thank You, Lord for granting my request, I deposit this prayer in my prayer bank that sicknesses like high blood pressure, diabetes and Alzheimer's disease, Parkinson's and loss of sight shall never come near my dwelling. I am thanking You, Lord in advance, for Your faithfulness and Your mighty hand of protection in my old age, in Jesus' name I pray, Amen.

PRAYER AGAINST ERRORS

Word Bank Sample

1 Samuel 15:27-28
2 Samuel 6:6
2 Kings 1:2
Ecclesiastes 5:6
2 Peter 2:18
2 Peter 3:17

Prayer Bank Sample about Error

Lord, prevent me from committing any errors that may cause problems in my life or the lives of others around me. Blessed Savior guide me when I am driving, or operating a machine, in the use of a gun or any other mechanism that could bring adverse effects to my life or the lives of people around me. You, O Lord are wonderful in Your doing, because the error of Uzzah became a blessing to Obed-edom and his household. As I record this prayer in my prayer bank before You, I understand that what the enemy meant for evil could turn out to be for good. Therefore the errors that others will commit will turn out to be a blessing to me, and my own errors will surely bring me favor. Through Jesus Christ, I shall not make any error that will send me, my wife and children to jail. Thank You, Lord for my answered prayer. Thank You again for Your power for victory. This prayer I pray through Jesus Christ our Lord and Savior, Amen.

PRAYER AGAINST SPIRITUAL BLINDNESS

Word Bank Sample

Isaiah 6:10
Isaiah 29:10
Mark 4:12
John 12:40

Romans 11:25
Ephesians 1:17-23

Prayer Bank Sample against Spiritual Blindness

Dear Lord, You made it clear in Your Word that the light of the body is the eye. I reject spiritual blindness and also reject physical blindness. Since a blind man cannot lead a blind man, I cannot lead Your people when I am blind, then we both shall fall into a pit. Therefore Lord, let me see both in the realm of the natural and in the realm of the spiritual, especially regarding Your glory so as to reveal the same to Your people. As I record this prayer in my prayer record, I take authority in the name of Jesus and attack every spirit of blindness and all such spirits that darken vision. Lord, Isaac, through the blindness of his eyes gave the blessing he wanted to give to Esau to Jacob. Therefore I record this prayer in my prayer bank and bind every sickness associated with blindness. I ask that the God of our Lord Jesus Christ give me the spirit of wisdom, and revelation in the knowledge of Him. And that the eyes of my understanding be enlightened that I may know what is the hope of His calling, and what the riches of the glory of His inheritance are in the saints, and what the greatness of His power toward us is. Thank You, Lord, for honoring my prayers. This I pray in Jesus' name. Amen.

PRAYER AGAINST CONTAMINATION/POLLUTION

Word Bank Sample

Deuteronomy 23:13, 18
Numbers 25:6-8
2 Chronicles 15:8
1 Corinthians 10:14
2 Corinthians 6:14-18

Prayer Bank Sample against Contamination/Pollution

Holy, most sanctified Lord, Your word tells us to live in the world but not to get mixed up in it. Like a lotus plant that grows in the mud but is not touched by the mud, let me thrive in this contaminated material world without becoming contaminated myself until the day You will take me to join You in Your purest abode. Lord, You are the Purest of the Pure. Like a red-hot burning rod, whatever it touches catches fire. Let Your purity touch me that I may catch Your fire and become pure like You. Because You are holy, You also want us to be holy. Because You are clean, You also want us to be clean. Every spirit of pollution, immorality and contamination that could drive away Your spirit from me is rejected, and cast out of my body and camp. I deposit this prayer in my prayer bank against the day my mind shall be tried with all manner of evil thoughts, wrong intentions and contaminations. May Your Word and this prayer bring a remembrance of this record before You and prevent me from falling into the trap that the devil sets for me to trap me and bring me into condemnation. Thank You, Lord, for answering my prayer, in Jesus' name I pray. Amen.

PRAYER FOR PROTECTION AND DEFENSE IN WEAKNESS

Word Bank Sample

2 Samuel 21:15
Isaiah 35:3-4
Joel 3:10
Romans 14:1
1 Corinthians 15:43
2 Corinthians 12:9-10
Hebrews 11:34

Prayer Bank Sample for Protection and Defense in Weakness

Father, in the name of Jesus, I thank You who have been with me all my lifetime and I appreciate You who have delivered me from all my enemies. This day I pray that You continue to extend Your hand of protection over me especially when I am weak in the flesh. You did say that the battles that Your children are going through are Yours and that we should hold our peace; therefore, let God arise and let His enemies be scattered. I deposit this prayer in this prayer bank against the day my strength will fail me. It happened to Your servant David, but there were faithful men around him so that he was not cut down by the giants and put Your name to shame. Let such faithful men be around me and help me through Your spirit so that Your name will not be ridiculed among the heathens. I stand upon Your promises one of which is, "behold I am with you always, even unto the of time." When I am weak, there is assurance that You are with me according to Your word. Thank You, Lord, for honoring Your word, in the mighty name of Jesus I pray. Amen.

PRAYER AGAINST CHARM / SPELL

Word Bank Sample

Numbers 23:23-24
Deuteronomy 18:9-12
1 Samuel 28:11
1saiah 8:19
Isaiah 54:17
Micah 5:12-13
Acts 16:16

Prayer Bank Sample against Charm/Spell

Dear Lord and King of the universe, You say that we should not use any other power or make for ourselves graven images. For this is an abomination in Your sight. I use the authority in the name of Jesus to bind all the powers of charms and spells cast into the air to afflict my life and that of my family. Those spells will not affect me in any way. I return them back to the sender. Your Word says we should do unto others as we would expect them to do unto us. I therefore decree that whatever anyone wishes me, he/she shall receive the same for himself and his household. In Your infinite mercy allow all spell casters to repent when they see the power of the Almighty God. Give them opportunity to give their lives to Jesus when the spells and charms that they cast begin to afflict them. Let them come to a conclusion that this is the finger of God. But let those who favor my righteous cause shout for joy and be glad. In Jesus' name I pray, Amen.

PRAYER AGAINST FORNICATION / ADULTERY

Word Bank Sample

2 Samuel 11:3-4
2 Samuel 13:12-14
Acts 15:20
1 Corinthians 6:13, 18
Colossians 3:5
1 Thessalonians 4:3

Prayer Bank Sample against Fornication/Adultery

My Father, to You alone I give all the praise. I thank You for who You are and for Your work of redemption. Holy Father, keep me daily from the evil spirit of lust and immorality. Help me to daily declare my body as Your sanctuary. I've been bought with a price; I am not my own, may the spirit of Jesus dwell in me. I know that the seducer may attempt to knock me off my perch and my flesh may be enticed, but with my prayer in my prayer bank, I will draw strength from You. Cause me to always see every elderly woman/ man as my mother/father, middle-aged woman or man as my sister or brother, and a younger woman or man as my daughter or son. Prevent me from any carnal affairs with any sheep of Yours that I am shepherding. Protect me from all forms and manner of bestiality, pornography and immorality that I am constantly surrounded by. Never allow me look at a woman or man lustfully, neither should I entertain any evil thought in my heart. Thank You for helping me to overcome this spirit of whoredom in the mighty name of Jesus. Amen.

PRAYER AGAINST ENVY

Word Bank Sample

Genesis 37:10-11
Psalm 37:1
Proverbs 3:31
Proverbs 14:30
Mark 15:10
1 Corinthians 13:4
Galatians 5:26

Prayer Bank Sample against Envy

Father God, I declare this day that You will not bring me into fellowship with those that envy me. Your word has made it clear that envy is one of the works of the flesh and whoever envies is a murderer. Every one called a brother or a sister or a friend or a neighbor or even a colleague who shall harbor evil intentions and the spirit of envy in order to destroy my life shall be exposed and removed out of my way. I also pray that You, Lord, clothe me with a sound spirit to not envy anyone for any reason but rather give praise to You at all times. Thank You Lord for answered prayer, in Jesus' name I pray. Amen.

PRAYER FOR DELIVERANCE FROM DANGER

Word Bank Sample

Psalm 37:28
Psalm 91:3
Proverbs 2:8
Isaiah 41:13
Isaiah 43:2
Matthew 8:23-26
2 Timothy 4:18

Prayer Bank Sample for Deliverance from Danger

Great God of wonders, You that led Israel as a flock for forty years in the wilderness and sent Your dread to overwhelm the inhabitants of the land so that they could not do them any harm, keep me Lord out of danger that might come my way in the course of my daily service before You. Whenever You know that there is danger in the place I walk into, order my foot steps to the direction of peace and safety. I deposit this prayer in my prayer bank before You so that at any time there is a sense of danger before me, Your angels will go ahead and dismantle those dangers. Thank You Lord because I have assurance that You are with me always and even forever more, this I pray through Jesus Christ my Lord and Savior, Amen.

PRAYER AGAINST FALSEHOOD AND LIES

Word Bank Sample

Genesis 3:4
Matthew 4:9
Luke 21:8
John 8:44
Galatians 6:7
Ephesians 4:14
2 Timothy 3:13

Prayer Bank Sample for Protection against Falsehood and lies

Father, in the name of Jesus, I reject every spirit of deception and lies perpetrated by the enemy, the lying devil. I record this prayer against all forms of deception, through false prophets, dreams and vision, and through ignorance in interpretation of the Word of God. Lord, let lies and deception be exposed and defeated. Manifest Yourself, Lord, to those who take the Word of God for granted and make merchandise of people because of their greed. Prove to them that You are the only wise God and there is none beside You. May Your mighty hand arrest those false apostles, deceitful workers who transform themselves into the apostles of Christ, and also those ministers of satan who transform themselves into ministers of righteousness. May the seed of deception not be sown in the heart of any member of my household particularly my children by their colleagues in their places of study. May those that double money and are dubious not succeed to deceive mine and claim their valuable treasures. I thank You, Lord, for using this prayer to prevent all forms of deception, in the Mighty name of Jesus. Amen.

PRAYER AGAINST DISOBEDIENCE

Word Bank Sample

1 Kings 13:21-22
Genesis 3:6
2 Corinthians 10:6
Ephesians 5:6
Colossians 3:6
Hebrews 2:2
1 Peter 2:7-8

Prayer Bank Sample against Disobedience

Dear Father in heaven, cause me to obey Your words and walk in obedience as Jesus Christ my Lord and Savior did. A time shall come when my obedience shall be tested. Lord, I am asking You not to depart from me. Clothe me around about You like a garment and cause me to obey You in everything. Keep reminding me concerning this prayer bank and use it to destroy the spirit of disobedience in any form it might try to infiltrate into my mind. At very critical times that it seems difficult to obey under the power of man, compel me through Your power to obey You and keep all Your precepts and commandments. Thank You Lord for letting me know that obedience is better than sacrifice and that it was through disobedience that king Saul was rejected. Thank You, Father for answering my prayer. This I pray in Jesus' name. Amen.

CHAPTER 6

WHY GOD MAY BYPASS OUR PRAYER BANK

Prayer banks are meant to prevent major catastrophes from occurring or minimize their impacts if they occur at all.

A prayer bank gives us something to fall back on when there is news or rumors of impending tsunamis, tornados, wars or earthquakes and other natural disasters. Prayer banks also help us handle unexpected man-made disasters such as wars, arson, theft, murders, robberies and accidents.

Nevertheless, sin and evil intentions of man may hinder the hands of God from moving; pride, boastfulness of man and not giving God all the glory in every achievement might stand as a hindrance and prevents our prayers from being answered.

Behold the LORD'S hand is not shortened, that it cannot save; neither His ear heavy, that it cannot hear: But your iniquities have separated between you and your God, and your sins have hid His face from you, that He will not hear.
Isaiah 59:1-2

Yeask, and receive not, because ye ask amiss, that ye may consume it upon your lust.
James 4:3

The following are therefore some of the reasons why God may bypass our prayer banks.

FIRST REASON

Here is Paul the Apostle:

And lest I should be exalted above measure through the abundance of the revelations, there was given to me a thorn in the flesh, a messenger of Satan to buffet me, lest I should be exalted above measure. For this thing I besought the Lord thrice, that it might depart from me: And He said unto me, My grace is sufficient for thee; for my strength is made perfect in weakness.
2 Corinthians 12:7-9

Apostle Paul besought the Lord thrice that the thorn on his flesh be taken away. But all that the Lord said to him was:

My grace is sufficient for thee: for my strength is made perfect in weakness.
2 Corinthians 12:9a

In accordance with God's purpose and bigger plan for Paul, God reminded Apostle Paul that He has bestowed upon him with abundance of anointing, strength and the power of God to cope and to do ministry. (God was telling him that he already had the victory over the situation). The Lord saw in His infinite wisdom that Paul, an apostle to the gentiles, who then were weak and full of infirmities, should not boast of himself and his own personal power but the power of God in his situation.

The Apostle Paul accepted the Lord's decision gracefully and came to this conclusion:

Most gladly therefore will I rather glory in my infirmities that the power of Christ may rest upon me. Therefore I take pleasure in infirmities, in reproaches, in necessities, in persecutions, in distresses for Christ's sake: for when I am weak, then am I strong. I

am become a fool in glorying; ye have compelled me: for I ought to have been commended of you: for in nothing am I behind the very chiefest apostles, though I be nothing. Truly the signs of an apostle were wrought among you in all patience, in signs, and wonders, and mighty deeds.
2 Corinthians 12:9b-12

God speaking through prophet Isaiah said:

I am the Lord: that is My name: and My glory will I not give to another, neither My praise to graven images.
Isaiah 42:8

God wants us to come to the point whereby we give Him preeminence in all things. Wherever we go, we must talk about Him; His power, His glory, His strength, His might and whatever He stands for. We must present Him as the only hope and solution to man's suffering and drawing people's attention to Him like John the Baptist: *..Behold the Lamb of God, which taketh away the sins of the world,* **John 1:29**. We must let people know that it was for their sake that Jesus left His throne in heaven and came down to the earth. He willingly laid down His life as a ransom for all by accepting freely to die on the cross to save mankind from eternal destruction. When we begin to talk more about God and His power and His saving grace, He will continue to do more and show up in our crusades, revivals, churches, lives and homes.

SECOND REASON

The child born through adultery by Bath-Sheba, the wife of Uriah the Hittite to King David died despite David's intercession unto God to save him.

David therefore besought God for the child; and David fasted, and went in, and lay all night upon the earth. And the elders of his house arose, and went to him, to raise him up from the earth: but he would not, neither did he eat bread with them. And it came to pass on the

seventh day that the child died. And the servants of David feared to tell him that the child was dead: for they said, behold, while the child was yet alive, we spake unto him, and he would not hearken unto our voice: how would he then vex himself if we tell him that the child is dead?
2 Samuel 12: 16-18

It does not matter how much fasting and praying we do, if we try to force the hand of God to do things that are against His will, He will not grant our prayers, and if we fail to live a life that is pleasing to Him, our prayers may not be answered except the prayer of repentance.

Many people today have not fully comprehended the implication of what God was doing by allowing this child to die. The child being born through adultery was only a contributory factor to his death, but the principal reason for his death was because this child-man would have carried the genealogy of king David and carried the Abrahamic Covenant through to Christ. God knew that the seed of David through Bath-Sheba would sit to judge His people Israel. He did not want a child without a name; that is to say, without a foundation and continuity to be a future King and a successor to King David. This is what the Bible says about the after effect of the death of the child:

And David comforted Bath-Sheba his wife, and went in unto her and lay with her: and she bare a son, and he called his name Solomon: and the Lord loved him. And He sent by the hand of Nathan the prophet; and he called his name Jeliliah, because of the Lord.
2 Kings 24-25

The northern kingdom lost its genealogy and kingship linage through sin, but God's covenant unto David was as follows:

And thine house and thy kingdom shall be established for ever before thee: thy throne shall be established for ever.
2 Samuel 7:16

It was in the light of the above covenant that God rejected the child without a name, foundation and continuity.

THIRD REASON

Disobedience to God's Word or instruction: Even a full prayer bank will fail to save one when one blatantly or through manipulation fails to listen to the voice of God or goes contrary to His directive like the disobedient prophet.

WHAT SHOULD WE DO NEXT?

One may have money in one's bank account and still be denied a loan. Conditions for securing loans do not depend solely on the amount of money that one has in one's bank account. One's past payment history may be called to question. The current economic climate may make giving you a loan foolhardy.

Therefore, when a person is walking in sin and in disobedience he does not meet the requirement for God to answer his prayer except the prayer of repentance.

At the same time, there comes a time in a believer's life that he rejoices and the scripture enjoins us to rejoice with those that rejoice, and to sorrow with those that sorrow. If a brother or a sister is in sorrow, God allows His grace which is already sufficient unto us to abound and to be extended to a brother or sister in need. And He also makes His Words available to enable us go and comfort the one in sorrow while dealing with the uncomfortable event.

This gives us an opportunity and enables us to select a different set of words and store them in our " Word Bank" for use in our prayers and counseling for those who go through difficult situations in their lives.

It is our place to create as many "Word Banks" as possible that can conform to our needs and help us comfort those in our midst who are in distress. If we do this, then when the need arises we do not have to scramble and be perplexed, but the words will readily be available for our use.

SAMPLE EVENTS AND WORDS OF COMFORT

FOR COMFORT

Word Bank Sample

Isaiah 51:3
Matthew 9:22
Isaiah 12:1
John 14:18

Prayer Bank Sample for Comfort

Dear Father, in the name of Jesus, thank You for giving me the opportunity to come and comfort my fellow brother or sister at this critical time. Thank You for Your love and for the finished work that was wrought in us at the cross of Calvary by Jesus Christ our Lord and Savior. As You, O Lord, have instructed us to comfort each other with Your word, I pray for the comfort of the Holy Spirit at this critical time of need and difficulty for this household. I pray that they should not lose hope but realize that You are able to do exceedingly and abundantly above all that they think or ask according to Your power that is working in them. I pray Your words keep reminding them that in this world we are bound to have tribulations, but that we should also rejoice because You have overcome the world for us. I pray that the hope of eternal life be released upon every member of this household to enable them come to term with the fact that there is a better place and a better life than here. Thank You, Lord for your love and for answered prayer. This I pray in Jesus' name, Amen.

FOR FORGIVENESS

Word Bank Sample

Ephesians 1:7
2 Samuel 12:13

Psalm 51:5-12
Psalm 78:38
Psalm 103:4
Isaiah 44:22

Prayer Bank Sample for Forgiveness

Dear heavenly Father, thank You for counting me worthy to stand before You and pray this prayer for Your children (this family). They were shapen in iniquity and in sin did their mothers conceive them. But You, O Lord, have not considered all these, but with Your steadfast love have blotted out, as a thick cloud, their transgressions and cleared the cloud of their sins. You have put forth Your hands and embraced them. Cause them also to forgive others as our Lord Jesus taught us to do. As they receive this assurance of forgiveness, may they forever stand and minister in Your presence. May they never be remembered of their past which You already have cleansed them of and have counted them worthy to minister in Your presence. In Your presence in fullness of joy, and at Your right hand are pleasures forever more. I pray that You create in them a clean heart, and renew the right spirit within them. Make them to hear joy and gladness and uphold them with Your free spirit. I pray this prayer in Jesus' name believing that they are healed and restored. Amen.

FOR RESTORATION

Word Bank Sample

Isaiah 57:18, 19
Hosea 14:4
Romans 11:5
Jeremiah 3:21-22

Prayer Bank Sample for Restoration

Thank You Father for fetching these ones back from their wanderings. Their hearts had departed from Your precepts and they had failed to say "Good morning, Daddy." But today You have searched and brought them back unto Yourself. You have called them Your children and have begotten them this day forward. When they kneel down trembling in fear, Your word says to them, "I love you my beloved children, do not tremble but go and change your garments, bathe yourselves and come and take your rightful place, for I have restored you." The veil of blindness is put away from them and now they can see Your glory. The wax of deafness is removed from their ears and they can hear Your tender voice clearly. As they read and study the scriptures, they can hear You minister into their hearts the understanding and joy that once were lost. Their dreams are true revelations of You, and their visions are Your plan and purpose for them. Thank You, Daddy, for who You are, and thank You again for counting them worthy to be called Your children. I pray this prayer believing that these ones are permanently restored. In Jesus' name I pray. Amen.

FOR CONSOLATION

Word Bank Sample

Psalm 119:50
Isaiah 30:19-21
2 Corinthians 13:4
Romans 15:4

Prayer Bank Sample for Consolation

Everlasting Father in heaven, I stand before You this day to pray for those in tribulation, in need and in sorrow. Reach out, O Lord unto them so that they may know that You are the God of all flesh though they do not know You and Your Holy Son, Jesus Christ. I pray this day that You send help and support and bind up their wounds and heal their bruises. Good Father, for the loss that they have already suffered, make necessary provisions through Your angels to reach them even as I stand praying. Through the consolation of Your spirit let them come to understanding and acknowledge You as their Lord and Savior, in Jesus' name I pray. Amen. I also pray for Your own children that are going through difficulty at this very hour. Let Your mighty hand of comfort reach out unto them and console them by taking away their heavy burdens from off their shoulders and the yokes off their necks. Let those burdens and the yokes be destroyed because of Your anointing upon their lives. Let them see You in their dreams as You go before them and lead out of their tribulations into a place of safety. Speak to them that their weeping has come to an end and that although they have been given the bread of adversity and the water of affliction, their teachers shall not be removed. And that they also shall hear the words of their teachers behind them saying, "here is the way, walk ye in it." Then shall they rejoice and glorify Your name. Thank You, Lord, for consoling Your people, in Jesus' name I pray. Amen.

FOR PEACE

Word Bank Sample

John 14:27
Psalm 29:11
Roman 8:6
Psalm 119:165

Prayer Bank Sample for Peace

Dear Father, our Lord and Savior, thank you for this day that You have made that we should rejoice and be glad in it. Thank you for sending Your Son, Jesus Christ, the Prince of Peace, to bring peace from heaven into our hearts here on earth. Help us to keep the peace and remind us to know that the kingdom of God is not meat and drink, but righteousness and peace and joy in the Holy Spirit. Lord, bring peace upon our nation, and upon our state. Let Your peace reign in Your church and in the homes of those that love peace and earnestly pray for it. I pray particularly for this family or couple that the enemy has been fighting. I bind the spirit of confusion, intimidation, trouble and fighting in their lives. I command, as Jesus spoke peace to the troubled waters and there was calmness, that peace be still in their home and surroundings, Amen. Thank You, Lord, for honoring Your anointing in me, and answering this prayer for Your own glory so that our joy may be full. May the peace of God that supersedes all understanding be with us; body, soul and spirit, in Jesus' name I pray. Amen.

PRAYER FOR THE BEREAVED

Word Bank Sample

Psalm 116:15
Eccl. 7:1
John 14:1-3
1 Corinthians 15:19
1 Corinthians 15:51-58
1 Thessalonians 4:13-14
Hebrews 4:9-11

Prayer Bank Sample for The Bereaved

Dear heavenly Father, blessed is Your name. As it is written, in everything give thanks, I give thanks unto You today because of who You are, and because of what You do and will continue to do. You created man in Your own image and breathed through Your nostrils the breath of life and man became a living soul. It also pleases You to take man home at the completion of his work on earth, for this place is not our home. Thank You Father, because there is hope of eternal life because when the trumpet shall sound the dead in Christ shall arise first and we that are alive and remain shall be caught up together in the cloud, and there shall we ever be with You forever. Having this hope therefore, comfort our hearts not to weep like those that have no hope. I pray for the family that one of their own has departed into heaven. I pray that You comfort their hearts and remind them that the one that sleeps in the Lord is not lost but shall awake in the last day into the resurrection of joy. Comfort and remind them that the departed shall not go through any pains again but has entered into eternal rest. Thank You, Lord, for comforting us at this very hour of pains and desolation. In Jesus' name I pray, Amen.

COUNTERING WISHES OF YOUR ENEMIES

Word Bank Sample

Exodus 15:9-10
Numbers 23:23
Isaiah 54:17
1 John 4:4
Luke 10:19

Prayer Bank Sample to Counter the Wish of Your Enemies

My Father, my Lord and my God, blessed be Your Holy name for all things You have done. Thank You for You have the whole world in Your hand, as You have never released any of Your children into the hands of their enemies to afflict them. I use every spiritual weapon available to me; the name of Jesus, the blood of Jesus, fire of the Holy Spirit and the Word of God to bind all the forces of darkness and destroy all the weapons of those that fight against me. You have said that not a single hair on Your children's heads will fall without You knowing the reason. I am therefore confident in Your Word that not a single hair shall fall off my head and the heads of all those who trust in You, without You knowing the reason. I also pray according to Your word which says that we should pray for those who persecute us and afflict us. My prayer therefore is that my enemies do not die without repentance. Let them live and join me in spreading the Good News of the kingdom of God. Turn their names from Saul the persecutor of the way, to Paul the defender of the way. I pray this prayer knowing that what the enemy thought for evil, You Lord have turned for good to the glory of Your name. I pray this prayer in Jesus' name. Amen.

FOR DELIVERANCE (ESCAPE)

Word Bank Sample

1 Samuel 19:10
Ezra 9:8
Psalm 55:8
Psalm 124:7
Obadiah 1:17
2 Chronicles 20:15

Prayer Bank Sample for Way of Escape

Most Holy Father, thank You because as the keeper of Israel, You will neither slumber nor sleep. I thank You much more, for the death of Your Son on the cross was not in vain. It was for my salvation and deliverance. Your mighty hand is upon me because You have anointed me to preach deliverance unto them that are bound. As You prayed for Peter when the devil went after Him and You told him that when he was healed, he should strengthen his brethren. It is the same way that You delivered me to strengthen my brethren. Your word in my mouth is not in vain, the blood of Jesus was not shed in vain, the Holy Spirit was not sent in vain and the name of Jesus was not given in vain. Father, in the name of Jesus, I use these weapons that You freely gave to us to destroy every power that put Your people in captivity and in bondage. I shell and destroy the power of sin and shatter the dungeon and the coven built by the enemy to imprison Your children. I declare that if the Son has set them free, they are free indeed. Through the shed blood, I pronounce them delivered and also make them sit with Him in heavenly places far above all principalities and powers and every name that is named, not only on earth but also in heaven. And by this deliverance I can rightly say that Your people shall possess their possessions. And finally, I say unto these that are liberated, go and sin no more. This I pray through Jesus Christ our Lord and Savior. Amen.

SECURING MY OPENED DOOR

Word Bank Sample

Genesis 22:17
Genesis 26:12-14
Psalm 1:3
Psalm 24:7-8
Revelation 3:8

Prayer Bank Sample to retain My Opened Door

Dear heavenly Father, the maker of all things, the Creator of mankind who hangs the earth upon nothing but the Word of His mouth. You that open and no man can shut, and shut and no man can open. Let it be known unto all people that the Creator of heaven and earth is not a man that He should lie, neither the son of man that he should fail. You have the power to kill and to make alive, to wound and to heal. Arise and show Yourself strong on behalf of Your people. Move in a very special way so that the whole world will come to acknowledge You as God. Let all the doors that You have opened remain opened and let no man be able to shut them, and those You have shut should remain permanently shut and no man should be able to open them. May Your people prosper where others have failed, and may they not labor in vain. Let the door of ministry be opened for them to walk in, from nation to nation and from kingdom to kingdom. I bind the powers of hindrances that might try to block their ways by making them stagnant and unproductive in ministry. I take authority over every spirit of blockage and setback. May the doors of marriage, business, prosperity, favor, etc. that You have opened for Your people remain permanently opened. I pray this prayer in Jesus' name. Amen.

DELAY IN CHILD BEARING

Word Bank Sample

Genesis 1:28
Genesis 21:1-2
Deuteronomy 28:4-5
1 Samuel 1:9-16
Luke 1:36
Luke 22:42

Prayer Bank Sample to Strengthen Those Experiencing Delay in Child Bearing

My Father, faithful Father, blessed Father, all knowing Father, Father to the fatherless, husband to the widows, it is written, "forever, O Lord, Thy word is settled in heaven." You that keep covenants, even a covenant unto Your people Israel that there shall not be found among Your people any that shall be barren, neither shall their vine cast off their fruits before time. Therefore, whose report shall we believe? It is the Lord's. The Bible says this concerning Elizabeth, "And, behold, thy cousin Elizabeth, she hath also conceived a son in her old age: this is the six month with her, who was called barren." This was the confirmation of Your word by Your prophet that a barren woman shall be a happy mother of children. Lord, I do not call this barrenness but a delay, because there is no barrenness among Your people. At this time of delay, help Your people (daughter and son) that are going through it to be at peace and also keep their faith. Lord, I prophesy that by this same season that this prayer is read and prayed, next year, this woman/man shall be a happy mother/father of children. They shall be lively children that will know You and praise the beauty of Your holiness. Is it not written that those that fear Your name shall still bear fruit even in old age? Therefore, there is hope for this woman/man because they trust in Your word. Thank You because the confidence that we have is that if we pray according to Your will, You hear us and also grant us our petition. Blessed be Your name, Lord, in Jesus' name I pray. Amen.

LIFTING THOSE CAST DOWN

Word Bank Sample

Exodus 15:2
Job 22:29
Isaiah 40:31
Nehemiah 8:10
Mark 11:22

Prayer Bank Sample to Strengthen Feeble Knee and Lift Those Cast Down

Father Divine, my rock, my shield, my strength, my redeemer, my hope, and my dwelling place, take all the glory, honor, adoration, majesty, dominion and might, Amen. Lord, touch Your people with strength as I release them into Your able hand. Clothe them all around with Your shield of faith to enable them quench the fiery darts of the wicked and to triumph over sin that weakens them and make their prayer lives dull. This is a critical moment in their lives and that of their families. It is a time that the wicked one has gone all out to test the faith of those that worship You. As he tries the faith of Your people, let them come out pure and clean as gold tried in the fire seven times and purified and made to stand the test of times and seasons. At any time that the enemy tries to pull them down in order to destroy them, Lord, for Your name's sake, arise and protect them. Let not the weakness of their flesh translate into weakness in their spirits. I also take consolation in Your word that says, "Let the weak say I am strong." I, therefore, openly declare that I am strong as they individually also declare, they are strong! Thank You for clothing us with Your strength. I pray this prayer in Jesus' name. Amen.

FOR MIRACLES

Word Bank Sample

Genesis 21:19
Exodus 14:16
2 Kings 7:1
Mark 7:37
John 6:1-13
Acts 3:6-7

Prayer Bank Sample for Miracle

My miracle working God, the Rock of my salvation, I ascribe all glory unto Your name, Amen. If it had not been You, O Lord, who was on my side, men would have swallowed me up. I would have been a reproach and a wanderer to and fro in the land of the living. When I call to remembrance all Your faithfulness to me and how You delivered me from the violent waters that had almost dragged me into the sea, Your praise will not depart from my mouth. You also miraculously saved me from head-on collisions which would have taken my life. Your daily provision for me and my family is beyond my explanation. First of all I am asking You to bless Your ministers with the gift of miracle and the anointing to bring people to Your kingdom. Let salvation be preached from the altar and let the hearers mourn for their sins and repent and give their lives to You. Let them make You the Lord of their lives. Except the people see signs and wonders they will not believe. Let therefore our preaching not be with the enticing words of man's wisdom, but with the demonstration of Your power and Your Spirit. Lord, bring miracles of finance, favor and of health. Let not Your people spend the blessing You bless them with in the hospital. Bless them with miracle children, homes, jobs and connections. Thank You for answering my prayer as we continually sing this song: "He's a miracle working God, He's a miracle working God; He's the Alpha and Omega, He's a miracle-working God." I am praying this prayer in Jesus' name knowing that He is faithful that promised. Amen and Amen.

WITCHCRAFT TRANSPOSITION, MANIPULATION, FAMILIAR SPIRITS AND SPIRITUAL HUSBAND/WIFE

Word Bank Sample

Genesis 27:18-29;
Genesis 30:37-39;
Judges 14:15-18;
1 King 3:16-27;
Isaiah 29:6-8;
Hebrews 1:7;
1 John 4:4

Prayer Bank Sample against Manipulation and Transposition

Most Holy Father, the Maker of the heavens and the earth, mighty in power, mighty in battle, the Great I AM THAT I AM, to You be the glory for ever and ever more. Amen. Let Your Spirit bear witness with my spirit that I am a child of God. I bind every transposition of any kind that the witches might want to use to deny me of my right in life, my admission into the school of my choice, the titles to my property and my certificates after my studies. I reject, refuse, resist and destroy all the activities of the witches. Whenever my name is mentioned, let fire burn. Whenever my exam number is invoked, let thunder strike. I destroy their seducing and manipulating power, their charm and spell, their tricks and all other devices used by the witches to deceive people. I also destroy the special code assigned to my name and exam number to be used against me. I release the fire of God to destroy the kingdom of witches, wizards and all dark powers. I bind incest spirit, dog spirit, pig spirit, peacock spirit and the spirit of the last days. I destroy all blood sucking and blood tapping agents and command the fire of God to burn around me and my bed at all time. I pray that any blood of mine that falls into their hand shall turn to acid and burn them. I become a flame of fire when I am sleeping, in my home, hotel room and any other place, and I completely block them from coming, and also blind their eyes from seeing me. I bind all the activity of spiritual husband/wife. I declare that my body is the temple of God and the spirit of God dwells in me. Who therefore shall try to seduce me to commit fornication with him/her shall be exposed and defeated, in Jesus' name. I cover myself with the blood of Jesus and clothe upon myself the whole armor of God. As I deposit this prayer in my prayer bank, I am calling unto the Lord so that He will answer me and show me great and mighty things that I do not know. Reveal clearly to me everyone that I work with and reveal me to those that You send to work with me. Thank you for giving me victory. I pray this prayer in the name of Jesus Christ. Amen.

CHAPTER 7

KNOWING WHY YOU HAVE TO FIGHT SATANISM, PAGANISM, OCCULTISM AND WITCHCRAFT: MAJOR CAUSES OF CRISES

It is very important to know why you have to wake up and deposit your prayers in your prayer bank against satan, his agents and all their activities. Satan has a well-organized system of government, which he strategically divides into four categories, controlled by his major princes.

For we wrestle not against flesh and blood, but against principalities, against powers, against the rulers of the darkness of this world, against spiritual wickedness in high places.
Ephesians 6:12

It is also very important for us to know the operational capabilities, the personnel and strategies employed by satan and his agents in his war against us individually and the Body of Christ as a whole.

Satan's power structure

1. **Principalities**: These are the next highest in rank of invisible authority after Satan. A prince is the son of a king with certain

rights and privileges. Their names indicate their stations and ranks, as well as their geographical control or municipalities. For example, the Bible talks about the prince of the power of the air in **Ephesians 2:2.** It shows that this prince controls other forces and powers in the air (the lower atmosphere). He is called the prince of Persia in **Daniel 10:13.** He had the power to retain angel Gabriel for twenty-one days until Arch-angel Michael was sent to release him. There is also the prince (god) of this world, who is in charge of the ungodly world systems as indicated in **2 Corinthians 4:4.** He is in charge of all that is in the world: the lust of the flesh, the lust of the eyes, and the pride of life, **1 John 2:16.** This takes charge of what is called the earth, which includes both the land and the sea.

2. **Powers (Authorities):** These are spirit beings or demons vested with authority and power to carry out attacks and also supervise lower powers and grant them back-ups during deliverance activities. They form a link between principalities and rulers of darkness and communicate decisions to all organs of satanic authorities. They motivate these rulers into inhumanity and ungodliness of all kinds.

3. **Rulers of darkness of this world**: Some have erroneously claimed that this refers to world leaders revolting against God. This cannot be so since the Bible has already announced that we wrestle not against flesh and blood, rather it refers to wicked spirits that rule over certain places, continents, nations, provinces, towns, cities, and even streets. There are certain streets or communities that are being ruled by spirits of drugs, spirits of prostitution, or even spirits in charge of suicides. One may not dare send one's precious daughter or son to reside in such a place, unless one is spiritually strong. For example, certain waves of crime in a specific neighborhood can only be accounted for in the light of the presence of "rulers of darkness." These rulers take command from the powers or authorities of darkness which cause havoc by bringing youths in one street against others in another in the name of gang activities, and watch them fight and

kill one another. Gang terrorism is a world phenomenon since the middle of 20th century. African universities are repeatedly interrupted with bloody gang fighting and killing while many streets in America and other places are declared too dangerous for the sake of young adults who operate gangs.

Whatever spirit that rules an area that is what the lives and behaviors of the children and even adults in those areas would reflect. The only way to deliver anyone living under any of these rulers is to relocate them. A child addicted to drugs must be relocated, sometimes to a church environment where prayers are constantly offered and the Holy Spirit of God is in operation. Understand that God is Omnipotent, Omnipresent and Omniscient, but He uses willing vessels, His anointed children to manifest God's power and presence in these places. Where there are no praying people to resist the devil, he will not flee, but rule, **James 4:7.**

4. **Spiritual wickedness in high places (heavenly places)**: These are called the operational spirits. We should not forget that all the spiritual blessings that God has blessed us with are in heavenly places in Christ Jesus, **Ephesians 1:3.** It is therefore not surprising that satan has chosen the lower atmosphere, (the air), to launch his attack against us in order to try to hinder, block, and terminate our prayers that are sent to the throne of God. These are extremely wicked spirits that fly to and fro the face of the earth. When someone is delivered and relocated as suggested in number three above, the principalities or powers send these spirits to win him or her back. They are the source of major accidents in the air, water and land. Witches are categorized in this group; demons that dwell in people are also part of this group. Wherever the principalities in the air assign these operational spirits to carry out operation on a given day, they are always at that point.

A deeper reading of **Deuteronomy 18:9-12** will bring more understanding of the activities of these spirits. They also disguise themselves as apostles of Jesus Christ and as the angels of light and ministers of righteousness in order to penetrate the rank and file in the hierarchy of Church leadership.**2 Corinthians 11:13-15.**

Satanism, paganism, occultism and witchcraft practices are rebellion against God, His Word and His anointed. These practices took their origin with Lucifer when he rebelled against God with his angels and he was cast down to the earth with other spirits (demons) who joined him in his rebellion.

For rebellion is as the sin of witchcraft, and stubbornness is as iniquity and idolatry…
1 Samuel15:23

This is God comparing Saul's rebellion to witchcraft. Some of the time, it is called familiar spirits, those that operate them have the power to tell fortunes and even give counsel. Witchcraft is the most wicked of all the operational spirits as their assignments are to kill, maim and destroy.

MY EXPERIENCE LIVING WITH A WITCH

As a refugee during the civil war in my country, I happened to serve as a house help under a man whose mother was a witch. I was *sold* to him by a man who also sold other members of my family, my mother, two sisters and a brother after he picked us from the road and promised to help us. (This selling was not a general slave trading but was carried out by a few individuals who capitalized on the unfortunate hunger situation that ensued during the civil war and traded children and adults that they picked by the road sides for money). Looking at the members of my master's family with ordinary eyes, they seemed great, rich, and educated. In fact their town, the particular community where they lived had the same name as their family name. This meant that their great-grand father was the founder of the town. But looking within this family, there was immense sadness and sorrow. Almost every member of the family was a drunkard or jobless. During the day I hawked goods from street to street selling whatever wares were given to me to sell and at night we went fishing in the Atlantic Ocean with a shallow wooden canoe. No jobs, no growth, no progress! Why? It was because their mother, who could not see very well physically but was very lucid in the witchcraft world, sold the entire family, children, grandchildren, etc. to witchcraft. Without being told, I was very afraid of my master's mother. She was terrible.

My instinctual fear was confirmed when my master who happened to love me dearly warned me to never eat any food from the mother. He warned that if she gave me food, I should respectfully receive but not eat because, according to him, the longer I stayed with them, the greater the chances of my being absorbed into the family and seen as a member of the family. One day my master took me aside and began to narrate to me how prominent their family was and how through witchcraft in the family, the once prominent family was wasting away. He strictly charged me to be careful and to not receive any food, cooked or raw, from anybody except his wife. He explained that there was no family in that whole town without a witch. He said that witchcraft had become an emblem in the life of every family in that town, a form of defensive armor. It was necessary, according to him, without which others would wipe out that family with witchcraft. The only way to survive was either to relocate or get involved.

FOUR TYPES OF WITCHES

Witchcraft could be categorized into four major types or categories, the blind, deliberate, white, and black. These will be elaborately discussed in the subsequent sections. My experience living in a witchcraft-infested family and other experiences with communities of witches through my years in ministry in various African countries have enabled me to gain sufficient firsthand information and given me the impetus to include this section. I feel this section will help Christian parents to learn to lay hands on and pray for their children as they depart to go to school and as soon as they return from school, since most witchcraft initiations occur in schools. And if possible parents should be advised to monitor how children sleep and also listen to their communications in their sleep. We know that the early missionaries who first came to the continent of Africa nicknamed it

"The Dark Continent" considering the prevalence of and ubiquity of these practices. They were not referring to the color of the skin of the inhabitants but these salient facts. Of course, witchcraft is found all over the world.

1. Blind Witchcraft: A blind witch is a witch who does not consciously submit herself to be initiated into witchcraft, and may not even know that she is a witch. Her friends in school or through any other social activities she might be engaged in could introduce her to the rituals. This is often done with gifts of morsels of food or even special candy or sumptuous feasts. Also those who go to psychics for help and are given "holy oil" to drink or "holy water" or are engaged in certain rituals such as cuts in the skin in the name of spiritual help could likely be initiated. The person infected with witchcraft might suspect that something is wrong through her dreams. This could be flying in the dream (though not all flying in dreams indicates wizardry because in some cases you might be taken away from danger zone by being given a wing to fly away). Others signs are, eating in the dream, love making and lots of romantic situations in the dream, swimming in dirty waters in the dream, partying in the dream and constantly going on tours in the dream and finding oneself at the airport ready to travel or in a hotel or in a strange land and sometimes on high hills or mountains. Some of the time it could manifest in the form of constant confusion in examination hall or outright failure. You will find that by the time you get to the place of your examination you are already late and as you try to write, your pen or pencil is nowhere to be found or is broken, you may never know what to do before the examiner stops the exam. This happens because your mind has been altered and you are not in control of decision making. As all these are happening in the dream, you are encountering downward and steady failure in all aspects of your endeavors in life.

Often one initiated may begin to have rashes on her skin after the initiation. Initiations may also take place in dreams without one knowing. I recall having a dream once where I was offered a sumptuous plate of fried rice. The plate had delectable condiments and was topped by an aromatic baked chicken. The food was presented to me in the dream. I raised my hand over the meal and no sooner did I utter the words "in the name of Jesus..." did the chicken transform into a serpent and began to dance away right before my very eyes! If as a minister of God I was being tempted to be initiated, and was only saved by my habit of regularly praying before eating food, then be warned, you believers and the self-righteous who regularly eat any food placed before you in real life, much less in a dream without the remembering of the name of Jesus. The suggestion then is that anyone who experiences these kinds of symptoms should seek spiritual counsel before they get promoted to a post in the witches' kingdom. A deliverance minister with knowledge in witchcraft matters could help them with deliverance and after deliverance programs.

2. Deliberate Witchcraft (witches by oath and assignment): These are witches who deliberately seek and initiate themselves into witchcraft. Some of them join through occult associations or gangs. These have sold themselves consciously to the devil and are always stopped by the mighty hand of God through constant prayers. Most of the times they undertake to visit churches and can even suppress the worship, making it dull. This happened in one of our Friday revival services and such a witch was exposed and she began to confess her atrocities.

On another occasion, there were three prayer warriors engaged in an all-night prayer vigil at our local church. After having prayed and bound demons, witches and wizards for most of the night, they took a short break at around 3.00 a.m. to rest for an hour. When they awoke approximately an hour later, they found a fourth person slumbering with them. The doors of the church were securely shut. No windows had been left open. How did this individual suddenly enter the church and was now sharing the same sleeping space with them? When he was awakened and asked to explain how he got into the church, he promptly confessed. Right there we began a powerful deliverance process on him. He recanted the secrets of his world, surrendered to Jesus and was baptized.

He said that he was a member of a marauding brood of agent witches and wizard regularly dispatched by their master to infiltrate local churches. Usually he and other agents are able to depress the mood of a prayer vigil, disrupt it, or in fact render it ineffective by countering it with séances. But this particular night, he instead fell into a stupor, was unable to cast countering spells and then realized he must have fallen asleep! He asked if there were others who also had been captured by the spirit of holy slumber. When told that he was the only one, he confessed the name of Jesus and was converted, for he knew he could no longer go back to face his master! I am a living witness to this event for I was the one who interviewed him, gave him money and released him. My prayer team suggested we notify the police, but I told them a soul won for the Lord is worth many more in jail. This was not a police matter, but a spiritual one. We all gave the glory to the One who sets a gentle trap to lure a dynamic soul to the service of the Lord. I stated that henceforth, just like the Apostle Paul, he would do exploits for the Lord, and not satan.

3. *White Witchcraft: This type of witchcraft is so called in some parts of Africa because it takes its root from and is associated with inventions, science, philosophy, stargazing, astrology palm reading, (psychic), and monthly prognostications, **Psalm 99:8; Isaiah 47:13; Colossians 2:8; 1 Timothy 6:20.** Through these inventions, the practitioners seem to have concluded that there is no God and that science is their god thereby rebelling against their Maker. A little knowledge is sometimes worse than no knowledge at all. With a little scientific discovery, many scientists claim that there is no God. In the meantime, the greatest scientist is God Himself. He can make gigantic planets float in a vacuum, or create something as complex as the human eye without any experiments but by just speaking them into existence. There is no evidence in the Bible of God having a laboratory where He tested and retested various hypothesis and theories before creating the cosmos. He simply willed and spoke them into existence. Denying this simple fact is usually the first basis for white witchcraft, after all, witchcraft is rebellion against God, and being in denial that God does exist is witchcraft.

4. *Black Witchcraft: This name was given because this practice was/is associated with human sacrifices, necromancy, divination, charms, magic, consulting with familiar spirits, and flesh eating wizardry, **Deuteronomy 18:9-11.** These are dangerously wicked and are involved with all kind of invocation, necromancy (bringing back the spirits of the dead and talking with them.) And all kinds of wickedness, ritual killing, voodoo, charms and spell casting.

*Please note that the names: **black and white witchcrafts** are not based on the color of the people that practice them. Rather the names are designations indicating the manner and style of witchcraft.

WHY MANY DO NOT BELIEVE IN THE EXISTENCE OF WITCHCRAFT

If you ask people if they believe in the existence of witchcraft they will answer that they do not believe in that nonsense. Some may say, "Yeah, I believe witches exist, but they cannot harm me." If you dig deeper and deeper you discover that the same people who claim that there is no witchcraft are the very ones being oppressed or suppressed by the powers of witchcraft making them to lose their discerning abilities. As we will see later, it is a tactic called "shielding" used prominently by witches and wizards to cover the eyes of a blind witch.

But if our gospel be hid, it is hid to them that are lost: In whom the god of this world hath blinded the minds of them which believe not, lest the light of the glorious gospel of Christ, who is the image of God, should shine unto them.
2 Corinthians 4:3-4

The Bible has not been silent about these heathen practices and even warns of the serious consequences for those that practice them. These are some portions of the Bible that confirm the existence of witches and wizards and other occults.

Thou shalt not suffer a witch to live.
Exodus 22:18

When thou art come into the land which the LORD thy God giveth thee, thou shalt not learn to do after the abominations of those nations. There shall not be found among you anyone that maketh his son or his daughter to pass through the fire, or that useth divination, or an observer of times, or an enchanter, or a witch. Or a charmer, or a consulter with familiar spirit, or a wizard, or a necromancer. For all that do these things are an abomination unto the Lord: and because of these abominations the LORD thy God doth drive them out from before thee.
Deuteronomy 18:9-12

And it came to pass, as we went to prayer, a certain damsel possessed with a spirit of divination met us, which brought her masters much gains by soothsaying.
Acts 16:16

Saul, the first King of Israel, when he was in a desperate situation consulted the infamous witch of Endor.

Then said Saul unto his servants, Seek me a woman that hath a familiar spirit, that I may go to her, and enquire of her. And his servants said to him, 'Behold, there is a woman that hath a familiar spirit at Endor.
1 Samuel 28:7

Jezebel the wife of King Ahab was seen as the leader in witchcraft practices. Those with her type of wicked spirit were barred by God from teaching in the church of God.

And it came to pass, when Joram saw Jehu, that he said, Is it peace, Jehu? And he answered, What peace, so long the whoredoms of thy mother Jezebel and her witchcrafts are so many?
2 Kings 9:22

Notwithstanding I have a few things against thee, because thou sufferest that woman, Jezebel, which calleth herself a prophetess, to

teach and to seduce my servants to commit fornication, and to eat things sacrificed unto idols.
Revelation 2:20

Today witchcraft is changing in form and mode and is openly practiced. In the past witches were dreaded and often times stoned to death. The modification of witchcraft to look like any other religion does not make it a religion. Those that practice it will tell you that it is the oldest of all religions, older than Judaism and Christianity. What they fail to acknowledge is the true origin of witchcraft. It began when angel Lucifer rebelled against God and was expelled from heaven. It is only God that is Alpha and Omega, the beginning and the end. He is the only Omnipotence, Omnipresence and Omniscience. Therefore before the expulsion of Lucifer for rebellion, Judaism and Christianity had existed in God even before Lucifer was created.

How art thou fallen from heaven, O Lucifer, son of the morning! How art thou cut down to the ground, which didst weaken the nations! For thou hast said in thine heart, I will ascend into heaven, I will exalt my throne above the stars of God: I will sit also upon the mount of the congregation, in the side of the north: I will ascend above the heights of the cloud; I will be like the Most High, Yet thou shalt be brought down to hell, to the sides of the pit.
Isaiah 14:12-15

Witchcraft builds it foundations on lies, deception and misinformation. One of these such lies is their rules in the so-called "wicca" which states that whatever you do to someone will come back to you three times, good or bad. They fail to make it clear that a witch can destroy the lives of their children, grandchildren and close family members that are blood related. That is why the Bible says this to those willing to listen:

Ye are of your father the devil, and the lusts of your father ye will do. He was a murderer from the beginning, and abode not in truth,

because there is no truth in him. When he speaketh a lie, he speaketh of his own: for he is a liar, and the father of it.
John 8:44

For the son dishonoreth the father, the daughter riseth up against her mother, the daughter-in-law against her mother-in-law; a man's enemies are the men of his own house.
Micah 7:6

When people say they worship nature and do not worship the Maker of nature, that is deception. When people worship fish and not recognize the fish Creator, that is a lie. When people worship a tree and not the tree Maker, it is ignorance and confusion. Hear what God has to say:

I am the LORD, there is none else, there is no God beside me...I form the light, and created darkness: I make peace and create evil: I the LORD do all these things. Woe unto him that striveth with his Maker! Let the potsherd strive with the potsherds of the earth. Shall the clay say to him that fashioneth it, What makest thou? Or thy work, He hath no hands? Woe to him that saith unto his father, What begettest thou? Or to the woman, what hast thou brought forth? For thus saith the LORD that created the heavens; God Himself that formed the earth and made it; He hath established it, He created it not in vain, He formed it to be inhabited: I am the LORD; and there is none else.
Isaiah 45:5, 7, 9, 10, 18

Who hath formed a god, or molten a graven image that is profitable for nothing? Behold, all his fellows shall be ashamed: and the workmen, they are of men: let them all be gathered together, let them stand up; yet they shall fear, they shall be ashamed together... He feedeth on ashes: a deceived heart hath turned him aside, that he cannot deliver his soul, nor say, Is there not a lie in my right hand?
Isaiah 44: 10-20

Verse 20 again: "He feedeth on ashes: a deceived heart hath turned him aside, that he cannot deliver his soul, nor say, Is there not a lie in my right hand?" Can someone see a similarity here? When God cursed the serpent for deceiving the woman, the curse was that he would walk on his belly and eat dust (ashes) all the days of his life. These ashes are people created by God who chose not to obey Him but chose the path of rebellion and formulate lies to deceive the weak and make disciples for satan. The people who foolishly follow them do not say, "Wait a minute, how old are you my deceiver? From where did you get your knowledge?" Rather, they allow their hearts to be deceived and continue to live in deception and transfer same to their children and children's children.

CHILDREN IN WITCH CRAFT PRACTICES AND EXPLOITATION

In African countries, children are being exploited and involuntarily initiated into witchcraft, most of the time, by step mothers and care givers. These step mothers or care givers are usually the second wives of their fathers where real mothers of these children might have died or have been divorced. Therefore if a man brings in a second wife who will be a step mother to the children of his ex-wife, chances are that 50% of those children are always in captivity through witchcraft by the new wife. Some of these women might have used some evil powers to arrest the men in the first place and blind them to do away with their first wives, in the case of divorce. Or they might have used similar influence to take over in the case of the death of the former wives. Then to make the men to focus on them and love them more than their children they use some outside influence which later turns counter to their actual plan through the deception of the witchcraft priests, satan's agents. It should be the responsibility of the church not to forget the orphans in their daily prayers.

In the Western world, many children are unknowingly introduced to witchcraft through some popular ceremonies, movies and books. The Internet wizardry, and spiritism has recently increased the number of media infecting children with witchcraft. America is one place where celebration of witch or spirit day has come to stay in the name of Halloween, with all its fun fare.

During a recent Halloween celebration, a man of God came home one day to find out that his neighbor had decorated not only her side of the apartment with pumpkins, ghouls and skeletons and spider webs but also hung the same decorations over his rail and door step as they shared an adjacent but common entrance. Now this neighbor has several young children who delight in dressing up in the attires of demons to play trick or treat. The man of God felt this was an opportunity to have a much needed conversation about the topic with his neighbor. He knocked on her door and when she came out, said to her "Madam, we are sorry we do not practice Halloween and as Christians we certainly do not encourage the celebration of witches and wizards."

"This is their day", she replied. "This may be their day, but why dress up as a witch even if it is for playtime? Strangely enough you never see anyone dress up as Jesus on Halloween! Please remove the spider web from my door post," he insisted. "Moreover, he continued, "as a stranger from a foreign land why have you adopted the strange practices of your land of sojourn?"

The lady responded that she was a Christian too and that it is a harmless holiday for kids to have fun and be merry. The man retorted, "I'm happy you are a Christian, I believe you understand what I'm saying. The Bible states unequivocally in **Deuteronomy 18:9** that:"When thou art come into the land which the LORD thy God giveth thee, thou shall not learn to do after the abominations of those nations." This warning which was for the house of Israel has today become a warning to the church. Halloween, and similar practices observed by various people should be your concern as a stranger and as a Christian. By putting the mark of the devil on one's door post, or wearing it over one's countenance, one proclaims to the passing demons one's acceptance of their creed. And because of these heathen practices many of our children are dominated by violent spirits. As long as those decorations hang over the houses of those that celebrate them and the children put on the terrifying masks of demons, ghosts, and lords of the underworld, parents are readily creating an avenue for witches to penetrate and have influence over those children. The children themselves take on these personalities and delight in acting out their fantasies. How easily have parents opened the door to spirit possession of their children through this seemingly benign practice? This is an example of the blind witch or children being possessed with familiar spirits. Ignorance is not an excuse. Whether one believes there is electricity or not, and touches a live electric wire, one will receive a shock. One will not be excused of the shock due to one's ignorance of the laws of how electricity works. The woman had nothing to say than conclude that the kids must have fun. Though my friend's neighbor believed it was a harmless festive practice, as can be seen, this is far from the case. Many children have been initiated through festival foods and candy.

The latest and very popular child induction into witchcraft could be traced to reading weird books and watching weird movies. One of the books that have recently attracted huge popularity and also criticism for its heavy adaptation of witchcraft and wizardry is the Harry Potter's series. Parents were reported to be found waiting at major booksellers' doorposts many hours before its release to buy copies for their impatient children in London, New York and other major cities of the world. The same spontaneous crave for Potter's films was reported by many media. It is right now the best-selling children's book and most widely discussed and patronized film in the Western world. The Harry Potter craze became child frenzy, which infected many parents who did not care to look closely at the material content of the books and movies.

The author, J. K. Rollings, a struggling single mother at the time of writing the book is now one of the richest women in the world by Forbes' rating, courtesy of the Harry Potter's series. The attraction is the supernatural elements! Biblically speaking, I would tell you that the condemnation is the unconscious induction of innocent children into subtle satanism where key actors and actresses fly and hurt like wizards and witches. Fearful and strange sites on the internet excite young adults as much as pornographic sites. Some sites now teach acts of magic and wizardry to the young ones.

WITCHCRAFT MOTIVATION AND GAIN

Why would a parent sell his or her children into witchcraft? Why is witchcraft attractive to its practitioners? Why do witches delight in killing their own children or grandchildren or members of their own household? What do they stand to gain? After all a parent's love is supposed to be the strongest natural bond that exists in the material world. What corrupts this impulse and makes it diabolical? The answer is simple. We will explore some of these questions in this section.

First let us pray. Our Father in heaven, the Creator of heaven and earth, You are the Author of all knowledge, wisdom and power. Reveal Yourself to every reader of this book as we stand to expose all the activities of witches and wizards. I cover the minds of all the readers with the blood of Jesus, and I bind every spirit of fear and affliction as You begin to expose the hidden truth about all forms of witchcraft, wizardry and the occult, their operations, and the solutions. This I pray in Jesus' name. Amen.

Embracing witchcraft practices or joining a coven is like joining any circular social club. One could be poisoned through food by being a friend to a witch or through invitation and initiation or through sexual intercourse or a blood covenant. Once one is initiated, given a name and signed-in, one can impulsively and involuntarily have an out of body experience where one finds themselves in a gathering of devoted people in a feasting ceremony. An out of body experience indicates that the person now has left their body while sleeping and traveled to the remote location where the witches meet. It should be made clear that these meetings could be held in an actual physical location. They could also be held in a world similar and adjacent to ours but completely different in composition. And one can only enter this world in a spirit body. Therefore the first understanding in spiritual warfare is that *you are not this body alone, you are also spirit and soul.* **Genesis 2:7**

As soon as the welcoming festivities are over for the newly initiated witch or wizard, one begins a process of training. Once one partakes in their communion, which is made up of "flesh and blood", the brainwashing begins. A guard is assigned to lead the new captive and to guide him/her through the rules, regulations, benefits and entitlements of their kingdom. Unlike a circular social club, secrecy is the guiding principle, but as in any social club, there is always a lot of eating, drinking and merriment.

The following portions of the Bible are turned upside down and used for their benefit.

And all that believe were together, and had all things in common; And sold their possessions and goods, and parted them to all men, as every man had need. And they continuing daily with one accord in the temple, and breaking bread from house to house, did eat their meat with gladness and singleness of heart. **Acts 2:44-47; Acts 4:34-37**

Soothing and lofty words such as togetherness, fellowship, protection, security, comfort, and happiness are the common phrases used at the beginning of an initiation. But these words later will be changed to: oppress, destroy, enslave, usurp, suppress, ensnare, murder and kill as the guiding principles. When this change occurs it is usually unbeknownst to the captive because it is part of the mind warp he comes under by the subtlest of means.

They practice a form of government similar to socialism, *one for all and all for one*. Once the captive accepts the lavish lifestyle provided there for him and enjoys it, he is hooked. He begins to accept life in his spirit body to be reality and life in his corporeal body to be the illusion. He may live a relatively benign, even wretched life in all apparent indications, but becomes king of the castle and lord of the manor in his nightly adventures. He begins to look forward to his nights. He may rise to a position of great wealth, enjoying unimaginable delights, amenities, comforts, and luxury that far surpass anything this world can offer him. And he usually purchases these luxury resources with either the sweat equity or life of his children or relatives whom he has authority over in this natural world.

Once at this level, one has become a hardened witch or wizard usually losing any sense of mercy or compassion for his relatives or offspring whom he now uses to fuel his lifestyle in the witchcraft world. It becomes akin to drug addiction, as we know it. Just as a drug addict would act contrary to common moral sense, a hardened witch or wizard does not think twice before committing his children as collateral to purchase his or her enjoyment in the witchcraft world. Finally, the time has come for him to offer the same goods he has been enjoying to his compatriots. This is usually when the trouble begins. The wizards' bonded children or relatives begin to experience all sorts of difficulties depending on the contract that the wizard negotiated at the initiation time. Difficulties may include daughters unable to find husbands or men unable to find wives. Or if they do, perhaps the wizard has mortgaged the wombs of his daughters. In such a case, repeated and unending miscarriages and spontaneous abortions. Other kinds of difficulties span the known miseries known to mankind. Accidents, joblessness, insanity, lack of progress in ones chosen career path and even death are some of the bonded contract points witches and wizards use to extract enjoyment, position and power for themselves.

METHODS OF WITCHCRAFT OPERATION

There are basically four types of witches as stated earlier with different modes of operation. The following patterns of devilish operation are noticeable.

1. FLESH-EATERS(FLESH DEVOURERS)

Initially, these witches and wizards are told that they are in for their protection and not to harm anyone. But in the signed form the witch has to list the names of all the people in her household under her authority or influence. Since satan cannot give anything freely, a day will come when it will be her turn to entertain the "congregation" or the "faithful" as she also has eaten from others. Therefore the first category of witches is the soul killing or flesh eating witches. They are very poor and wretched in the physical world and cannot afford to provide all that is needed for the daily feasting. Therefore they have no other alternative than to surrender one of their children, one who is more intelligent or has good standing or is more valuable than others to be the *sacrificial lamb* for the moment. But the nature of death will be determined by the leaders (whether by accident, strange and sudden sickness, dying in one's sleep through spiritual spear, etc.).

2. LABOR-DESTROYERS (ENEMIES OF PROGRESS)

The witch or the wizard might enter into negotiations with the occult authorities and decide not to permit any of their children to be killed, and then the contract point might be as follows: "I have five children who are well to do, let's not kill any of them but all their labor or fruit or marriage is handed over to you." As negotiated and agreed, soon afterwards, the first son working with an oil company is fired, the next day the second child loses his high powered job on Wall Street and is now receiving unemployment. Or perhaps a mysterious fire consumes the skyscraper that houses his daughter's business. And before one can gather one's wits about him, these prospective young millionaires become prospective beggars, living from hand to mouth. Or worse still they may go without children or even without marriages based on conditions during negotiations. It is termed, "Let them live as though they are not." Many of these people under the second category do get deliverance as they begin to run around seeking spiritual help and answers to their unexplained downfall.

3. THE AFFLUENT

The very materially rich and prosperous among the witches or wizards are deceived into thinking that witchcraft could be used as a mark of protection over their children and members of their household if they are readily able to provide whatever is needed for the sacrifices and for the feasts in the witchcraft world. They are forced to make periodic sacrifices according to their negotiation agreement to provide merriment and feasting to the faithful. And yes, this may come as a surprise to many, the witches use the same words Christians use to corral and keep their flock such as "faithful" "brethren" etc. They even have "congregations" and "churches" and can quote Bible verses and mount hermeneutical discourses to defeat the very best pastors of the churches in support of their activities and to legitimize their causes! This category of wizards and witches are usually the politicians, the very wealthy amongst us belonging to secret societies with exotic names. And because they are rich, they have no problem providing whatever is required of them to pay for their feasting. Their children hardly fall sick, they emanate position, power, vibrancy and they live a very peaceful and quiet lifestyle. We are not suggesting that every wealthy and successful person is a witch. Wealth, position and success are blessings and gifts from the Almighty God as it ought to be and often is. The Bible sheds light on some of these occultists that enrich themselves not of the blessings from God but through practices disapproved of by the Lord.

For I was envious at the foolish, when I saw the prosperity of the wicked. For there are no band in their death: but their strength is firm. They are not in trouble as other men; neither are they plagued like other men. Therefore pride compasseth them about as a chain; violent covereth them as a garment. Their eyes stand out with fatness: they have more than heart could wish. They are corrupt, and speak wickedly concerning oppression: they speak loftily. They set their mouth against the heavens, and their tongue walketh through the earth. Therefore his people return hither: and waters of a full cup are wrung out to them. And they say, How doth God know? And is there knowledge in the Most High. Behold, these are the ungodly, who prosper in the world; they increase in riches.
Psalm 73:3-12

These wizards willingly are involved in the flesh eating of others and in the feasting but have power and resources through their wealth to be protected by the law of substitution. At their death, their wealth vanishes and their children become vagabonds and strange death sets in. Their offspring begin a terrible downward spiral through drugs, addiction, sometimes prostitution, homelessness, and finally death.

4. SOUL-SELLING FOR FAME

This is the deliberate seeking out of the occult by persons seeking fame, wealth or other achievement. This aspect of witchcraft is often known by the general public as "selling one's soul to the devil." A musician seeking fame, a politician seeking power, a business man seeking wealth all sometimes deliberately seek out witches (occult) to get these temporary benedictions. Upon being initiated into the society, the captive usually would experience a sudden and dramatic increase in their desired goal. Sudden and astronomical fame as an entertainer, great power as a politician and victory over one's opponents all occur in quick succession. Great and sudden increase in one's business acquisitions will shortly follow. Those who subscribe to these temporary benefits are usually ignorant of the everlasting promise of life in abundance by the Lord Jesus. We must know that that which is sweet in the beginning and bitter in the end is usually in the mode of ignorance. Some Pastors and men of God have also fallen into this trap. They initiate themselves to acquire mega churches using the powers of the devil. Usually such contracts have a short duration and in the midst of the fame or wealth the recipient dies suddenly. It is usually a violent and unexplained death. There are instances where famous pastors have confessed right from the pulpit of engaging in witchcraft to help build their churches.

The power of witchcraft is an inheritable commodity. A passing down of the guard to future generations. It is akin to one leaving their home or bank account or car in a will to their children at the time of death. Similarly when a witch or wizard dies, they usually pass the skill to one of their offspring to carry on the practice. They may not pass it to all their children, but will endeavor to pass it to the most beloved of the children. It is considered a priced commodity to be given only to the most loved child as it confers powers, position and influence on this special child to rule and if possible dominate over their sibling. It is a practice similar to a king dying and the scepter passes onto his specially chosen child. This is the beginning of generational bondage. Witches and wizards rarely die without first initiating one or several of their children into the practice. To fail to do so is considered an utter failure of one's mantle of duty as an occultist. Therefore, once the offspring of the family of witches has identified the existence of witchcraft in their family, a household deliverance is necessary to terminate the handing of the baton down the generations. It is also worth noting that a stubborn child or stubborn children are rarely accepted as sacrifice or for transfer of this inheritance initiation to continue the practice.

As has been stated before, people get initiated into witchcraft at the beginning through deception by satan or his agents. Just as in the beginning in Genesis, satan tempted Eve by telling her that the fruit of the tree will *actually* bring her wisdom if eaten and not death, the evil one still uses this time-tested deception to win recruits for his kingdom. He starts by telling the potential recruit about the enjoyments of the kingdom of witches and wizards. Satan's agents tell them that they should join to receive protection from their enemies, to get power and prestige for themselves and their children so that one is not hurt by other forces. Secondly, satan approaches the very poor and assures them and actually shows them a life of plenty in the very beginning by having them participate in lavish initiation ceremonies and merry making.

But just as our Lord Jesus resisted the devil when he took Him up into an exceeding high mountain and showed Him all the glory of the earth and offered everything to Him in exchange for His worship, we must similarly reject any offer from the devil no matter how enticing it may appear! Because usually after one has been lured in and has accepted the "apple" and has eaten of the fruit of the forbidden tree, the time will now come for them to pay a ransom for all that was offered. Usually one pays dearly with one's own life or onc's children. And God does not forgive deliberate witch as long as they continue to carry out witchcraft practices, hence He says "suffer not a witch to live!" **(Exodus 22:18.)** If many today in the occult had known how the end would be for their children and their posterity, they might not have joined, but there is a way out if one could run to Jesus and forsake satan and all his lies, deception and evil association.

Ye are of your father the devil, and the lusts of your father ye will do. He was a murderer from the beginning, and abode not in truth,

because there is no truth in him. When he speaketh a lie, he speaketh of his own: for he is a liar, and the father of it.
John 8:44

WHAT IS IN A NAME?

The deceptive names that the witches answer help them not only to operate but also to use the power or nature of that object to deal with their captives. If someone is called, "Beggar" all his captives may become beggars. Names like "Flush" may help to flush children out of women's wombs through miscarriages. It may also result in empty treasuries. "Fly" may indicate one with the ability to swat humans as easily as one swats or squashes a fly. And there are others such as "pumpkin," "rat," tortoise (crafty) and so on. The first order of business when a person is initiated is to assign the person a pseudonym appropriate to the person's powers in the evil kingdom. As noted above, one technique of liberation is to "listen," "investigate" and "discover" the given name of a witch to liberate him/her from the clutches of the demons.

An anecdote is proper here. One day, as we gathered to pray, a young lady that I would like to call "Grace" was brought and laid by the front door of the room we were using for fasting. When we opened the door we beheld someone lying by the foot of the door. We shut the door again and called our leader to come and investigate. When she came she identified her as someone she used to know but had not seen for a very long time. The woman could not speak and her body emanated a terrible odor. Our leader commanded that she be brought in. Our prayer team all fell backwards from the strong smell and her almost lifeless body. But I went forward, picked her up as one picks a new born baby and brought her inside. When we examined her, there were no signs of beating or anything of that kind, and then we understood that she had been "caught" as a "captive" by the evil ones.

Two Types of Captives: There are two types of captives, *the prey* and the *lawful captive*.

Shall the prey be taken from the mighty, or the lawful captive delivered?
Isaiah 49:24-25

The prey is also called the *unfortunate or wondering captive*. He could easily be set free at the judgment of the elders. These are captives who disobey their parents by not staying home and wandering with friends and colleagues from home to home, get poisoned or initiated by friends' parents. The lawful captives are blood related or covenanted people and it takes only the mercy of God for them to be set free.

But thus saith the LORD, Even the captives of the mighty shall be taken away, and the prey of the terrible shall be delivered: for I will contend with him that contendeth with thee, and I will save thy children.
Isaiah 49:25

Grace was a lawful captive and had been kept roasted, waiting until December of that year for her to be used for the Christmas feast. She would swell up in the early morning hours of 4:00 and 6:00 a.m., ballooning to about 200lbs. However, at noon time, she would suddenly lose the weight and shrink to a mere skeletal 100 lbs.

Our leader examined her and decided we take up her case. "No more going home," declared our leader, "fasting and prayer has begun," she concluded. We began a three day fast without food and water and on the third and final night of our fast; we were so weak that we had no more strength because we were just coming out of one fast to join another. I had finished cleaning Grace's face as I took upon myself to do because the ladies in our group were not willing to do it. When I looked through the room everyone was already asleep except our leader, she was awake encouraging me to be strong. As soon as I poured the water that I used to clean Grace's face out, I fell on my feet and began to sleep. Suddenly, a mighty sound like that of a great storm began to hum; it hummed and hummed and before I knew it I was taken in the spirit to where Grace was being roasted. There was a serious celebration in the camp. Grace was placed on an old bamboo bed and an old woman was assigned to fan the flames of fire and add more firewood while others continued in their celebration. Somebody I knew came in, lifted up his left hand and they all greeted him in their unique way. They began to praise him with his given name and each time they praised him, he rejoiced and rejoiced, danced and danced.

The angel of the Lord that took me there stood with me and I was very strong. It was now time to recess; they left one by one with instruction to come back quickly. The old woman in charge of Grace fell into a deep slumber while I loosed Grace and ran with her. I ran and ran holding Grace's left hand with my right hand. Our leader knew that something was happening; she saw how there was a struggle in my sleep and how I uttered some words while sleeping. I woke up with a shout, "Grace is back, Grace is back!" Today, Grace is a happy mother of many children. Praise the Lord!

Grace was favored to meet with praying people that God used to set her free. To avoid going through what Grace went through, a prayer bank is very much recommended so that your enemy will not even have the opportunity to look at your face, not to speak of touching you or taking you captive.

ANOTHER WAY THAT WITCHES AFFLICT PEOPLE

One of the ordinances that God gave to Moses clearly spelled out that anyone involved in witchcraft or sorcery or fortune telling should be stoned to death so as to remove abomination out of the land; hence the statement: "Thou shalt not suffer a witch to live," **Exodus 22:18.** It was then possible to do that because the government was a Theocracy and the land was ruled by God through His appointed messengers. But the more the population of the world grew, the more people rebelled against God and the more various nations of the world made laws that permitted everyone to live together not minding the influence these occult associations had on the populace.

Apostle Paul writing to the Corinthian church strictly charged them as follows:

Be ye not unequally yoked together with unbelievers: for what fellowship hath righteousness and unrighteousness? And what communion hath light and darkness? And what concord hath Christ with belial? Or what part hath he that believeth with infidel? And what agreement hath the temple of God with idol? For ye are the temple of the Living God; as God hath said, I will dwell in them, and walk in them; and I will be their God and they shall be my people. Wherefore come out from among them, and be ye separate, saith the Lord, and touch not the unclean thing; and I will receive you, And will be a father unto you, and ye shall be my sons and daughters, saith the Lord Almighty.
2 Corinthians 6:14-18

Therefore, because we are unable to follow the biblical injunction to not have anything to do with the wicked ones, we the believers become victims and captives or prey.

AN AFFLICTED YOUNG MAN FROM OVERSEAS

One day a young man travelled from his base in a foreign country where he lived, studied and worked to his native country in Africa. He had been away from his homeland a long time and was excited to meet old friends. One day as he took a walk with one of his brothers along an old track behind their home, he met an elderly woman on the street and recognized her as a neighbor whose children he used to play with in the sand before he left for overseas many years back. He went, bowed down according to custom and greeted the old lady. He willingly introduced himself to the old lady who became very happy to see him again while she was still alive. He brought out his wallet and gave the elderly woman some money. This young man never realized he had sold himself to a witch. The old woman received the money and thanked him for his kind gesture.

That night, the old woman took the same money that the young man had given her to their witchcraft occult meeting and reported the young man claiming that she had been insulted. "He mocked me and tried to prove to me that he is better and well-dressed, and more educated than me. I never asked him for anything, not a penny, but since he saw me to be wretched, he must be made wretched, too."

A day for a hearing was fixed because according to their practice, witches must first justify themselves that you instigated war and insults against them and therefore you were at fault for deliberately going to mock a senior witch. Within an hour, a decision had been reached. The young man was found guilty as reported. "Make him wretched, penniless and miserable," they all chorused in one accord.

No sooner had the young man arrived back at his base where he had lived and worked the past fifteen years than he received a letter from his employer that he was relieved of his position as a manager in a pharmaceutical company because something had gone missing when he was away. The wife took offence and did not even want to hear her husband's part of the story, and left him. The following week, he received a court summons to appear before a district judge for default in some loan payment. The young man began his downward trend in every aspect of his life.

Thank God for praying parents. His mother was in a prayer meeting back home when everything that took place was revealed to her. Prayer warriors went into a seven-day fast and one of the prayer warriors was taken in the spirit realm, to where the young man's money was changed into pennies and spread on the floor to be trampled upon. Sometimes a penny would be cast into the sea and left to sink, thereby sinking the financial fortune of the young man. At other times a few pennies would be put in a bag and hung on a tree and made to toss with the wind, thereby tossing the financial stability and life of the young man. Whatever thing they wanted to happen in the life and finances of the young man would happen through the actions performed with those pennies that represented the young man's finances.

THERE IS POWER IN THE WORD OF GOD, NAME OF JESUS AND BLOOD OF JESUS

If only believers knew the power that they have through Christ Jesus, they would not bother about the activities of the wicked people but would rather use their good works and the prayers that follow their good deeds as traps to bring the wicked to the Lord. In the case of the young man, it took a man of understanding to deposit money in God's tray kept in the altar of the Lord and prayed upon for a period of time. While that was going on, prayer and fasting was also on so that those pennies in the witchcraft camp, water and those tossed by the wind lost power in representing and directing the young man's finances. This system is termed, "Disconnecting from the source of affliction." Anyone whose good deed is used against him has to be prayerfully "disconnected and reconnected." Using those portions where the Lord commanded us to do good to others, as we will see later, the devices of the wicked was turned against the wicked. The money from the presence of the Lord that was prayed upon was given to the young man to start a new life and prosper. But the pennies in the witchcraft camp were converted and used as bullets against the wicked. The pennies became a hail of stones raining down onto the camp of the wicked. That made that particular meeting place dangerous for the witches and prompted them to clean up their camp and do away with those pennies. While there was confusion in camp of the enemies, the young man began a process of recovery. (Always pray for confusion in the camp of the enemies). A portion quoted below is very appropriate:

Let God arise, let His enemies be scattered: let them also that hate Him flee before Him.
Psalms 68:1

Should events like the one above stop believers from doing good work and showing mercy? No. But the Bible says we have to be wise.

When somebody comes to borrow or ask of you, do not say, "I don't have" if you do have, because that will make you go against

God's Word. There are many portions in the Bible to use as a foundation for lending and giving. **Matthew 5:42** is very appropriate.

Give to him that asketh thee, and from him that would borrow of thee turn not thou away.
Matthew 5:42

But if it happens to be a sudden gift like that of the young man in the story above, a prayer bank takes care of that. The daily deposit of prayer into you prayer bank with verses like:

Blessed are the merciful: for they shall obtain mercy. **Matthew 5:7**

And the parable of the Good Samaritan in **Luke 10:30-37,** which concludes with the word: ***"Go, and do thou likewise."*** The Lord is sending us to go and do good things to others and help the poor and needy.

The young man in this story lost in the judgment of the witches because, first of all, while the old woman in question did not ask him for money, he did not have a preventive prayer bank. Such a prayer might go like this: "May I never be held captive for showing mercy to people who have not sought my help". Secondly, he did not listen to his spirit to hear what the Lord was saying to him before he rendered what he thought was a help. Or simply, when you give always remember to give in the name of the Lord, for whatever is given in the name of the Lord is safe from wizardry.

There are certain things that should always accompany our proclamations: "I love you in the name of the Lord", "I give you in the name of the Lord, "I greet you in the name of the Lord", and so on. Do all you do in His name, remembering Him always and never forgetting Him. "And whatsoever ye do in word or deed, do all in the name of the Lord Jesus, giving thanks to God and the Father by Him," Colossians 3:17. With Him all things are possible, by ourselves nothing is. If you always perform your deeds in the name of the Lord and leave the consequences of your actions to Him, you will never live to regret any pious action turned on its head by evil doers.

Prayer Bank Sample

Most blessed Father, I thank You for giving me the opportunity to be who You want me to be. I stand by Your Word and make this declaration: I shall not be held captive for showing mercy to people. I shall not be in bondage and in captivity when people borrow from me. I allow Your Word to play a part in everything that I do with the finances that You give me. I ask the fire of the Holy Spirit to burn around the money that I give out to people. Let the monies be a blessing to everyone that receive them to use according to the intended purpose, but let them become "bullets of fire and hails of fire" in the witchcraft camp and destroy all their wicked devices and plans against me and my finances. Since I am following the directive of the Lord to do what I do, the Lord will fight for me at all times. And because I give, it shall be given unto me, good measure, pressed down and shaken together and running over shall men give into my bosom. I shall receive far and beyond finances but everything that I give that involves giving: love, mercy, faithfulness, peace and every good thing shall I receive back. Dear Lord, I am hated because you were hated for doing good. May You, O Lord, arise and may your enemies be scattered. You have promised to be an enemy to my enemy and love them that support my righteous cause. Show Yourself strong on behave of those that love Your Holy name and keep You commandments. I pray this prayer in Jesus' name. Amen.

HOW WITCHES PENETRATE THE HIERARCHY OF THE CHURCH

It is important to warn church leaders to abstain from eating food that members cook in their homes and bring to the pastor. In a previous example given in this book, a sister in my congregation kept trying to feed me with food she would prepare at home and bring especially for me in church. When she noticed that I was not eating her food, she approached me one day and said. "Pastor, the Lord has asked me to cook for you! Would you come to my home for dinner?" That night in a dream Iwas invited to a church function with many people in attendance, some of whom I could identify. Suddenly a plate of rice was handed over to me with a big leg of chicken, commonly called a drumstick. If I were the type that eats without praying, today I would be singing the blues. As soon as I collected the plate of rice I proceeded to bless it. I raised my right hand over the meal and no sooner did I say, "Father, in the name of Jesus..." the drumstick sprang up and became a big cobra (serpent).

I threw the plate on the floor as people scattered in all directions and the place erupted in confusion. When I woke up I understood what the sister wanted to do with me. If I, as a minister of God, was being tempted to be initiated and was only saved by my habit of regularly praying before eating, then it is a serious problems for all those believers and leaders who regularly eat any food placed before them in real life without first praying, as they could easily be initiated through food in their dream. Because how can someone who does not pray in the natural world pray in his or her dream world?

Another incident worth noting during my years of ministry was when certain female members of the choir decided to "test the power of God in their pastor!" As I was getting ready for an all-night prayer vigil one fateful Friday afternoon, I went to my office to meditate but promptly fell asleep. In a trance the Lord showed me that it would be a tough night ahead as He revealed three girls in the choir who had gone to contact four more girls outside the church and invited them to come to church because, according to them they were going to test the power of God in their pastor that night. I quickly sent for my wife and told her my vision and we got ourselves ready. That night power actually surpassed power as the saying goes and they were all subdued and confessed.

Here are some points to note:

- Lack of preparation in advance of any major program will allow witches and occultists to come and have a field day in the church unhindered. After all, they do have their leaders backing them and may send reinforcements if they sense danger.

- Sexual relationship with women or girls in the church by the pastor or the church leader weakens him and opens the church hierarchy to witchcraft manipulation and contamination.
- Witches work harder than ordinary members of the church and are quick to seek promotion so as to get close to the leadership. It is the place of the pastor to hear from the Lord before appointing anyone to any position in the church.
- Above all, the church should have a standard prayer team groomed and nurtured by the pastor with a standing rule not to admit anyone except as directed by the Holy Spirit. Members of this prayer team should fast constantly and intercede for their pastor and the membership.
- Many pastors allow members who are also members in secret societies and occult organizations to take leadership positions in their churches and from there they see opportunity to initiate other members through communion and the giving of sacrament.
- Some pastors who have escaped initiation by witchcraft members through food and sex could be seduced through other ways and rendered weak and feeble and made to lose their sense of discernment and weakness in their prayer life.
- Money changing in the church during offering time is not acceptable and should be discouraged. When someone gives an offering unto the Lord and someone else brings money and says, "Give me change." and somebody's offering is given to him without first being blessed, the person whose offering is used for making the change may not receive a reward from God and may suffer a downward trend financially. This is so because the money received has not yet been blessed by the authorized person in the church. But after the money is blessed and handed over to whoever is authorized to make expenditure for the church, whatever change that is given out does not affect the giver because the Lord has received it. Many witches use money exchange in the church to render church members poor by taking members' offerings to witchcraft coven for sacrifices.

Note also that some pastors and church leaders have been used by the devil to attract congregations whose salvation is in the balance. Many pastors have been in absolute witchcraft and occultism for years, but after they have transferred a lot of these spirits to their congregations through laying of hands and impartation, they come to confess their past. At this time, many members of their local congregation may leave, but with something in them while the devotees will remain and back their pastor because their names have already been short-listed and their hearts bought. Those who leave those churches should seek deliverance or stand the risk of lusting throughout their entire life while some backslide and turn hostile to the church without restoration.

It is therefore the responsibility of every believer to always have a personal and devotional time with the Lord who will reveal to them what is going on in the church and the leadership.

*See also, “Rape through Manipulation” in the next chapter.

For such are false apostles, deceitful workers, transforming themselves into the apostles of Christ. And no marvel; for Satan himself is transformed into an angel of light. Therefore it is no great thing if his ministers also be transformed as the ministers of righteousness; whose end shall be according to their works.
2 Corinthians 11:13-15

It is advisable for one to prayerfully seek the face of the Lord in everything he is involved with in life; whether church or club or marriage, etc.

SOLUTIONS AND HOW TO EXPOSE WITCHCRAFT ACTIVITIES:

As could be seen, there are four methods of operations and everyone does not fall under the same pattern of arrest and affliction. The only solution that people who fall under method 1(flesh-eating witch) have is to have their prayer bank fully loaded. The daily recording of prayers in their prayer bank will break the yoke of untimely death and witchcraft manipulations through arrest, lock-ups and killings. One should also live a clean and pure life devoid of lying. This will help neutralize the power of the witches.

If one finds that they fall within method or category 2 of arrest, where all your labor is without fruit with serious hardship, one does not wait until one is completely drained before beginning to fast and seek the face of the Lord. Many people only know how to pray the prayer of asking, but not many seek the face of the Lord concerning changes that they begin to experience in any aspect of their lives. Above all, people who begin to suffer in the hands of the witches are also being veiled so as not to be aware of their surroundings. When a man is veiled, anything black may appear red or yellow. A captive may unconsciously be very mad with anyone who suggests a person to him or her with regards to his or her problem. Therefore the only prayer that could help these people are, *seeking, targeted* and *specific* prayers.

1. **SEEKING**: Whenever someone seeks the face of the Lord, he delights in knowing the will of God for his life. He also delights to know why his businesses or finances are going down and why strange things are happening to him.

Call unto me, and I will answer thee, and show thee great and mighty things, which thou knowest not.
Jeremiah 33:3

At the time of seeking God's face, all dreams, revelations and visions must be closely documented and observed. Joshua sought the face of the Lord to know why Israel was defeated by Ai.

2. **TARGETED:** God answered Joshua that Israel was the reason for the defeat. Joshua's target area was then the house of Israel. He had to target all the tribes of Israel. Another name for this is casting of lots. This was the system used to identify Achan who entangled himself with the accursed things in Jericho and led to the defeat of Israel's army in Ai.

3. **SPECIFIC:** A detailed prayer is a prayer that is divided into different aspects. People and things shown you in a dream or the target revealed must further be broken down so as to arrive at a specific person or place. You do not ignore anything, no, not an inanimate thing, not a lamp post, not a piece of clothing, nothing. Everything, every article is subject to intense scrutiny because the witches like to camouflage and take on other people's postures, faces, and countenance. Specific prayers asking the Lord to unmask these chameleons will expose the masked wicked.

Going back to the story of Achan in **Joshua chapter 7** lets us see how Joshua combined these three approaches to achieve his goal. Israel has been defeated in the battle with Ai and what did Joshua do? He sought the face of the Lord.

And Joshua rent his clothes, and fell to the earth upon his face before the ark of the LORD until the eventide, he and the elders of Israel, and put dust upon their heads. And Joshua said, Alas, O LORD GOD, wherefore hast thou at all brought this people over Jordan, to deliver us into the hand of the Amorites, to destroy us? Would to God we had been content, and dwelt on the other side of Jordan! O Lord, what shall I say, when Israel turneth their back before their enemies! For the Canaanites and all the inhabitants of the land shall hear of it…?
Joshua 7:6-9

Joshua began seeking the face of the Lord. He cried to God and made his case to God based on God's own Words and promises. Let's hear what God said to Joshua:

And the LORD said unto Joshua, Get thee up; wherefore liest thou thus upon thy face?
***Israel hath sinned**, and they have also transgressed my covenant which I commanded them…*
Joshua 7:10-11

God has now revealed to Joshua where the defeat came from; the house of Israel. The house of Israel is the target, not the Canaanites, not the Amorites and not even Ai that defeated them. Once your target is revealed, the details or the specifics will easily be arrived at. One may pray a general prayer for a whole year without arriving at something, but once your prayer is streamlined and concentrated the result is near. Joshua's target was the house of Israel.

In the morning therefore ye shall be brought according to your tribes: and it shall be, that the tribe which the LORD taketh shall come according to families thereof; and the family which the LORD shall take shall come by households; and the household which the LORD shall take shall come man by man.
Joshua 7:14

So Joshua rose up early in the morning, and brought by their tribes; and the tribe of Judah was taken.
Joshua 7:16

The house of Israel has been targeted and the tribe of Judah has been found. Now is the time to be specific so as to arrive at who the culprit was.

And he brought the family of Judah; and he took the family of the Zarhites: and he brought the family of the Zarhites man by man; and Zabdi was taken: And he brought his household man by man; and Achan, the son of Carmi, the son of Zabdi, the son of Zerah, of the tribe of Judah was taken.
Joshua 7:17-18

This is the type of prayer that exposes and defeats the enemy and his agents-the witches and wizards.

People in method three, that is the affluent, who grow up to realize that their parents sold them to witchcraft should without delay seek the reliable services of an authentic man of God, anointed within the Christian Body of Christ, qualified to intercede and pray for a name change, breaking of curses, breaking of soul ties and renunciation of the devil's society. If this curse is not destroyed out of this family, there may be a perpetual and generational imprisonment. All the members of such a family can come together and have what is called: "family liberation." Here **Ezekiel 18,** "Personal or Individual Responsibility should be used to disconnect the past from the present.

It is important to inform those suffering from witchcraft oppression to seek the Lord in order to know the operational name of the witches or wizards that oppress them, as this is one of the quickest ways to get delivered from this terrible spirit. The Lord might take you in the spirit to a hiding place in the convention camp of the witches and once the witch's name is known you will now pray invoking that name. The witch will become feeble and exposed and will also be discharged. It is one of the quickest ways to get liberated from the power of witchcraft. Knowing the name with which a witch operates is similar to when Achan was identified by name. It helped Joshua take care of him in one day, and he went ahead to defeat Ai and restored Israel's glory.

When the Spirit of the Lord takes you to the "convention camp" of the witches, like prophet Ezekiel was taken in the Spirit from Babylon to the temple in Jerusalem to be shown the abominations that were being perpetrated by the Jews left behind in Jerusalem after the captivity, **Ezekiel chapter 8** there you will learn things that could beat your imagination. It is the Lord's personal design that He takes you to witness the amazing things that go on daily in the coven, especially those who have sought Him diligently with a strong will to bear what they see. You will be surprised to see a very trusted family member, a beloved church member, or a close friend displaying the type of dance steps that you cannot imagine. These dance steps will accompany serious praise based on the coven's assigned or operating name. It is at this time that you learn of the operating names that various members of the coven bear and use in their witchcraft activities. All that you witness in the witchcraft coven becomes a weapon in your hand in helping you to defeat the witches that afflict you and others and put them in bondage and in captivity.

Those in the category of the fourth method of witchcraft operation should follow the same pattern of deliverance prescribed for those under method three. Whenever you see a very influential political family or a family of a renowned artist beginning to fade and losing fame and family recognition, then know that something is wrong somewhere. Deliverance should be sought as prescribed for method three above.

In the final analysis, there is individual will and freedom to opt out of any occult society upon accepting Jesus as Lord and Savior. Usually the occult authorities would try to keep such an individual in perpetual bondage by threatening dire consequences for renouncing their society. But anyone with strong faith, will and conviction in Christ Jesus is free to leave after submitting oneself to the protective arms of the power of the Holy Spirit and public confession of Jesus Christ as Lord and Savior of his or her soul.
Romans 10:8-11

CHAPTER 8

FURTHER STUDY ABOUT WITCHCRAFT, OTHER RELATED AGENTS AND THEIR TACTICS

DEALING WITH SPIRITUAL HUSBAND / WIFE, MARINE SPIRITS, FAMILIAR SPIRITS AND SERPENTINE SPIRITS

The concept of spiritual husband or wife is something that a lot of people do not really believe in or understand. Whether it exists or not is to be seen in the context of what a victim of a spiritual marriage has to say. Spiritual husbands or wives are male or female spirits that come regularly to have sexual relationship with their human partners in their sleep. Usually an individual's family background plays a major role in the issue of spiritual marriage. For example, if a family had been involved in idol worship prior to joining a church, and perhaps without actually being born again, the family spirit (familiar spirit) continues to be a part of that family. The male spirits get married to the female children, while the female spirits get married to the male children with regular visits for friendship and sexual purposes.

Another major source of the introduction of these spirits to families is through a common practice during child birth ceremonies. In some typical African families, when a child is born many guests come to the new born parents' home. White powder is usually put in a plate at the reception point where guests will drop some money and take some quantity of the powder. They will rub this powder on their faces and around their necks as a mark of celebration with the family for their new born baby. Inadvertently, such parents open the door for witches and wizards to deposit evil money which they regard as bride price (money that is paid by a man to marry a woman) for the engagement and marriage of that child from his or her infancy. And as soon as the child becomes an adolescent, he or she starts having visitations of male or female spirit partners coming to have sexual relationships with them. Another source of spiritual husband or wife is usually where the parents or one of the parents was involved in occultism, secret society or witchcraft activity and had enrolled their children in their secret society by submitting their names during registration or initiation. These children automatically will have visitations by these spirits. Yet, another very important source is the child care providers or babysitters. Many babysitters are crown witches, marine witches, spiritists, or are possessed with familiar spirits, serpentine spirits or are actual witches. They will initiate the children under their care at their infancy without the knowledge of their parents. Also, children who carry out some traditional dances during festivities or get involved in eating things sacrificed unto idols or used for occult festivities are usually married to spiritual wives or husbands. These are the spirits that control the activities that these children performed during the dance. These children become engaged and married to these spirits, which pay them regular visits and sometimes have sexual relationship with them.

Furthermore, mothers that are frequent visitors to cemeteries during pregnancy expose their unborn babies to spirits who engage and later marry or possess those children. Furthermore, another reason for having a spiritual husband or wife is due to soul ties with a departed husband or wife that has not been severed. This is further explained under the subheading, "Spiritual Husband/Wife and Soul Ties." Yes, a wandering spirit resembling a departed partner could constantly visit his or her living partner for sexual purposes, especially where the departed partner was not born again and the living partner is not filled with the Holy Spirit. **Genesis 6:1-2**

EFFECTS OF SPIRITUAL HUSBAND / WIFE

Ladies and men who have spiritual husbands or wives find it difficult to find real physical husbands or wives. They may always get close to getting married, be engaged for a long time, but as discussions for marriage progresses, disagreements ensure and the relationship comes to an abrupt end. For those who have succeeded to marry, miscarriages become a common phenomenon. The night before a miscarriage occurs, the woman is most likely to be approached by a man in the dream, who would resemble her husband and will have sexual relationship with her in the dream. After the relationship, the woman may awake hemorrhaging or with pains that would later result in a miscarriage. On the part of the man with a spiritual wife, his living pregnant wife could find herself fighting with other women in her dream who would hit her stomach and the results would be serious pains, bleeding or a miscarriage.

People with a strong prayer base can overcome this as they start praying as soon as they wake up with pains or bleeding. Another effect of spirit spouse possession is an often recurring uncontrollable anger. A spiritual husband or wife uses anger to send away those who would have considered their captives for a wife or husband. Another effect of the presence of a spiritual husband or wife is fluctuations in business undertakings. You may record quick success in any business you are engaged in, but may suddenly become penniless if you make any effort to get married. This is because spiritual husbands or wives are very jealous. A prospective husband or wife could suffer some losses because some wicked spiritual husbands or wives could go after the would-be partner's wealth or businesses to prevent him or her from marrying. Marriage proposals or weddings are usually met with cancellations due to some unfortunate circumstances. And a man with a spiritual wife may regularly experience bed wetting due in part to the fact that he becomes romantic and give in to a woman in his dream. A woman may experience irregular menstruation which makes it difficult for the woman to get pregnant. You may have problems similar to these problems described above that are not as a result of a spiritual spouse. But once you are involved in a romantic situation or sexual relationship in your sleep, then your problem is a spiritual husband or wife.

SOLUTION TO SPIRITUAL HUSBAND / WIFE

The major solution is in your knowledge of the Bible. The unmarried female and male should apply the following portions of the Bible amongst others before they go to bed: **1 Corinthians 3:16-17; 1 Corinthians 6:15-20,** for their daily declarations. **Ezekiel chapter 18: 1-20** is another appropriate scripture to apply, it is termed, "Personal or Individual responsibility." It is used during prayer declarations to disconnect from the past that has to do with generational spirits, ancestral spirits, curses and soul ties. Ezekiel Chapter 18: 1-20 is especially relevant for breaking of bondages, strongholds and all forms of idol worship and witchcraft practices by one's family. Praise and worship must be regarded as a priority. Reading and studying the scriptures is also highly recommended. Having regular prayer time and daily meditation of the Word of God, especially in the morning (morning devotion) and spirit-filled prayer before bed must be observed.

Married couples that are afflicted with spiritual husbands or wives have an advantage because the scripture says, "two are better than one..." Their closeness in relationship is a great tool in sending away a spiritual husband or wife. The couple must learn to eat together and to pray together holding hands. They must apply the following scripture verses in addition to the ones named above: **Matthew 19:4-6; Proverbs 18:22; Eccl. 4:9-12; Proverbs 5:15-20; 1 Corinthians 7:3-5,** etc. My suggestion is that since spiritual husbands and wives are sometimes stubborn due to individual's inability to take authority over them, married couples should make their daily declarations as if they are retaking their marriage vows. While they kneel by their bed for declaration before going to sleep, the husband should take the wife's hand and declare thus:

"This is my wife (say her name). She is my legally married wife before God and many witnesses. Her body belongs to me alone and mine belongs to her. I have no other relationships, physical or spiritual besides her. Anyone who tries to carry-on asexual relationship with her in the physical or spiritual realm apart from me, goes against the Word of God that says, 'What God has joined together let not man put asunder,' and, 'Thou shalt not covert thy neighbor's wife.' Such a spirit therefore must face the wrath of God, in Jesus' name. Amen. No one comes in my likeness or resemblance to commit abominable acts with my wife against the Word of the Lord. May we prosper in our relationship. If she had knowingly or by error taken anything from any man in the physical or in the spiritual which could be used against her and put her in perpetual bondage, we collectively return such a gift in Jesus' name, Amen." And the wife will also pray similarly using the name of the husband in her daily declaration.

Concerning family idols or gods or worship in the past, reading aloud this portion and declaring its content is very effective. "...The soul that sinneth, it shall die. The son shall not bear the iniquity of the father, neither shall the father bear the iniquity of the son: the righteousness of the righteous shall be upon him, and the wickedness of the wicked shall be upon him." **Ezekiel 18:1-20**

The above prayer is just an example of how spiritual husband/wife prayer should be worded. One is free to word his or her prayer the way he or she wants, but let your prayer come from your heart.

SPIRITUAL HUSBAND / WIFE AND SOUL TIES

A soul tie is when the souls of two friends or partners like husband and wife, mother and child, and father and child knit together and are in bond in the spirit that make them inseparable in the physical **1 Samuel 18:1.** This is usually so especially with regard to a departed husband or wife.

Recently a woman whose husband traveled for medical treatment somewhere and did not return because he died there, experienced constant visits by the familiar spirit of the husband who also engaged her in sexual relationship every night in her sleep. Her friend who knows me suggested to her to call me which she did. My wife and I went to see her and were moved by her tears. They had been deeply in love and she has three young children for him. She explained what usually occurs to her when she goes to sleep. She regularly has sexual intercourse with her dead husband in her sleep. She even brought a friend to spend some nights with her and her children but the spirit of the man still came. In her dream it would look real and she would not be able to resist him.

Well, as a minister of the Word, I know that the Word of God is everything and can solve all of man's problems. I began by putting together the four pillars that are the corner stone of all other armors that the Lord has given to us His children for our spiritual battle. These are the name of Jesus, **Philippians 2:5-11**; the blood of Jesus, **Revelations 12: 11**; Holy Spirit and fire, **Luke 3:16** and the Word of God, **Isaiah 55:10-11; Jeremiah 1:12; 23:29, and Hebrews 4:12-13.** I made her confess to the Father in Jesus' name and brought her in good relationship or standing (righteousness) with Christ Jesus. Reading **1 Corinthians 7:39** (the only ground given by the scripture for freedom from old marriage and for remarriage) and with a short prayer, I commanded the spirit of the husband in the house to "Go." The ring also that bound them together was removed and the covenant of the ring destroyed. From that day henceforth, the lady ceased seeing the familiar spirit of her late husband in her dreams and having sexual relationship with it.

Most soul ties relationships and familiar spirits have to be severed through a strong knowledge of the Word of God and a beyond average prayer life. Constantly depositing prayers into one's prayer bank is recommended.

MARINE AND MERMAID SPIRITS

Marine or water spirits are also called mermaid spirits. These are spirits that afflict or possess young ladies that live close to coastal or mangrove areas of a country. These spirits are directly the opposite of "desert spirits" which are spirits of violence and sickness. They produce sicknesses like leprosy, blindness, stubbornness and arsons. But marine spirits bring delays in marriage. They are responsible for prostitution, lusting, lying tongues, false prophecy and divorces. These could be contacted through the sacrifices that fisher men make to the water spirits to help in their fishing businesses and other personal undertakings. Some barren women living in these areas make sacrifices to these spirits believing that through them they could be blessed with children. Most of the time, these children become possessed by evil spirits because of the activities of the parents. They later become what is called in some African languages, "Ogbanje or Abiku," (children with evil spirits who will soon return to where they came from). **Matthew 13:38; John 8:44; Acts 13:10; 1 John 3:10; Hosea 5:7.** These are children that do not live long because they are offered to the devil with their destiny destroyed. The short time that they live, they usually spend it in wickedness, destruction and wastage. If they succeed to live long, they usually are violent and die violently and most of the time, take many lives with them. Ladies that are possessed with these spirits love churches that are not spirit-filled and can be used for divination and fortune-telling. They can also be used as prophetesses and for money making by their owners. **Acts 16:16-19**

Those possessed with these spirits usually have long delays in marriages and most of the times die during child birth leaving their children behind with a transfer of the spirits. They could also be delivered by strong word-based preachers with knowledge on how to handle this type of deliverance.

FAMILIAR SPIRITS

Familiar spirits are basically spirits that have been in someone for a very long time, probably from birth or childhood, and have now made that body their home. Spiritual husbands and wives, marine and mermaid spirits can become familiar spirits. If it is about a location, they are called, "territorial spirits." **Deuteronomy 18:10-11** further explains other types of familiar spirits in operation. Examples are the spirits of divination, observer of times, enchanter, witchcraft, necromancer, and fortune telling. The Bible in the New Testament calls it, "the unclean spirit", **Matthew 12:43-45.** Those with familiar spirits can turn the possession into a church where they claim to help people with spiritual problems and counseling. It is in places like these that many miracle seekers are initiated into witchcraft through, palm-reading, anointing oil or holy water. Many popular mediums have turned their possessions into lucrative businesses. Some have appeared openly on national TV shows to talk about their sorcery.

If they decide to operate on their own in their home, they usually have a sacred place in their homes; have a small table covered with white cloth and a bell and a Bible where they divine for people. These so-called psychics can be seen on any given day in a city such as Manhattan inviting people as they pass by for readings. King Saul when confronted with a situation where he could no longer hear from God turned to a witch or a woman with familiar spirits for consultation**. 1 Samuel 18:7-19**

SERPENTINE SPIRITS

These are exactly like spiritual husbands or wives. They visit and could craw all over their lovers without harm while they are sleeping. *Mammy water* (a goddess of the sea or river that operates and befriends people mostly in the Niger Delta part of Nigeria) does this and brings much fortune to those that befriend them. But when the serpent comes as a spell from the witches and takes habitation inside one's body, one has to be ready as one may experience strange movements all over one's body. These can also be the spirits that the family used to serve or worship in the past and have been abandoned, and now have found one of the members of the family to be loving. These are lustful spirits that turn their captives into sex maniacs. Ladies with serpentine spirits could get involved in sexual activities all day without getting tired. Their bodies could move like caterpillars. If they get angry and bite you with their teeth, you have to seek for medical treatment as the venom from them could cause serious harm as it is equivalent to a bite from a python. They are very unstable as no one man can satisfy them sexually. They have special likeness for those that they love and can work for or take from other men to take care of their lovers. But the day they are disappointed by their lovers, those men are in danger of death. Those women that their men cheat on them with or whom they perceive as their replacements could also be in danger of attacks and persecution. They can somehow pretend to be good and yet be terribly bad. When they are good they are very good, but when they are bad they are deadly. Many men have been found dead in their beds after having sex with such women. One reason for this would be that the serpentine girlfriends found out that these men have other girlfriends and so would kill them with poisons from within them during love making. Another area where one may not be able to defeat these women is their wisdom and craftiness. It is only with the wisdom of God and the help of the Holy Spirit that those with serpentine spirits could be delivered or defeated.

In seeking deliverance, the person has to completely abstain from sin and sexual activities. My personal suggestion is for the person to read and study the Bible daily with the help of his/her pastor. Declare a period of fasting for praying and seeking the Lord. Dedicate your body as a living sacrifice, holy and acceptable unto God, **Romans 12:1.** Break bread at the end of each daily prayer session and ask to be anointed with holy oil dedicated by the pastor from the altar of the Lord at the end of the fast. **James 5:14-15.** The snake will leave, but one must continue with his/her daily declaration after the fast to keep him away completely. Declaration such as, "My body is the temple of the Holy Spirit. I was bought with a price. I am not my own. The blood of Jesus cleanses me from all sin. I am washed, renewed, adopted, predestinated for heaven, sanctified, consecrated and a joint heir with our Lord and Savior Jesus Christ."

Finally, the person may receive some attacks in his/her dream. In the dream, the person who used to come for love making may become an adversary; fighting and throwing things at him or her. This is a good sign that the person has been delivered. Also, not long afterwards, the person may begin to witness in his/her dream a woman or a man begging from afar to be allowed to come back. In nightly prayers, before going to bed, the person should ask the Holy Spirit to help him/her overcome weakness by giving him/her the understanding not to allow wicked spirits back in his/her life. After some period of time the begging and the pleading will come to an end and the person may never see or experience these spirits again. Hallelujah!

My analysis above is very helpful for the person who does do not have an experienced deliverance minister that can cast out these spirits and banish them from him or her and prevent them from coming back. And even when a deliverance minister has completed the deliverance process, the person still has to do his/her daily declarations and consecration.

TRANSPOSITION AND MANIPULATION BY WITCHES

Witches are known to cast spells and place charms. They do real harm to their captives by interchange or transposition and manipulation. Transpositions are practices whereby witches interchange people's blessings or positions or documents or results or school admission slips with negative ones. These make their captives to suffer losses or miss opportunities. Results of transpositions are always sadness, tears and desperation in the lives of their captives and their families. Apart from direct transposition by witches as a punishment on any child that they choose to punish, transposition is mostly used by rich parents who are members of occults and whose children are not bright enough to pass examinations or pursue a specified course of study in higher institutions. The children from poor families do gain from the children from rich families by borrowing books and other personal needs from them. Most of the time, the rich children take their poor friends to their homes where they are fed and at times blessed with money and made to pay with their talents. Transposition has been on for a long time. The Bible gives us an account of two harlots in the days of King Solomon. The one with a dead child went and interchanged her dead baby for the living when she saw that her friend was fast asleep. It took the wisdom of God in King Solomon to return the living baby to the rightful mother, **1 Kings 3:16-27**. It also will take the righteous judgment of King Jesus for anyone who suffers transposition to recover.

Witches have been known to interchange or transpose. You may be the most intelligent person in the class and may want to read a course of your choice, but you may be shocked by not receiving your examination number with your examination center. Many a time a call for prayer pays off as the slip arrives late. Sometimes it is declared lost in transit or you may receive another person's with which the exchange was made. All these happen to destabilize and send the spirit of desperation and confusion upon the person oppressed. One may make it to the examination and at the end his or her name may be missing from the lists of those that pass or fail, or the admission slip may not be received or one could find the word, absent against his/her name. While one is going north and south, east and west to try to sort out what went wrong, he or she may likely miss the registration and forfeit his or her chances of admission for that period. As a consolation, one may end up reading his/her second or third choice. This happens because a witch has succeeded to transpose the name, slip or course of study. Prayer bank is a necessary tool that can deal a blow and bring defeat to an act of transposition by the witches.

MARRYING THROUGH DREAMS AND NOT THE WORD

Marriage should be based on the Word of God, not on a dream. The Word of God is where the mind and the will of God are found. The foundation for a successful marriage must be built upon God's Word. Abraham in searching for a wife for his son Isaac sent his servant across the desert to *his own family* to search for a rightful wife for his son. According to **Genesis chapter 24,** the would-be wife must possess certain basic qualities, one of which was her root and origin, without which she was not qualified to be the bride. Abraham in the above mentioned passage represents God the Father. The Father will like the bride to come from His root, the family of God. She must not be a stranger or a visitor. She must be a "well goer", where she would draw the water of life. She must be generous, giving the water that she draws from the well to a thirsty stranger and his camels. She must be sincere (transparent or with a fair countenance) and must be a virgin (without defilement). She must invite her new converts home and feed them and nurture them to grow. All these qualities were found in Rebekah who later became Isaac's wife. God later made this a statute to the children of Israel through Moses saying, "...neither shalt thou make marriages with them; thy daughter thou shalt not give unto his son, nor his daughter shalt thou take unto thy son." **Deuteronomy 7:1-3.** The "them" in the above passage refers to the unbelievers. The Scribe, Ezra, enforced this statute to the letter when he commanded that those who had married strange wives should send them and their children away as the only condition under which God would be appeased and their sins forgiven. It was also the only qualification for their return with their brethren back to Jerusalem after 70 years in captivity. **2 Corinthians 6:14-17**

Many men and women end up marrying witches and wizards because they see them in their dreams. Some of the time people see themselves involved in very lavish and expensive wedding ceremonies. Most of these marriages take place between members of the same faith, mostly from the same church or neighborhood. When that happens, the man or the woman quickly concludes that their prayers have been answered. But truly speaking such marriages are usually staged. The enemy assumes the face of someone familiar to you or whomever they want to use, but in actuality they are presenting one of their own. This man or woman will appear with you in a gathering, dressed up in marriage apparels and made to exchange "rings of bondage and captivity." Then the manipulation begins. Manipulation works with spell and charm to make the man or the woman conclude that the person in the dream is the right partner. Relationship and marriage plans soon begin. The engagement usually does not last long before a wedding such as was revealed in the dream, takes place. Watch, you have been manipulated to marry a witch or a wizard! The main targets are usually the "born again, spirit-filled and tongue-speaking active members of the church. Through the marriage vows and exchange of rings, one automatically becomes a lawful captive and may later backslide or even gets killed.

Yet we cannot discount the fact that God does speak to us through dreams. The challenge now is to differentiate when the Lord is genuinely directing us through a dream and when we are being manipulated. The answer to this is, when one has a dream such as one where a marriage proposal is given and rings are exchanged, the dreamer should not immediately wake up and pronounce the person seen in his/her dream as his or her spouse sent from God. First he/she must check to see if the dream is in line with the Word of God. Try as much as possible to remain neutral and seek the face of the Lord with fasting and prayer. During the prayer sessions, stand against every manipulation by the witches. Then ask God for confirmations if the dream is God'swill for you. "Lord, I ask that this dream be repeated two or three times because in the mouth of two or three witnesses every case is established". **Matthew 18:16.** During this period keep your mind pure and if possible, avoid sharing the dream with friends.

What should follow is if this was of the Lord or from the Lord, the Lord will honor your request. He will send "Word confirmations" and will also confirm with signs and follow-up dreams as requested. But if during this time that you wait to hear from the Lord, you have a follow-up dream that is contrary to the one you had and the would-be spouse is now abusive, and you experience disappointment while at the altar, or strange appearances or events occur which are contrary to God's Word, then know that it was a witchcraft manipulation. This same process can be used for all other dreams and desires that we encounter and need to hear from the Lord.

Again I say unto you, "To overcome manipulation by the witches, every revelation or dream must be kept secret, and targeted prayers must be made until a Bible based confirmation is received, at least twice because the Bible says, 'At the mouth of two or three witnesses, every matter is established.'" **Deuteronomy 19:15; Matthew 18:16; John 8:17**

RAPE THROUGH MANIPULATION

A young pastor who was single once lived in a studio apartment next door to a witch. This witch tried to befriend this pastor and would often ask if he needed help which he would bluntly refuse. Any time she saw the young man she would say, "Pastor I am praying for you," and he would answer, "Thank you." She cast a spell on the pastor to get him to have sex with her, but she did not succeed. She also failed in the area of food since the pastor was not yielding to any of those things. She became very frustrated and reported the matter to her witchcraft group. She was mocked and booed. Their leader scorned her and asked if she indeed was fit for the position that she held in the witchcraft society. "Send your underage daughter to befriend him and work through her with patience," she suggested. "As soon as he walks in let your daughter follow behind, he will not drive her away. Let her make it a habit until she becomes familiar with the room and knows the position of things. All I need from her is his underwear, and if she can bring that to me, your problem will be solved." The witch's five year old girl was already initiated and had been enrolled as an agent and trained on how to seduce. She became very active as she always waited at the door every time the pastor returned from church. As soon as the pastor unlocked his door, she went in first and put on the television. She would reach into the refrigerator and give the pastor water to drink. She did it with all diligence and craftiness. One day she saw an opportunity to complete her mission. The pastor came in tired and sweating. He went to his bed area which was curtained off from the sitting area, undressed and tied a towel around his waist and headed for the bathroom to take a shower. The little girl who had a mission wasted no time but went straight behind the curtain and picked the underwear and quickly ran to their own apartment, dropped it and came right back to the pastor's studio to continue watching the television. As soon as the pastor came out of the bathroom the girl went home.

That night the underwear was handed over to the leader-in-charge. She worked with it for a week and returned it to the woman to bring it back to her daughter for return to the pastor claiming, "The trap is set." At this time the girl had become a part of the pastor's life. One morning the pastor did not go to church. The girl spent half of the day in his room watching television. She even fell asleep and the pastor picked her and put her in his bed to sleep. He then stepped out to buy something at the gate, the little girl awoke and ran straight to their apartment and brought back the underwear and put it into a cabinet where the pastor has all his underwear. The next day the unsuspecting pastor wore and immediately started lusting. As he began to pray, everything seemed to be calm. When he returned home, he met his young friend standing by his door, he opened the door as usual and they both went in. He suddenly became dizzy, feeling intoxicated and tormented. And before he knew it, he raped the five year old girl. The girl began to cry and raised alarm.

Her parents came in and found out what the pastor had done and got him arrested. The news spread quickly, his church closed while he was sent to prison.

Let us not forget that the dancing of the daughter of Herodias, Herod's wife led to the execution of John the Baptist **Matthew 14:1-11.** Children have been used both in biblical times and in our contemporary world to destroy mighty men and women. Through manipulations, many pastors have been caught with prostitutes and many have fallen from the faith. One may wonder why the young pastor did not know that this woman was a witch. Let us not also forget that during Apostle Paul's second missionary journey, a damsel tried to seduce Apostle Paul and his team at Philippi. I am also a witness where a minister was seduced by a lady who invited him home after preaching in a revival program in a church. The minister fell that night and the same lady who made him fall brought the report in the morning. The mistake that the young pastor made was allowing a neighbor's child, who was not his biological child to get too close. In deliverance ministry, there is no permanent friend and there is no permanent enemy. Everyone is a suspect, but a friend. Pastors themselves need prayers more than the flock. And men and women of God need to be careful who they welcome into their homes because every minister of God is a target. Above all, men and women of God should learn to follow the Word of God strictly and not wait until they receive fresh new revelation. Fresh new revelations are good but at times God remains silent directing us back to the Bible, because most of what He has to say have already been written in the Holy Scriptures.

WITCHES AND TRICKS

Witches like to play tricks with people. Their trickery is like the casting of dice. For example, witches like to play tricks with students' scores after examinations. Many lecturers dabble into the occult and know who is who in their class. Sometimes if a lecturer hates you for no just cause, there could be more to it than is apparent. Your paper could be selected and grouped among those to be used for witches' tricks. When the dice is cast whatever number comes up could be your score. Samson used a riddle at Timnath because of the woman that he desired to marry. But his in-laws used tricks, threats, and manipulations to get the answer, **Judges 14:12-18.** There are many ways to play tricks; casting of lots is one of them. But when the witches play tricks, they go all out to ensure that one's destiny is affected. It is important to understand that a believing and praying student is a problem to a teacher involved in witchcraft and vice versa. A student that is involved in witchcraft activity can trick his or her way to a higher score than he or she merits. But they do so usually at the expense of one or two of their colleagues. Students that are Christian believers should take authority over every power that could wreak havoc with their scores and store up prayers in their prayer banks before the examination season as well as enter into praise after the examinations. Many intelligent students fail exams not because they do not know what they are writing but because they are a target of satanic forces and have been listed among those whose scores will be tossed.

When satanic forces are at play, students may receive poor scores due to the examiner's inability to read or understand the students' writings. The real paper they submitted will be substituted with another and the replacement papers will appear dull, full of inconsistencies, dark and incomprehensible. How these papers are taken from the bulk of other papers is difficult to explain, but those that are familiar with the magic of witchcraft will know that it is a very simple thing to "conjure" up papers based on names, examination numbers and special codes allotted by the witches to those papers they wish to tamper with.

Prayers that will disrupt and destroy the powers of the forces of darkness and prevent them from tampering with your scores must cover your name, examination number, your scores and the dismantling of the special codes assigned to your papers. But with the anointing of God upon your life, what happened to King Saul could happen to you. God also can transpose, transform our "term papers" or even ourselves to protect us from harm or danger. At times God can transform you to appear as someone entirely different from the person your enemies are seeking. Your enemies on a mission to kill you might even approach you asking if you know someone by your name! For example, Prophet Samuel told Saul that when he met with some prophets, he would become like them, be transformed into them and begin to prophesy just like them. This was one of the indications that Saul had been anointed. More so, it was to bring confusion into the minds of those who would have opposed him and to produce obedience in the hearts of his faithful followers. So, though the witches can perform these apparent tricks of transposition, God, who is the creator of all including the witches, can transform whatever your enemy has transposed for the glory of His name. So we should put our trust in His powers and stock our prayer bank:

...when thou art come thither to the city, then thou shalt meet a company of prophets coming down from the high place with psaltery, and a tabret, and a pipe, and a harp, before them; and they shall prophesy. And the spirit of the Lord will come upon thee, and thou shalt prophesy with them, and shalt be turned into another man. 1 Samuel: 10:5-6

BLOOD SUCKING AND BLOOD TAPPING WITCHES

This is a branch of witchcraft that specializes in cutting the skin of those that they attack and sucking their blood. Those who are afflicted by this group of witches may wake up to experience some excruciating pains and some cuts on the surface of their skins. Most of the time one may think that his/her cuts are from the finger nails especially those who have long finger nails. The truth is that these categories of witches/wizards are referred to as "Blood tappers." Their major work is to plant all types of sicknesses and diseases in people's bodies and to cause disappointments in business undertakings, failure in examinations, and divorce in marriages. They also specialize in causing miscarriages, weakness of the male organs and low sperm count, fibroid implantation, brain tumor, cancer, eye diseases, barrenness and hemorrhages in women. If you give them opportunity to come repeatedly you may likely come down with high blood pressure that can lead to heart attack.

They usually announce their arrival with a bang on the roof of the house. The bang is accompanied with a sleep spell and fear, then weakness follows immediately and everyone in the room sleeps off. An hour after the bang, a cricket-like creature comes into the room with a flashing light on its tail. It circles the room many times to ensure that everyone in the room is asleep. It alights, transforms into human form and the process of blood tapping begins. This is not unlike the modern fascination with vampires in western culture. This fascination has spawned uncountable TV series and books on this subject. But blood tapping is not just a hip TV depiction of suave charismatic individuals who subsist on blood, it is actually a life changing and life affecting phenomenon that needs and requires the intervention of God.

Some of the time, the blood tapper could suppress the victim under an invisible weight. The victim usually begins to struggle for breath and feels being suppressed in their sleep. This victim despite super human effort is usually unable to wake up, utter a word or escape from the suppression. Most Christians, if they succeed in just uttering the name of Jesus they can then escape from this attack and the witch will then take off. The witches perform this suppression to test ones spiritual strength and the more they perceive one to be weak and feeble, the more visits one will receive. The witch/wizard could be arrested if someone with a higher spiritual power and understanding is in the room. When arrested he/she will beg not to be made known. He/she will show a hole in the wall and beg to be let go through the wall and not through the front door. But if one forcefully sends him/her away through the front door, his/her end has come. Once arrested and exposed, he/she will be dis-fellowshipped from the coven and his/her health starts immediately to deteriorate. He/she may start to lose his hairs and may not live much longer. My father actually arrested one in our presence while we were young. He begged to be let go through the wall but was forced out through the front door. It was not long we received the news that the man had died.

Since his/her major assignment is to plant sicknesses and diseases in people's bodies through their blood and blood vessels, it is advisable to not allow these witches to visit you or your home twice. My recommendation is "dangerous prayer." This is returning "Superior Fire for fire." Go all out hunting the hunters, destroy the destroyers, etc.

The Bible says, "Thou shalt not suffer a witch to live". Therefore, turn God's natural resources that they use for their daily living, (sunlight, moonlight, rains, water, sand, air, etc. against them, except they repent). The air, the sea, the land, the mountain, the valley and the forest which they use for their meetings should be soaked with the blood of Jesus and made to become uninhabitable and desolate. The sand on the earth must be made too hot for them to tread on. The air they breathe and the water that they drink must not pass peaceably into their system except they repent. If you are oppressed by witches, do you think they will spare you no matter all your begging? A witch will not spare a captured victim. Then why should we spare them when they fall into our trap? We should use the authority we have through Jesus Christ to bring them to their knees and make them confess and repent or die.

Combining all the activities of witchcraft transposition, manipulation, marine spirits, familiar spirits and blood sucking and tapping witchcraft together, below is the prayer bank sample.

Word bank sample

Genesis 27:18-29
Genesis 30:37-39
Judges 14:15-18
1 King 3:16-27
Isaiah 29:6-8
Hebrews 1:7
1 John 4:4

Prayer bank sample

Most Holy Father, the Maker of the heavens and the earth, mighty in power, mighty in battle, the Great I AM THAT I AM, to You be the glory for ever and ever more. Amen. Let Your Spirit bear witness with my spirit that I am a child of God. I bind every transposition of any kind that the witches might want to use to deny me of my right in life, my admission into a school of my choice, the titles to my property and certificates after my studies. I reject, refuse, resist and destroy all the activities of witches. Whenever my name is mentioned, let fire burn. Whenever my exam number is invoked, let thunder strike. I destroy their seducing and manipulating power, their charm and spells, their tricks, and all other devices used by the witches/wizards to deceive people. I also destroy the special code assigned to my name and examination number to be used against me. I release the fire of God to destroy the kingdom of witches, wizards and all dark powers. I bind incestuous spirit, dog spirit, pig spirit, peacock spirit and the spirit of the last day. I destroy all blood sucking, blood tapping and vampire agents and command the fire of God to burn around me and my bed at all time. I pray that any blood of mine that falls into their hand shall turn to acid and burn them. I become a flame of fire when I am sleeping, in my home, hotel room and any other place, and I completely block them from coming, and also blind their eyes from seeing me. I cover myself with the blood of Jesus and clothe myself with the whole armor of God. As I deposit this prayer in my prayer bank, I call unto the Lord so that He will answer me and show me great and mighty things that I do not know. Reveal clearly to me everyone that I work with and reveal me to those that You send to work with me. Thank you for giving me victory. I pray this prayer in the name of Jesus Christ. Amen.

MY EXPERIENCE WITH A WITCH WHILE SHOPPING FOR A PUBLISHER

Recently while shopping around for a publisher for this book a friend referred me to a brother who works with him who also has published two books so that he would help me. After talking with the brother that I was referred to he also gave me a name and phone number of a lady whom he claimed has published more books than he had and also knew more publishers. I contacted the lady. Three days later, I got a call from the lady telling me where and when we could meet.

That fateful Thursday, I found my way to the public library that we agreed to meet. She had told me that her place was five minutes from the library. She also told me on the phone that she used to pastor a church but had developed a high level of knowledge that is beyond the ordinary. I took note of that. I got there before her, dressed in African attire for easy identification. Fifteen minutes later she arrived and went straight to the computer to show me some of her works. She was tall with blond hair that reached to her waist. She began to tell me how she loves nature and takes care of animals. "That's good," I replied. "You see all these deliverances going on, many only cast more spell on the people and claim to deliver them, this is what I know very well because I've been there," she added. She insisted that we go to a Diner to talk because the library would not be a convenient place. Before I could say yes or no, there came a mighty thundering from heaven. It thundered and thundered so much that she was afraid and said to me, "I have not seen anything like this all my life." Following the thundering was lightning that seemed to be penetrating through the windows right into where we sat, and then followed a heavy rain. Each time the thunder and the lightning struck, she became very uncomfortable and would mumble some words.

We left where we were sitting and went and stood at the veranda of the library as she was still trying to see if we could get to her car in order to get to the Diner, but the lightning, the thundering and the rain increased. She then turned and said to me, "come with me to the basement", and I followed her as we descended into the basement of the library. She opened a door and we entered into a big but empty hall where one part of it had light and the other part was dark. There were three tables joined together with three chairs in the area where there was light and a table and two chairs in the area with on light. She went to the dark part of the hall and sat on one of the chairs and said to me, "I am diabetic, can you please pray for me?" "Yes I can pray for you but I do not want to sit down", I replied. I opened my mouth as I raised up my right hand to heaven and ask God to send down more rain, thunder and lightning. I applied **Isaiah 29:6** asking God to punish the wicked with thunder, earthquake, great noise, storm and tempest and with flame of devouring fire.

She asked me to stop, "Please stop, that is not what I want." I cut in quickly, "Why are we in the dark and not in the light? Let's move to the area with light. She retorted, "I don't want people that pass by to see us, I am well known in this area." "Good, but we have to come under the light," I replied. I took the two chairs and brought them under the light and placed them a distance apart and asked her to sit. She resisted for a while and then sat down. While she was talking, I was walking around the hall going through all the pictures hung on the walls around the hall. "I want to show you how to pray for me, don't be afraid, we will get there," she said. "Surely we are already there, but you don't teach me how to pray for you," I replied. "I would love to help you with your book but you don't seem to cooperate with me, I don't know what to do now," she added. "You don't have to worry about the book, it will be published, I want to know who you are," I demanded. She became confrontational as I began to pray again. She began to cast spell, her lips shook and shook and smoke was coming out of her mouth. "Stop, don't pray while I'm praying. You asked me to pray for you, you must be silent while I pray," I commanded. "I can't come under your authority; I refuse to surrender to your authority," she screamed. "You must surrender to the authority of our Lord Jesus Christ," I replied. She headed for the door, opened it and walked out, ran upstairs and ran straight across the road under the rain. As she went, she was looking back to see if I was coming behind her. But I stood at the veranda of the library praying in the spirit and watching her as she walked to her car and took off under the heavy rain.

This is what God says concerning these liars:

Thus saith the LORD, thy Redeemer, and He that formed thee from the womb, I Am the LORD that maketh all things; that stretcheth forth the heavens alone; that spreadeth abroad the earth by Myself; That frustrateth the token of liars, and maketh diviners mad; that turneth wise men backward, and maketh their knowledge foolish; That conformeth the word of His servant, and performeth the counsel of His messengers…
Isaiah 44:24-26

This lady must have initiated a lot of people for her occult masters. Do not forget that she was once a pastor while in the occult. She saw one to be more lucrative and profitable than the other and she opted for the more profitable one, witchcraft. That day she thought she had caught a big fish for her promotion, but she failed for various reasons. One of the reasons why she failed is that my prayers in my prayer bank moved the hands of the Almighty God to send down the rain without me even asking. Secondly, she miscalculated. It seemed she lost her mind because she looked confused and did not know how to proceed in every step of our discussion. And thirdly, I took over and became her boss with the help of the Holy Spirit.

Witches love to boss and dominate in order to weigh down people's spirit and cast spell, but from the time we met I was on top, I talked with authority like someone who knows what he is doing. I frustrated her and weakened her spirit to cast spell, I walked around while praying in the spirit.

My advice to men and women of God is that they should never be afraid of meeting with all categories of people, after all, our work is to minister to people. But know who you are in Him; your stand and understanding of His word should not be in doubt. Always speak like someone having authority through Jesus Christ. And let your prayer bank never be empty. He is right there to back you up. If it had not been for the rain, thunder and lightning that the Almighty released to prevent me from going further, I think I would have been taken to a place where I would have come face to face with the "prince" and, make no mistake, I would still be alive today. But the battle would have been fought on another level. But the will of God for me that day was what happened; we should always allow the will of God to prevail at all times.

Like any other deliverance minister, I have had these confrontations hundreds of times during deliverance services. While delivering a woman in Togo, a knife that she buried in her skin in one of her thighs popped up and cut one of my fingers. She was right there on the floor moving like a crocodile. While bending over her to try to remove the knife safely, one of her companions that came to church with her that night came all the way from the back, forcing her way through the heavily congested church and landed a heavy slap on my face shutting my left eye. The ushers were taken by surprise. But the good news for that night was that both ladies were delivered and set free.

CHAPTER 9

SPIRITUAL WARFARE

In simple terms, I will define warfare as an engagement or involvement in a war or a battle. It is also a struggle or a fight against an opposing enemy, or against the will or authority of an oppressor. It could also be a war against deception, manipulation, slavery, or social ills like drugs, prostitution, etc. When the word spiritual (spirit realm) is added, what comes to mind is that the war is not fought in the physical realm or natural world, it is fought in the spirit realm. The two types of spiritual realms in existence are; realm of God (the Holy Spirit) and the realm of satan (evil spirits) where all evils are perpetrated.

For we wrestle not against flesh and blood… **Ephesians 6:12**

Since this is not the war that one is fighting against a physical human being, it is therefore inconceivable for one to think that a natural man in the flesh can fight against a spirit.

Spiritual warfare therefore is a human (a willing vessel) who is filled with the Spirit of God (Word of God) and equipped with the weapon or armor of God (Word of God); using both the Spirit of God in him and His weapons or armor to fight for his/her personal freedom, the freedom of his/her family and freedom from the control and the dominion of the power of darkness. Satan or evil spirit's operation includes but not limited to, lying, deception, oppression, wickedness, drug addiction, prostitution, the flesh, worldliness, sickness, and death.

Thou art My battle axe and My weapons of war: for with thee will I break in pieces the nations, and with thee will destroy kingdoms...
Jeremiah 51: 20-28

God was preparing the kings of the Medes, the captains and the rulers (human agents) for use in the destruction of Babylon. Babylon once a destroying mountain (nation) would soon become a burnt mountain because the mouth of the Lord had spoken it. God now prepares us, His Church for use in destroying the works of satan.

Wherefore take unto you the whole armor of God... **Eph. 6:13**

What the verse quoted above is saying is that you should "dress yourself up" with the appropriate Word of God which is able to help you stand and defeat the enemy. It is all about His Word. The heavens, the earth and all that are in them were made through His Word.

I will now break down the tactics and the implementation of the strategy of spiritual warfare.

For the Word of God is quick, and powerful, and sharper than any twoedged sword, piercing even to the dividing asunder of soul and spirit, and of the joints and marrow, and is a discerner of the thoughts and intents of the heart.
Hebrews 4:12

It is the spirit that quickeneth; the flesh profiteth nothing: the Words that I speak unto you, they are spirit, and they are life.
John 6:63

When the messengers of satan (false apostles) have succeeded in building strongholds in the hearts of their captives by making them to believe their lies and come under their influence or spell, it is essential for believers to awake and fight. Fight using the weapons

(God's Words) provided by God the Father, through Jesus Christ His Son in the wisdom and power of the Holy Spirit. Satan and his agents will be defeated and his power or influence, destroyed.

It is important for everyone reading this book or that is involved in helping others overcome spiritual problem to always pay attention to what the Holy Spirit has to say to them in every situation. If the Holy Spirit does not ask you to send out handkerchief, do not do it because Apostle Paul did it. Jesus, who is our example, did not use only one pattern throughout His healing ministry.

I have heard ministers criticizing others claiming that their pattern is better. There are some who claim that Jesus did not go out there to fight against territorial spirits; that He only dealt with the evil spirits in people. This is wrong altogether. Let us see what the Bible say about this:

And when he was come to the other side into the country of the Gergesenes, there met Him two possessed with devils, coming out of the tombs, exceeding fierce, so that no man might pass by that way. **Matthew 8:28**

The fact that these demons did not hinder those two men that they possessed only, but blocked the way for all the residents of that country, that makes them "territorial spirits." Territorial spirits are spirits or demons or evil forces that torment, afflict, or block access to prosperity or good things from coming into an area, or a community or a country. They also make the residents of those places to behave alike and practice a common sin. Jesus' success in driving out those demons helped set those men free and also opened doors to the inhabitants of that country to prosper. Each time Jesus carried out deliverance and banished those demons, He prevented them from becoming territorial spirits and afflicting other people in those places.

Many also have criticized prayer walks and the application of the blood of Jesus. If the Bible says men ought to pray everywhere lifting up their holy hands, is it then a sin if men walk in the street praying and binding demons if they choose to do so? Or, if the application of the blood of the lamb and goat to the door posts of the children of Israel in Egypt brought salvation unto them, is it a sin if a man applies the blood of Jesus upon his life, wife, children and all his possessions? What I say to you is that; to the pure, all things are pure. But run away from all kinds of sins. Pay attention to what the Holy Spirit says to you in any situation involving you or others that you help, and God will be glorified through His Son, Jesus Christ.

THE ARMOR OF GOD

These are the equipment, weapons and armory given by God to His children to be used in spiritual warfare. They could be used both for defensive and offensive purposes. The whole armor of God is categorized into three: purely defensive armor, offensive armor and defensive/offensive armor/weaponry.

In dressing up yourselves with spiritual armors (Word of God) before confronting your foes, there are a few things to **observe**, **identify,** and **apply**. They include the following:

(i) the weapons and the strength of your enemy;
(ii) the location or position of your enemy;
(iii) the equipment or weapons at your arsenal (knowledge of application of the Word of God in spiritual battle)
(iv) the position in which you will stand to battle your enemy; (that position is Christ Jesus);
(v) the right strategy and approach in spiritual battle;
(vi) the right method in applying the weapons at your arsenal. And
(vii) your reinforcement unit, the reserves, supporting units and the states of their preparedness.

Wherefore take unto you the whole armor of God, that ye may be able to withstand in the evil day, and having done all, to stand. Stand therefore…
Ephesians 6:13-14

The Bible in **Ephesians 6:14-18** identifies nine spiritual armors, while three of them are identified in **Revelation 12:11** and many more in other places as we will soon see. Some of these armors are for defensive purposes while others are for both defensive and offensive attacks. Let us take a look at these weapons:

Ephesian 6:14-18:

1. The first and the most important armor is, "Standing." I have never seen a man who does not stand going to war. Stand therefore and dress up yourself (you must be willing to confront the enemy, count the cost, must strategize, be battle ready, approach to the battle, no retreat, no surrender).
2. Loins girded about with truth (Jesus is the truth, reject every lie, confess the truth).
3. Breastplate of righteousness (go to battle not on your personal righteousness but righteousness of God through Christ Jesus).
4. Feet shod with the preparation of the gospel of peace (as the spiritual battle is ragging, the seed of the gospel of peace is being sown and deliverance is being released).
5. Shield of faith (every step of the way from beginning to the end must be by faith).
6. Helmet of salvation (assurance of salvation is necessary in spiritual battle, the unsaved cannot stand in the battle).
7. Sword of the Spirit which is the Word of God (the Word of God must appropriately be applied as a sword to cut every cord of satanic bondage and set the captive free).
8. Praying always with all prayer and supplication in the Spirit (all prayers must be in the Spirit, Who is there to help your infirmities).
9. Watching: with all perseverance and supplication for all saints (we do not only watch for ourselves but for all saints. This we do with perseverance and supplication.

Revelation 12:11 identifies three armor/weapons:

10. Blood of the Lamb (declare in the court of heaven that you are a winner through His blood. Anoint yourself, wife and

children regularly and apply the blood to your house, car, etc.)

11. Word of testimony (testifying to all that Jesus Christ is Lord and Savior, that He died and rose again)
12. They loved not their lives unto the death (be determined be steadfast, do not give up: because your willingness to accept to die for Christ is a strong weapon that will bring life to millions of souls.
13. Binding of the strong man, **Matthew 12:29.** (This is a powerful offensive weapon when you use the name of Jesus as authority of the believers)
14. THE NAME OF JESUS: **Philippians 2:10.** This is the ultimate armor/weapon for defense and for battle against all foes. His name brings every contending powers to their knee.
15. Praise: **2 Chronicles 20:21-22** (The more praise goes up, the more your enemies are being slain, etc.)

There are still many other armor/weapons in the Bible that you may likely stock in one's arsenal to be ready for use at any time as you continue to study the scripture, giving diligent to what the Holy Spirit says to you at any time during the battle.

DEFENSIVE ARMOR

This is the armor that you put on to protect yourself from the bullets of your enemies while you are in the battlefield. In spiritual warfare, it is advisable to begin first with the defensive armor. You dress yourself up with them before applying the offensive weapons. You cannot step into the battle unprepared. The defensive weapons include but are not limited to:

1. ***Loins must be girded about with truth:*** all lies must be confessed and repented of before going to confront your enemies.
2. ***Breastplate of righteousness***: This must be worn around the heart or the chest, back and front, which means that your heart must be in good standing with the Lord. Or pray David's

prayer before going to fight: "Create in me a clean heart, and renew the right spirit within me."

3. ***Helmet of salvation*** (you must be saved). Your mind must be free from pollution. Someone still nurturing sin will be defeated as soon as he steps into the battleground. As when the evil spirit said to the seven sons of Sceva: **Acts 19:15,** "...Jesus I know, and Paul I know, but who are you?" And the evil spirit proceeded to thoroughly beat, humiliate and defeat them. For the only prayer that God honors from an unbeliever is one of repentance.
4. ***The blood of the lamb*** played a major role in the protection of Israelites in Egypt against the angels of death, so ***the Blood of Jesus*** should play a stronger role in the protection of God's people. We have to use Jesus' blood to block access to heaven by satan so that he can no longer have opportunity to stand before our Father and accuse us. Every function of the blood, justification, redemption, purchased, washed cleansed, etc. has to be declared before descending into battle against your enemies.
5. ***The shield of faith*** will help us quench all the fiery darts of the wicked: the shield will stop all incoming bullets without giving them the chance to penetrate and hurt you. By faith we have already won and claimed the victory.
6. ***The Word of God*** is always available as a defense to everyone in spiritual conflict that trusts in the Lord. More so as it is available to avenge their enemies on their behalf. As you step into the battle continue to declare, "It is written..."

Now that we have completed suiting ourselves up with all this defensive armor, we do not just jump into the battlefield and begin to fight. We have to send spiritual spies. Moses and Joshua sent spies, spies are necessary for success in battle, and in this case, spiritual spies by praying investigative (seeking) types of prayer. God will reveal who our enemies are, where they are camped and what types of weapons they have.

While I was setting up a structure for a place of worship on a demonic street, I was very frustrated as all the bricks already built would be torn down by the next morning by an evil agent. With all patience and humility, I prayed and prayed until God revealed to me who was doing this. I made up my mind to challenge him.

One night at 2.00 a.m. when the night was still, I went and beheld a skeletal winged creature breaking down the walls of the church already raised to the window level. I walked towards him shouting, "Who are you?" Before I knew it, he jumped on me and wrapped his long nails around my throat. I lifted him up threw him to the ground and sat on him. He tore all my clothes and struggled to overturn me but the Lord strengthened me. I was cautious not to try to hit him but only tried to pry his two vise-like hands from around my neck. We rolled around the ground for a considerable time jostling for dominance, and it made every effort to be on top of me. The Holy Spirit helped me and he could not overturn me. After about two hours of struggling like this, help arrived. A street vendor who barbecued roasted meat (suya), a late night activity, walked by and saw us battling on the ground. I was applying all the weapons: the name of Jesus, the blood of Jesus, fire of the Holy Spirit, praying also in the Spirit. The man came close, and seemed to recognize me, having seen me work there every day. He picked up a bamboo cane and hit the demon who let loose of my neck and skipped away. The helper looked at me and proclaimed, "Why do you come here at this unholy hour of the night to build your church? Do you want to die? Go home!" From this day onward, the building of the church proceeded without further hindrances from demonic forces.

What I am trying to say is that through fasting and prayer the Lord had me go out in the middle of the night to confront the devil that did not want our church built. God knows the state of your mind, your strength and a way to handle things for each and every one of us. He gauges our faith and engages us accordingly. He knew my determination to openly confront the forces that were destroying our church building and He prepared me for the fight.

POSITION MATTERS

The next step in our spiritual warfare is locating one's position; the ground on which one must stand to battle one's enemy.

This is something very important which must not be overlooked. This involves taking a rightful position or standing on the kind of solid ground, which will not shake as one releases one's offensive weapons against the hosts of the enemy. What is that position and where is that ground?

And what is the exceeding greatness of His power towards us who believed, according to the working of His mighty power, Which He wrought in Christ, when He raised Him from the dead, and set Him at His own right hand in the heavenly places, Far above all principalities and powers, and might, and dominion, and every name that is named, not only in this world, but also in that which is to come. And hath put all things under His feet, and gave Him to be the head over all things to the church, Which is His body, the fullness of Him that filleth all in all.
Ephesians 1:19-23

This is the exalted position of victory that God the Father hath given to His Son Jesus Christ. Therefore Christ will not be up there and leave us alone to struggle with the devil down here. This is what the Bible says:

He hath raised us up together, and made us sit together in heavenly places in Christ Jesus.
Ephesians 2:6

Therefore the position for our ultimate victory over the forces of darkness is the heavenly place where we sit with Him and bring all powers of darkness under our footstool. Hallelujah!!! And this will not be possible without the application of ***the shield of faith*** as a defensive armor and later as an offensive armor. You must believe like David that you are able to confront this champion and also believe that God, through Jesus Christ, already overcame for us. We are only taking hold of what He has already wrought for us in Calvary.

Having dressed ourselves up with all the defensive armor and having also taken our rightful position with Him in the heavenly places, it is now time to rain down the fire of destruction with our offensive weapons directed against Satan and his kingdom. The Bible says in **Job 14:7** that there is hope for a tree if it be cut down because it will sprout again. Therefore, the only way to kill a tree is to dig it up from the root. Most of the deliverances that we do or receive are on the surface; the foundation or the root cause of those problems is not addressed. To destroy the powers of the rulers in our streets or communities we must go beyond those spirits that are used to attack us, and advance to where they get their power and support from. Principalities and powers must be dislodged. You must direct your weapons to destroying all the jets and helicopters in the air and their entire submarine under the water and ammunition on the land. We must use our spiritual bulldozers and earth moving equipment to mow down their structures. We must also seek the release of all the souls in captivity and under the spell of satanic manipulations.

OFFENSIVE WEAPONS

For though we walk in the flesh, we do not war after the flesh: (For the weapons of our warfare are not carnal, but mighty through God to the pulling down of strongholds;) Casting down imaginations, and every high thing that exalteth itself against the knowledge of God, and bringing into captivity every thought to the obedience of Christ; And having in a readiness to revenge all disobedience, when your obedience is fulfilled.
2 Corinthians 10:3-6

These are weapons given by God to His saints for use in spiritual warfare against all foes. Warfare is a daily battle that we fight against flesh, worldliness, satan and his agents. It is the implementation of the strategy given to us by Christ Jesus, who having spoiled principalities and powers, He made a show of them openly, triumphing over them in it. And we are complete in Him, which is the head of all principality and power, **Colossians 2:10, 15.** The offensive weapons include but not limited to:

1. THE NAME OF JESUS

The most important weapon that God has given to man to use in the destruction of the powers of darkness is the **"Name of Jesus."** The name is so powerful that the witches find it difficult to call that name in their meeting places. This name is everything: it is a defensive weapon; it is also an offensive weapon.

The Bible calls it mighty weapon: because it is the only weapon that can pull down strongholds, cast down imaginations and every high thing that exalts itself against the knowledge of God, and bring into captivity every thought to the obedience of Christ. The name of Jesus stands out as number one; it is the only weapon given to man by God the Father that will make every knee to bow both in heaven and on earth,

Wherefore God also hath highly exalted Him, and given Him a name which is above every name: That at the name of Jesus every knee should bow, of things in heaven, and things in earth, and things under the earth; And that every tongue should confess that Jesus Christ is Lord, to the glory of God the Father.
Philippians 2:5-12

Salvation is also through His name.

The name of the LORD is a strong tower: the righteous runneth into it, and is safe.
Proverbs 18:10

Neither is there salvation in any other: for there is none other name under heaven given among men, whereby we must be saved.
Acts 4:12

2. THE WORD OF GOD

You can never pray an effective prayer without the Word of God. This weapon with the name of Jesus brings every battle and every stubborn spirit to its knees. That is why word bank should not be taken lightly, as it is written:

Then said the LORD unto me, Thou hast well seen: for I will hasten My word to perform it.
Jeremiah 1:12

Put Me in remembrance: let us plead together: Declare thou, that thou mayest be justified.
Isaiah 43:26

So shall My word be that goeth forth out of my mouth: It shall not return unto me void, but it shall accomplish that which I please, and it shall prosper in the thing whereto I sent it.
Isaiah 55:11

Word bank will readily sharpen your spiritual sword and make the right word for the right circumstance available for use at all times.

Do not tell the Lord what the devil said to you or what the enemy said about you. What really matters is what God said. Then you send the Word of God back to Him, He will watch over His Word to perform it.

3. FEET SHOD WITH THE PREPARATION OF THE GOSPEL OF PEACE

As you begin to advance into your enemy's territory and gain more grounds, make sure that your feet are solidly fitted with iron shoes for the preparation of the gospel of peace. We are ready to march forward to release those bound at the other side of the isle upon girding our feet, **Isaiah 61:1-4.** The purpose for which you wage spiritual warfare will be defeated if all the captives of satan are allowed to remain in their captivity.

4. THE BLOOD OF JESUS

Knowing the functions of the blood of Jesus and applying them in battle is very important. It is another two-edged weapon: for defensive and offensive use during battle. Sincerely speaking while confessing all lies before going to battle against your enemy, you must constantly apply the blood and its function: "I'm redeemed, justified, washed, cleansed, saved, and shall overcome satan and his agents in heavenly court and in this world, by the blood of the Lamb."

And they overcame him by the blood of the Lamb and the word of their testimony…
Revelation 12: 11

This statement gives us a picture of the defeat of satan by archangel Michael and his angels by the blood of the Lamb. They have no more access to heaven where they can daily accuse us, their accusations of believers are rejected because of the blood of the Lamb. They cast them out of heaven into the earth (banished them from heaven) with courage, determination and perseverance. The Bible makes it clear in **Revelation 12:17** that the dragon went forth to make war with the remnant of the seed of the woman, which kept the commandment of God and have the testimony (the Word) of Jesus Christ. This clearly shows that every member of the Church of Jesus Christ will at one time or the other be subjected to constant attack until Jesus comes to take the faithful to Himself and establishes His Kingdom on earth and satan is bound and taken out of the way. These verses also give us a clue as to how we, the remnants will have to fight our battle to defeat satan and his army. We must apply the blood of the Lamb as we also apply appropriate words of God selected and deposited in our word bank, which must readily be available for use at critical times such as these.

5. WATCHFULNESS

Applying the weapon of God for battle requires watchfulness, less talking, focus and wisdom. The time for spiritual warfare is not the time to discuss business, personal matters, listening to the radio or TV, reading newspapers or having phone conversations. Whenever you are at the battlefront, open up your heart to hear what the Lord will say to you about the battle: its strategy, approach, changes in personnel and equipment. Each time we fail to watch, we receive a hit and may lose our focus. If we are praying against witchcraft power in the family, be very observant to see what is happening to each and every member of the family based on your prayer point. We should constantly watch, not only for ourselves, but also for all saints so that those who have already been delivered fall not back into captivity. The enemy we are talking about does not easily accept defeat, he may redouble and circle back to reclaim his lost ground.

A YOUNG WOMAN AND HER WITCHCRAFT MOTHER

A young lady who went to the village to bring her mother to come and stay with her began encountering problems as soon as the mother moved in. She got fired from her job, and started fighting with her husband and her health also began to deteriorate. Each time she went to church for prayer we would ask her to bring her mother and she would say her mother was too weak to walk to church. We even volunteered to send a car for her mother. But she vehemently refused to come to any church services. Each time we visited the house to pray she would tell the daughter to inform us that she was weak and sleepy and would not permit noise.

Eventually it happened that each time we prayed violent prayers in the church stretching our hands towards the lady's house, we specifically asked God for a sign. And by the time the daughter arrived home the mother's face would be swollen up and she would be rolling on the ground vomiting. The daughter immediately would call us to come to her house and pray claiming the mother was dying.

Even though we seemed to understand what was going on, we were willing to go along with her for a while. She did the same thing time and time again because according to her she could never believe that her mother had been initiated into witchcraft. One day we prayed "a specific and a targeted prayer" asking for a sign and when she got home, it happened as we had prayed. She called us and we went and rained down fire from heaven and she began to confess and was delivered. The power of watching or being watchful as a weapon should not be underestimated. When you pray, watch people around you, things around you, circumstances around you and changes that have taken place in your life and surrounding.

6. PRAYER

Prayer must go forth without ceasing; pray privately, pray corporately and pray at all times. Pray forcefully and with conviction. If it is a corporate prayer, make sure that there is agreement because the only defect to corporate prayer is when parties involved are not in agreement. If it is a private prayer, make sure that you are in the right state of mind, with the right intention, repent and forgive. Most of the time back your prayer with fasting and know exactly what type of prayer you want to pray: asking, seeking, or knocking? Learn to pray more at night and do the work in the day: pray at all time.

7. HOLY SPIRIT

Then all prayer and supplication must be made in the Spirit: the fire of the Holy Spirit has to be released. This is so powerful that during deliverance, the demon will openly cry out, "Please stop calling the fire, please, please stop!" As you speak you are also praising God in the Spirit: speaking and praising in the language your enemy would never understand. The Spirit of God will also help our weakness especially in areas that we do not know how and what to pray, the Holy Spirit will investigate, spy out, report, assist and give guidance on how and when and where to advance.

8. BINDING OF THE STRONG MAN

Then as we advance we are binding the strong man. Bind him, weaken him and make him feeble. This is possible through the power of a stronger man than the strong man. **Luke 11:21-22**

9. COURAGE

In spiritual warfare courage is essential. When the Bible says "...they love not their lives unto the death," **Rev. 12:11**, it goes a long way to show how the devil will do everything to frighten you and resist you, but when you stand your ground, you win.

10. PRAISE

In every step of the way we have to give God the glory even when it seems that we are defeated. Praise brings more confidence and courage and compels God to complete what He started.

11. WORD OF OUR TESTIMONY

The potency of our words is declarations made, example: "Jesus is Lord forever; through His death on the cross I am saved, His blood washes all my sins, greater is Jesus in me than satan that is in the world, etc."

12. HOLINESS

While the word of our testimony goes forth we must remember to keep ourselves pure and clean by being holy as our Father in heaven is holy. Without holiness, the wicked one will fight to return with seven more wicked spirits than he in order to keep us in perpetual bondage. But Jesus, the greater in us, has bruised the head of satan under our feet and will preserve us until He comes to take us to be with Him in His kingdom. And when He comes we shall be like Him.

When the unclean spirit is gone out of a man, he walketh through dry places, seeking rest, and findeth none. Then he saith, I will return into my house from whence I came out; and when he is come, he findeth it empty, swept, and garnished. Then goeth he, and taketh with himself seven other spirits more wicked than himself, and they enter in and dwell there: and the last state of that man is worse than the first. Even so shall it be also unto this wicked generation.
Matthew 12:43-45

13. ANOINTING

Many people do not realize that anointing is a powerful offensive weapon. Whenever we stand to fight we must be careful what word we pronounce with our mouth because that is what our Father in heaven will give us. I do hear people pray that they break all the weapons of their enemies, but every weapon broken could be mended. We rather should say we destroy those weapons because anything destroyed is good for nothing and it is only with anointing that bondage can be destroyed.

And it shall come to pass in that day, that his burden shall be taken away from off thy shoulder, and his yoke from off thy neck, and the yoke shall be destroyed because of the anointing.
Isaiah 10:27

No sooner than Prophet Samuel anointed Saul with oil that he prophesied transformation, favor and prophetic unction upon him, and all happened as the man of God had prophesied. Therefore anointing is a great weapon of spiritual warfare in our hand.

14. COVENANT/VOW

Thou art my battle axe and weapons of war: for with thee will I break in pieces the nations, and with thee will I destroy kingdoms. And with thee will I break in pieces the horse and his riders; and with thee will I break in pieces the chariot and his rider.. And I will render unto Babylon and to all the inhabitants of Chaldea all their evil that they have done in Zion in your sight, saith the LORD. **Jeremiah 51:20-24**

A covenant is a bond that comes with oath. Israel exists today because of God's covenant unto Abraham, Isaac and Jacob. While most of the time a covenant originates from God, a vow from man goes to strengthen a covenant. When the mark of the covenant is observed by the two parties, victory is assured in every battle.

And Jephthah vowed a vow unto the LORD, and said, If thou shalt without fail deliver the children of Ammon into mine hands, Then it shall be, that whatsoever cometh forth of the doors of my house to meet me, when I return in peace from the children of Ammon, shall surely be the LORD's, and I will offer it up for a burnt offering. **Judges 11:30-31**

Jacob vowed a vow when he was faced with reality of life and had to run away from his brother. And before Israel descended into a battle with her enemies they used to first make a vow unto God. God also honored them by giving them victory

We had seven major covenants that bound God and man and that brought us to the New Covenant through Christ Jesus, they include:

1. Edenic Covenant
2. Adamic Covenant
3. Noahic Covenant
4. Abrahamic Covenant
5. Mosaic Covenant
6. Davidic Covenant
7. The New Covenant- Through Christ Jesus.

Covenants and vows were and are still effective weapons that help us defeat our enemies. Once you cry to God in the midst of adversity and call on Him to remember His covenant unto you, it is done.

But our resiliency and resolve, determination and focus on what we are doing, while steadfastly avoiding distraction, will continue to keep the devil and his agents on the defensive. The Bible says that we should be vigilant to know the areas the enemy may want to re-launch with insurrections and refortifications.

Be sober, be vigilant; because your adversary the devil, as a roaring lion, walketh about, seeking whom he may devour.
1 Peter 5:8

Since we know that it is not yet his time to be arrested, chained and locked up, he must be fought back time and time again by being vigilant for his inevitable second, third or more attacks. But Jesus who had given us victory at Calvary through His blood is always there for us. Amen.

Finally brethren, in spiritual warfare, fear must be put aside. Our preparation to be warriors must involve training our heart, mind and stiffening our flesh. It is a fact that many times during deliverance sessions, the devil calls for reinforcements. There is nothing wrong if you inform trusted friends in advance to back you up. This does not negate what I said before about not picking up your phone when you are in motion. Note also that the battle of life is not a day's, a month's or even a year's affair. It is fought all through one's lifetime. Therefore if you are single, the day you marry, enroll your wife into the Lord's army. When you start producing children get them enrolled and trained also because if the enemy sees that you are too strong for him, he might pass through any of your dependents.

We should not forget this: Jesus was made to sit on the right hand of His Father in heavenly places far above all principalities and powers. He also elevated *us* to that position to sit with Him in heavenly places so that we might be able to triumph over all our foes. Even though we are here on earth, by His weapon, ***the shield of faith,*** we as believing Christians are exalted and lifted above all the powers and are made to sit with Jesus in heavenly places far above all the spirits of darkness. We therefore have easy victory because he that is above has the greater power than he that is beneath.

The position for our ultimate victory over the forces of darkness is the heavenly place where we sit with Him and bring all powers of darkness under our feet. Hallelujah!!!

Do not fight for yourself alone, but for other members of the body of Christ.

- We must also seek the release of all the souls in captivity and under the spell of satanic manipulation.

- Therefore when we stand to pray, because of the recognition of the presence of these spiritual forces and power of hindrances, we have to do much more than shouting and screaming. We have to first put on the ***whole armor of God.***

Prayer Bank Sample for Warfare and the Armor of God

Our Almighty Father in heaven, I come to You in the name of Jesus. I ascribe to You all glory, honor, adoration, dominion, majesty, power and might. You are the beginning and the end; You are our rock, our hope, our strength, and our dwelling place. Thank You, Father, for the gift of Your only Son, Jesus Christ who came and died and set me free from all curses, generational spirits, and powers of enslavement and captivity. I confess before You this day, all sins, known and unknown, generational, ancestral, personal, and parental. I confess before You all lies, cheating, and pollution. I wash myself in the pool of the blood of Jesus. I am washed, cleansed, renewed, sanctified and restored through His blood.

I now dress myself with the totality of the armor of God, defensive, offensive and counter offensive. I declare that Jesus is the truth, and I gird my loins with that truth. I am not going to this battle by my righteousness but by the righteousness of God through Christ Jesus, therefore I tie the breastplate of righteousness around my chest, around my back and shield my front. I put on my helmet of salvation by declaring that I am saved because He died to save me.

I take in my left hand the shield of faith which is my defense, and by faith I am seated with Jesus in heavenly places far above all powers and principalities; and in my right hand, I take with me the sword of the spirit, which is the Word of God, and I now declare emphatically thus:

It is written, touch not my anointed and do my prophet no harm; it is written, I have overcome the devil because greater is Jesus in me than the devil that is in this world. It is written, the name of the Lord is a strong tower; the righteous runs into it and is saved. It is written, I shall not die but live to declare the works of the Lord. It is written, the battle is not mine; the Lord will fight for me and the Egyptians that I see today, I will see them no more forever. I command the Spirit to help my infirmity even as I pray in case I do not know what to pray; as I pray in the Spirit, set a watch over me that no bullet of the enemy shall penetrate to harm me.

I now destroy all the powers of darkness and burn down the kingdom of satan, witchcraft and occult- set all their agents a fleeing. With my feet shod with the preparation of the gospel of peace, I go to his prison houses and release those souls in captivity and set them free; I command a new spirit into them and plant the love of God in their hearts. I bind all demonic forces and resist them from regrouping. I release the blood of Jesus into the air and dislodge all the spiritual wickedness from their habitations and from their strongholds.

I claim total victory to live and to continue to worship You, my Lord and Savior. Thank You, Father, as I put a seal upon this prayer and send it express to the throne of grace, and by faith I receive immediate answer now in Jesus' mighty name. Amen and Amen.

Benediction: *One who regularly girds himself with truth, and puts on all his spiritual armor; both defensive and offensive and fights shall never be defeated by satan and his agents, but shall by all means live a victorious Christian life in this world, and shall be called the greatest in the kingdom of God, for his faithfulness in the battle to liberate souls from the kingdom of satan and translate them into the kingdom of Jesus Christ our Lord and Savior. Amen.*

CHAPTER 10

CRISIS RESOLUTION

Crisis Resolution is putting a nail in the coffin of a crisis, burying it and preventing its resurrection. Crisis resolution is the end product of a good crisis management. And it is only God alone that has the ultimate power to resolve crisis.

"He maketh wars to cease unto the end of the earth; he breaketh the bow, and cutteth the spear in sunder; he burneth the chariot in the fire."
Psalm 46:9

Most of the time people think they have succeeded in resolving a particular crisis, but surprisingly the crisis springs forth from a different direction. When a crisis is resolved, the peace, the blessing and the assurances that follow will be overwhelming.

Go, and say to Hezekiah Thus saith the LORD, the God of David thy father, I have heard thy prayer, I have seen thy tears: behold, I will add unto thy days fifteen years. And I will deliver thee and this city out of the hand of king of Assyria: and I will defend this city. And this shall be a sign unto thee from the LORD, that the LORD will do this thing that He hath spoken; Behold, I will bring again the shadow of the degrees, which is gone down in the sun dial of Ahaz,

ten degrees backward. So the sun returned ten degrees, by which degrees it was gone down.
Isaiah 38:5-8

As Hezekiah was sick, God told him to prepare himself and put his house in order for he was going to die. When he cried to God, God did not only solve his immediate problem of giving him life, but also solved the surrounding problems that could become sources and agents of crisis in the future. He restored unto him peace, rest of mind, good health, and blessing and also stopped all wars throughout the rest of his life.

When we give God the opportunity to resolve our crisis He will not only resolve the immediate crisis but will go further than that, by making wars to cease to the end, breaking every bow aimed at us, cutting every spear asunder and burning every chariot in the fire. And we will live a crisis-free life through Jesus Christ our Lord and Savior. PRAISE THE LORD!!!

It is important to understand that when we stand to pray we should not have to ask God to break down things in the kingdom of darkness but to completely destroy things. The Bible says, "… and the yoke shall be destroyed because of the anointing," Isaiah 10:27. Whenever you break any weapon of the enemy, they quickly fix it and use it against you. Therefore, your prayer should be: "I destroy, I crush, and I dismantle every weapon of the enemy." These are the weapons that the LORD said He would use to punish the wicked: thunder, earthquake, great noise, storm and tempest and flame of devouring fire.

Thou shalt be visited (punished) of the LORD of host with thunder, and with earthquake, and great noise, with storm and tempest, and the flame of devouring fire.
Isaiah 29:6

These are instruments or agents of destruction in the hands of the Almighty God. Today God is still using these agents to pass judgment on wicked nations and people.

The powerful and effective prayer against the forces of evil will sound like this:

Father, in the name of Jesus, the name that is above all names I take my stand and get myself dressed up with all the defensive armor of God (you may name them). I saturate the air with the blood of Jesus and spray the air with the arrows of the LORD's deliverance and the arrow of deliverance from the prince of the power of the air to clear the air from the blockage of the prince of Persia so as to enable my prayers to reach up to heaven and my rewards to flow down freely unhindered **2 Kings 13:17; Daniel 10:12, 13.** With the instruments of the judgment of God, I strike the gathering of the forces of darkness and the witches with thunder; I command the thunder from the LORD to tear down the kingdom of Satan and his agents. I command earthquakes to sink down every stronghold that resists the power of God. Let the earth open her mouth and swallow every idol, and its makers. Every gathering of the witches and wizards, principalities and powers, rulers of darkness of this world and spiritual wickedness in high places must stumble. May the storm and tempest cut down their wings. I take authority over the sea, the mountain, the valley and the plains. I send lightning and tornadoes into the camp of the wicked and command the borders of the sea to release its tsunamis. Let the fire of God consume and destroy the remnants of their weapons and equipment while I declare peace unto the people of God, in Jesus' name I pray. Amen. **Isaiah 29:6**

CHAPTER 11

OTHER RELATED MATTERS

Pray and seek help to be loosened from diabolical soul ties, especially if you were in a relationship with someone who later died but once in a while in your dreams you see him or her still in a relationship with you. This could stand against your progress throughout your lifetime.

- If you had been involved in any blood covenant with someone; a childhood friend or former lover that you later separated from, this could have a terrible effect in your present social and marital life with regard to child bearing and other things.
- Is your family name associated with idol worship or something you are not comfortable with? It is wrong to wake up one day and change a name, as a name change has to be first done spiritually to break the covenant associated with the former name before a new name, which the mouth of the Lord should give. Therefore every change of name that did not take root in the spirit may not be effective, and after the change of name, the problem might still persist.

- **AN OFTEN ASKED QUESTION**:_Can a Spirit-filled, born-again Christian, be under any curse of any kind as against **Galatians 3:13:** "Christ hath redeemed us from the curse of the law, being made a curse for us: for it is written, Cursed is every one that hangeth on a tree."

- **ANSWER: YES!**

- **WHY AND HOW**? When we take the pains and time prayerfully to study **Ezekiel 18:1-32** we will come to understand that if an unbelieving father had taken someone else's land or anything by violence or through oppression and changed the title and claimed it to be his or his family's. If a believing son knowingly inherited that possession after the father without restitution, that property is accursed and the son automatically comes under that curse. The curse is upon that property because it was taken by false means. **Exodus 20:17; Hebrews 10:26.**

- **SOLUTION:** The solution to this is in repentance and **RESTITUTION**. Since the blood of Jesus justifies, it does not justify sin but the sinner. Therefore as long as we willfully retain the lies with us, there remains no more sacrifice for sin. For this very reason God had to separate Abram from: (i) his country; (ii) his kindred; and (iii) his father's house; to give him a new beginning, because if any man be in Christ, he is a new creature... **2 Corinthians 5:17.**

  Genesis 12:1, talks about separation. May we be separated from *accursed things* that tend to hinder our spiritual growth. Amen.

  Above all, the Bible in **Galatians 3:13** talks about "curse of the law." We are saved by grace through faith in Jesus Christ. He is the fulfillment of the law and through faith in Him we are saved. Apostle Paul asked this question to the Roman Church and to us today, in **Romans 6:1**, he asked: "What shall we say then? Shall we continue in sin, that grace may abound? The answer is not far-fetched as the Apostle Paul himself made the answer available in **verse 2**: "God forbid.

How shall we, that are dead to sin, live any longer therein?" Living in sin does not connote a continuous sinning only, but also includes retaining items or property acquired by evil.

Jesus said, Not every one that said unto me, Lord, Lord, shall enter into the kingdom of heaven; but he that doeth the will of my Father which is in heaven.
Matthew 7:21

If Jesus, Himself can say that not all those who call Him Lord, Lord shall enter into the kingdom of His Father but those that do the will of His Father, the question then is: What is the will of the Father? The will of God is the Word of God.

I once heard a pastor tell his congregation that Jesus did not mean to say so because the Bible also says, "...if thou shalt confess with thy mouth the Lord Jesus, and shalt believe in thine heart that God raised Him from the dead, thou shall be saved," **Romans 10:9.**

The two quotations are correct, and are from the Holy Bible. As soon as we come to Him as we are, He receives us, cleanses us and preserves us. We can now see what takes place at that one second that a sinner repents and gives his life to Him.

The Holy Spirit has convicted him of something. The conviction runs straight through his vein and sends a belief into his heart. The belief is processed through blood flow from the heart to the lips for sincere confession. But every confession that does not flow through the normal route, proceeding from the heart, and flowing with the blood through the mind does not lead to "godly sorrows" but mere deception and lip service.

Jesus also knew that accepting Him is just the first step and the beginning of a life long journey in Him. As one continuously sits before Him to learn from Him, He will step by step lead and open his/her eyes of understanding to see the wonderful treasures buried in His Word. The process and the teachings will help a beginner in Christ live a life that conforms to His image. Jesus knows better and will send the Holy Spirit to regenerate the heart of a new convert and nurture him to become adult in Him. At this point he is no longer a baby but adult and knows evil and good and also accepts responsibilities.

For God so loved the world, that He gave His only begotten Son, that ***whosoever*** *believeth in Him should not perish, but have everlasting life.*
John 3:16

With all the unconditional love that God loves the world by giving His only begotten Son, there is a condition in the middle: "that *whosoever* believeth in Him..." It goes to show that salvation is a free offer by God to the dying world, but not all will accept the offer. Those who reject the offer will not have it.

But as many as received Him, to them gave He power to become the sons of God, even to them that believe on His name.
John 1:12

Any gift that is not received cannot be owned. Jesus is a gift from the Father, and those who refuse to receive that gift are without Him.

ZACCHAEUS AND SALVATION

It was after RESTITUTION that Jesus pronounced salvation.

And Zacchaeus stood, and said unto the Lord; Behold, Lord, the half of my goods I give to the poor; and if I have taken any thing from any man by false accusation, ***I restore to him fourfold.*** *And Jesus said unto him, This day is salvation come to this house, forsomuch as he also is the son of Abraham. For the Son of man is come to seek and to save that which was lost.*
Luke 19:8-10

I wish Zacchaeus did not mention the aspect of restitution, then would we hear what the Lord would have told him. Today's believers refuse to restitute for some reasons; because of shame, because of fear, and due to misleading teachings by some. It is important to listen to what the Holy Spirit says to you. If He wants you to restitute, waste no time as failure to obey will hinder your prayers and spiritual growth. Many teachers who themselves failed to restitute and make many to believe that salvation is a license to either commit sin or live in sin.

But, if a witch or anyone wakes up to pronounce any curse on a believer without a reason, such a curse cannot and will never stand.

As the bird by wandering, as the swallow by flying, so the curse causeless shall not come.
Proverbs 26:2

A believer in Christ Jesus is free from every curse pronounced by anyone, or satan or a witch because the blood of Jesus has redeemed us from every curse.

But the God of all grace, who hath called us unto His eternal glory by Christ Jesus, after that ye have suffered a while, make you perfect, establish, strengthen, settle you.
1 Peter 5:10

He is a God of order, plan, purpose and a God of time. The Lord wants to know how, with patience, we do the works He committed into our hands and how we trade with His talents that He gave us to occupy till He comes and what gains we make. If we will accept to do first things first, money and other material needs will later beg us, not the other way round.

CHAPTER 12

DAILY PRAYER OF CONFESSION AND DECLARATION

PRAYER AGAINST ABANDONMENT, NEGLECT AND ISOLATION

Most Holy Father, I thank You for giving me my spouse to live, to love and to cherish all the days of my life until death do us part. Lord, help me to be the best that You made me to be in this relationship. I resist, I refuse and I reject the spirit of isolation, negligence, neglect and abandonment in our family. We shall stand for one another; to care and to help, to comfort and to love, in faith, in winter and in summer, in prosperity and against adversity. Lord, make me conscious of the need of my spouse and children. Give me a quickening spirit at all times to be willing to answer the call of my spouse and children. As I deposit this prayer in my prayer bank, give me more burning love for my spouse especially when he or she is sick or calls for help under any circumstance. May we love and submit to each other as did Christ for the church. Thank you Lord for my answered prayer, in Jesus' precious name I pray. Amen. **Ephesians 5:22-33; Proverbs 5:15-20; 1 Corinthians 7:3-5, 10-11; Proverbs 18:22; Ecclesiastes 9:9; Proverbs 19:14; Proverbs 31:10-31; 2 Samuel 3:15-16**

PRAYER AGAINST ANGER

Father, in the name of Jesus, thank You for sparing my life and giving me another opportunity to seek Your face. I confess all my sins before You and ask that You forgive them all. I resist, refuse and reject every invitation by the devil to live a life of violence and abomination. I am asking God through this prayer to control my temperament even when I am wronged or provoked. Your word is clear concerning anger; it says I can be angry without committing sin by not allowing the sun to go down on my anger. I also recognize that a prolonged anger can lead to murder, arson and all kinds of evil. Help me Lord because I am blood and flesh and can easily be tempted to live in it. In place of anger give me love, for love shall cover my multitude of sins. I declare that I shall not be angry with my wife, I shall not be angry with my children, and I shall not be angry with the government and with the authorities, and I shall not be angry with brothers and sisters in the church and with people around me. I deposit this prayer in my prayer bank before You and use it to fight against every spirit of anger that might attack me at any time. Thank You, Lord, for my answered prayer, in Jesus' name I pray. Amen. **Psalm 4:4; Psalm 37:8; Nehemiah 9:17; Proverbs 15:1; Proverbs 16:32; Proverbs 22:24; Matthew 5:22; Ephesians 4:26; Titus 1:7**

PRAYER FOR ANOINTING

Dear Lord, I am praying that You anoint me with Your oil of gladness. I understand that anointing is the mark of recognition, approval, acceptance, and empowerment. I stand upon Your promises that when I am anointed with fresh oil my horn shall be exalted above all my equals. I deposit my anointing prayer into my prayer bank with You, that the word of my mouth be anointed, the meditation of my heart be anointed, the ministration and the move of the spirit in me be with anointing. All the favors that follow anointing shall be my portion, and every yoke upon me shall be destroyed because of the anointing. Anoint my feet that you may order them where You want them to go. Anoint my head for sound memory.

Anoint my tongue to speak the mysteries of God, words coated with salt and honey in season and out of season, to satisfy the needs of the hungry souls. Anoint my hands for miracles and anoint my eyes for divine vision and direction. With the anointing that You anoint me, give me also self-control so that pride does not take hold of me. I know that when You anointed Saul to be a king over Israel, the prophecy upon him was that men would meet him and he would be favored with salutation and gifts. He was also told that when he met prophets prophesying, he would prophesy with them and he would be turned into another man. I sincerely believe this is what anointing can do, and, by Your anointing upon me, let me be transformed and used. Please Daddy let me receive favor that come with salutations and gifts and also be turned to into Your image when I am in the midst of people, whether they be friends or enemies alike. Thank You, Lord, for my answered prayer, this I ask and pray in Jesus' name. Amen. **Isaiah 10:27; 1 Samuel 10:1-7; Acts 10:38; 2 Corinthians 1:21; James 5:14; 1 John 2:27**

PRAYER AGAINST BARRENNESS

Most blessed father in heaven, I take my stand today against the spirit of barrenness. I reject all forms of barrenness; financial barrenness, spiritual barrenness, mental barrenness and barrenness in the fruits of my body. My plants shall not cast off their fruits before time, as there shall be no barrenness in my house. I bind the spirit of miscarriages in my family and among my children, male and female. My sons and daughters shall be fruitful in their marriages as Eliezer of Damascus shall not be the heir in my house. If I choose to adopt a child, it shall be out of love to help but not out of lack of children of my own. I sincerely believe that those Word collections are Your words concerning this issue and You will honor Your words on this subject matter. Since You are not a man that You should lie, and You have never lied and will never lie, I believe You sincerely that since I have hearkened unto Your words to observe and to do all Your commandments, the blessedness of obedience shall be my portion now and forevermore. In Jesus' name I pray, Amen. **Genesis**

15:4; Genesis 17:2; Genesis 24:60; Exodus 23:26; Deuteronomy 7:14; Luke 1:36

PRAYER FOR BLESSING

Father, I do know that You created me in Your image and after Your likeness and You blessed me from the beginning to be fruitful, multiply, replenish the earth, subdue it and to have dominion over all other creatures of Yours. Dear Father, that is who I am; I am blessed beyond the curse, with long life and prosperity will You satisfy me and bless all that belongs to me. It shall come to pass that after You have blessed me that the devil will come to try me so that I will not remember to thank You. He may also try to make me not to respond to You with my tithes and offering and may blind me to forget the poor in the society. I am asking that with the blessing You bless me, You will also take control of my heart, my soul and my mind so that I will love You with all my heart, soul and mind, and my neighbors as I love myself. Since You are a covenant keeper and there is no unrighteousness in You, I have assurance that Your blessing will make me rich and You will add no sorrows with it. Thank You in advance for answering this prayer, in Jesus' mighty name I pray. Amen. **Genesis 1:28; Genesis 22:17; Numbers 23:20; 2 Samuel 6:11; Job 42:10; Deuteronomy 28:1-13**

PRAYER FOR BREAKTHROUGH

Dear Father, my source and my provider, thank You for providing me with the key to success, Your word. You have made it abundantly clear that if I will hearken unto Your voice and observe to do Your will and meditate daily on Your word, Your blessings will come upon me and overtake me. Therefore my Father, help me to hearken diligently unto Your word. I truly need this breakthrough, this overtaking blessing in every aspect of my life. I shall have breakthrough in my Marriage, in my business, in my ministry and in every field of human endeavor. I thank You Father for keeping my heart in Jesus, and not allowing me to depart from His ways. In addition, You have assured me that if I will meditate on Your word, I shall be like the trees planted by the rivers of water that will bring forth their fruits in due season and their leaves will never wither and that I also shall have good success. Help me set Your word before me in order to claim these promises. I bind the spirit of setback that usually attacks at the time of breakthrough. As I deposit this prayer in my prayer bank, I have confidence that my breakthrough is at hand. I give You thanks, Lord, for answering my prayer, in Jesus' name I pray, Amen. **Deuteronomy 28:8; Deuteronomy 30:5; Joshua 1:8; Psalm 1:3; Ezekiel 36:30; Daniel 11:32**

PRAYER AGAINST CHARM / SPELL

Dear Lord and King of the universe, You say that we should not use any other power or make for ourselves graven images. For this is an abomination in Your sight. I use the authority in the name of Jesus to bind all the powers of charms and spells cast into the air to afflict my life and that of my family. Those spells will not affect me in any way. I return them back to the sender. Your Word says we should do unto others as we would expect them to do unto us. I therefore decree that whatever anyone wishes me, he/she shall receive the same for himself and his household. In Your infinite mercy allow all spell casters to repent when they see the power of the Almighty God. Give them opportunity to give their lives to Jesus when the spells and charms that they cast begin to afflict them. Let them come to a conclusion that this is the finger of God. But let those who favor my righteous cause shout for joy and be glad. In Jesus' name I pray, Amen. **Numbers 23:23-24; Deuteronomy 18:9-12; 1 Samuel 28:11; 1saiah 8:19; Isaiah 54:17; Micah 5:12-13; Acts 16:16**

PRAYER FOR CHILDREN AT SCHOOL, SPORTS AND THE MILITARY

Father, in the name of Jesus, the children that You give me shall be outstanding in every field of human endeavor. You blessed Abraham with Isaac and he grew up to continue in the covenant that You made with his father. You blessed Isaac and chose Jacob his son to further the covenant You made with his grandfather and his father. I therefore desire that my children are chosen to further the covenant You made with me. You blessed Jacob (Israel) with twelve sons who have become a force to reckon with world without end. Since I have become the seed of Abraham by faith, I claim all the promises of God that the generation of the righteous shall not have an end. I also claim all spiritual blessings in heavenly places to be mine and my children's and children's children for ever and ever. In sports they will be outstanding. In the military they will fight mighty wars and return home alive. And since my children are for signs and for wonders, they represent God's purpose in life and their names represent God's plans for my household. None of them shall be cut off in the midst of their years. They shall be free to choose any profession of their choice, but all shall minister before the Lord. The pilots among them shall retire at an old age and lecture other pilots. The soldiers shall retire at an old age and train other soldiers, and so shall it be with those in other professions. Thank You, Lord because none of my children shall be wayward. I record this special request in my prayer bank before You trusting that You will honor me according to Your words for me, in the name of Jesus I pray. Amen. **1 Samuel 10:23; Job 42:15; 1 Samuel 14:1; Isaiah 8:18**

PRAYER AGAINST CONTAMINATION / POLUTION

Holy, most sanctified Lord, Your word tells us to live in the world but not to get mixed up in it. Like a lotus flower that grows in the mud but is not touched by the mud, let me thrive in this contaminated material world without becoming contaminated myself until the day You will take me to join You in Your purest abode. Lord, You are the Purest of the Pure. Like a red-hot burning rod, whatever it touches catches fire. Let Your purity touch me that I may catch Your fire and become pure like You. Because You are holy, You also want us to be holy. Because You are clean, You also want us to be clean. Every spirit of pollution, immorality and contamination that could drive away Your spirit from me is rejected, and cast out of my body and camp. I deposit this prayer in my prayer bank against the day my mind shall be tried with all manner of evil thoughts, wrong intentions and contaminations. May Your Word and this prayer bring a remembrance of this record before You and prevent me from falling into the trap that the devil sets for me to trap me and bring me into condemnation. Thank You, Lord, for answering my prayer, in Jesus' name I pray. Amen. **Deuteronomy 23:13, 18; Numbers 25:6-8; 2 Chronicles 15:8; 1 Corinthians 10:14; 2 Corinthians 6:14-18**

PRAYER FOR COURAGE

LORD God Almighty, mighty in battle, the Rock of my salvation, thank You for all Your protection. I am asking You specifically for courage in the time of trial and temptation. I need courage, wisdom and power to take the gospel of our Lord Jesus Christ to the unreached. I need courage to fight and defeat all my enemies and remain steadfast in the midst of adversity. I need courage when I am faced with hostility even among Christians who will try to pervert the gospel of Jesus Christ for their selfish gain. Thank You for helping me to continue to deposit this prayer in my bank before You. Use it, Lord, at the appointed time to grant me the courage I need for daily victories. I need courage to be able to rebuke, reproof, instruct, encourage and correct with long suffering and perseverance. I need courage to lead God's people to the "Promised Land" which is Your eternal dwelling place. Let Your Spirit drive away fear out of my sight. Cover me with Your dread as with Your people Israel in the wilderness, so that no man with evil intent will be able to stand before me. I end this prayer by thanking You, Lord, for answering my prayer and giving me courage and boldness to take the race to an end in Jesus' name. Amen. **Numbers 13:20; Deuteronomy 31:6-7; Joshua 1:6-9; 1 Samuel 30:6; 1 Samuel 14:6; Ezra 10:4; Psalm 27:14**

PRAYER AGAINST CURSES

Father, in the name of Jesus, I reject any curse that anyone might bring upon my family and me. You have said that causeless curses shall not stand, therefore Jesus died to set me free from the curse of the law. All curses, whether they be from the witches, generational, through any property that I will purchase, curses by association, curses through marriage or curses through and from my parents, or from friendship, shall never cleave to me in the name of Jesus, Amen. Every action of mine that would have brought a curse upon me is covered by the blood of Jesus. I am redeemed, I am purchased, I am justified, I am cleansed and washed and I am forgiven through the blood of Jesus, Amen. I confess all wrong doings and move on because I have assurance that the blood cleanses me from all sins. This prayer bank stand as a reminder before God that through the blood of His Son, Jesus Christ, that was shed at Calvary, the curse of satan and his agents shall not come upon me nor all that pertains to me. I cover myself with the blood of Jesus, everyone in my family is covered with the blood of Jesus and the church of Jesus Christ is covered with the blood of Jesus. Thank You Father for Your divine hand upon my life, in Jesus' name I pray. Amen. **Genesis 8:21; Numbers 22:12; Galatians 3:13; Proverbs 26:2; Genesis 12:3; Numbers 23:23; James 3:9; Revelation 22:3**

PRAYER CONCERNING THE DAY OF CHILD DELIVERY

Dear Lord the covenant keeper, it is written in Your holy Word that children are an heritage of the Lord. I therefore share in Your inheritance with abundance of children and claim them as a reward for my marriage. Lord, let my quiver be full with God-fearing children. Lord, in the day that my child will be born, there shall not be any difficulty because of Your covenant with me. It shall even be like Hebrews' women in Egypt since we are children of Abraham by faith. There shall not be any hemorrhage after delivery. The placenta shall not be delayed after the birth but will be delivered as soon as the baby is born. There shall be great joy at our child delivery. As I open this bank to record this prayer, let it also be recorded in Your book that such an account is kept before You, Lord. The Bible says that the expectation of the righteous shall be granted him. Since through Christ Jesus I am counted righteous, this prayer is my expectation concerning my child delivery. I am certain that my petition has been granted through Jesus Christ my Lord and Savior. Amen. **Genesis 35:16-18; Exodus 1:19; Psalm 127:3; Psalm 127:5**

PRAYER AGAINST DEATH THROUGH WAR

Father, in the name of Jesus, it is certain that there will be war one day either in my life time or my children's as Your word has affirmed. It is even certain that one of my children might fight in a war to defend his or her country, my prayer and my request is that no member of my family shall die through war; either through friendly fire or the bullets of the enemy. Lord, I have seen You use wars to downgrade people and You have also used wars to upgrade people. Let every war that might come be a source of promotion for me and members of my family. I bring all members of my family into this prayer bank deposit and I degree that violent death shall not be our portion. Many have fought in battles and come back to tell their war stories and many have come back to rule. The dead cannot praise You, only the living can sing praises unto Your name. I therefore declare that my family members shall fight and live to testify and be decorated. Like King David, they shall come back to rule and even rule over their defeated enemies. In the times of war may we find peace, happiness and joy. I also recognize that there are other wars that we must fight; war against hunger, against drug usage, against prostitution, against sickness and against all manner of ills that the wicked one might unleash upon the earth. Yet we still have to fight against all kinds of sin. But in all these, I say, we are more than conquerors through Jesus Christ our Lord and Savior. Amen and Amen. **Joshua 23:3; Matthew 24:6; Ecclesiastes 3:8; Psalm 27:3; 1 Corinthians 15:32; 2 Timothy 4:7**

PRAYER OF DELIVERANCE FROM DANGER

Great God of wonders, You that led Israel as a flock for forty years in the wilderness and sent Your dread to overwhelm the inhabitants of the land so that they could not do them any harm, keep me Lord out of danger that might come my way in the course of my daily service before You. Whenever You know that there is danger in the place I walk into, order my foot steps to the direction of peace and safety. I deposit this prayer in my prayer bank before You so that at any time there is a sense of danger before me, Your angels will go ahead and dismantle those dangers. Thank You Lord because I have assurance that You are with me always and even forever more, this I pray through Jesus Christ my Lord and Savior, Amen. **Psalm 37:28 ; Psalm 91:3; Proverbs 2:8; Isaiah 41:13; Isaiah 43:2; Matthew 8:23-26; 2 Timothy 4:18**

PRAYER AGAINST DEPRESSION

Holy Father, thank You for the sound spirit that You have sent into my heart. There shall not come near me the spirit of stress, heaviness or depression as I will not open my heart to evil thought and worries. Lord, keep me focused on what You have me do and my mind active in all that concerns You. Let not the pressure of life overwhelm me and set my mind into much thinking. But let me be satisfied with the fullness of Your joy. Let the blood of Jesus wash me from all filthiness and contamination and let my soul sing You praise every day of my life. Give me the spirit of satisfaction and appreciation in all that You have done and remove worries and filthy communication from my life. Let me be content with what You give to me for godliness with contentment is great gain. Remind to live by faith for if You can take care of the birds of the air that sow not neither reap, how much more me Your child. Thank You, Lord, for the comforting of my spirit, thank You for the assurances through Your word. This prayer stored in my prayer bank shall awake for my defense and deal a heavy blow to the spirit of depression. I seal this prayer with the name of Jesus Christ of Nazareth, to Him be glory for ever and ever more. Amen. **Psalm 34:19; Psalm 119:28; 1 Samuel 16:14; 1 Kings 21:4; Judges 16:16; Matthew 11:28; James 4:9-10; 1 Peter 1:6-7**

PRAYER AGAINST DISOBEDIENCE

Dear Father in heaven, cause me to obey Your words and walk in obedience as Jesus Christ my Lord and Savior did. A time shall

come when my obedience shall be tested. Lord, I am asking You not to depart from me. Clothe me round about You like a garment and cause me to obey You in everything. Keep reminding me concerning this prayer bank and use it to destroy the spirit of disobedience in any form it might try to infiltrate into my mind. At very critical times that it seems difficult to obey under the power of man, compel me through Your power to obey You and keep all Your precepts and commandments. Thank You Lord for letting me know that obedience is better than sacrifice and that it was through disobedience that king Saul was rejected. Thank You, Father for answering my prayer. This I pray in Jesus' name. Amen.
1 Kings 13:21-22; Genesis 3:6; 2 Corinthians 10:6; Ephesians 5:6; Colossians 3:6; Hebrews 2:2; 1 Peter 2:7-8

PRAYER FOR DIVINE DIRECTION

Holy Father, I pray and ask that You divinely direct me to where You have determined for me. It is written that the steps of the righteous man are ordered by You, and that You also delight in all his ways. I therefore request that You order my steps and also delight in all my ways. Dear Lord, I reject the leadership of my senses and flesh, I have acknowledged You as my Shepherd, and also request that You go before me while I follow closely behind. May I not go ahead of You, Lord, so that I do not make a wrong turn, and may my sins not stand against me and prevent me from being focused, paying attention to Your divine direction and command. I request that You store this prayer up against that day that the deceiver will try to make me veer off from the path that You have me walk, and Lord, lead me to the Rock that is higher than I. I pray that You build me upon that solid rock where no storm can shake. You know me more than I know myself and can also keep my heart from pollution and evil work. I bind the spirit of contamination, wandering thoughts and diversions and I clothe myself with Your beauty and ask Your Spirit to permanently indwell in me, so that it shall be said of me, "Christ in me, the hope of glory." I pray that this prayer that is recorded in my prayer bank before You guide me to success in ministry and all other undertakings through Jesus Christ my Lord.

Amen and Amen. **Psalm 32:8**; **Proverbs 14:12**; **Isaiah 26:2**; **John 10:9**; **John 14:5-6**; **Romans 5:2; Revelation 3:8**

PRAYER AGAINST DIVORCE

Most glorious Father, thank You for the good spouse that I have found and married and will live with, all the days of my life. She/he is the spouse of my youth and shall be the spouse of my old age. She/he will not only be a wife/husband but a mother/father, a friend, a companion and a lover. If at any time our marriage goes through a test, Lord, give us the wisdom to get through it together, and may the grace to cope and bear with one another be sufficient unto us. I reject the spirit of separation and divorce in our marriage. I resist all outside influences that might cause confusion in our marriage. Mothers and fathers in-law, brothers and sisters-in-law, friends, relatives shall have no power to destroy our marriage relationship. This word of God prayed and deposited in my prayer bank shall fight for us and unite us together to the end of time. I shall love my wife as Christ loved the church and gave Himself for her, (I shall submit unto my husband as unto the Lord). We shall team up together and fight against the spirit of neglect, abandonment and unfaithfulness. I bind the agents of home invasion, lust, communication breakdown, dislike for each other and gossip. We shall be sincere to each other in everything and not give the enemy room to destroy our peace. We shall jointly raise our children in the way of the Lord, and not divide them between mother and father. We shall rebuke them jointly and also praise them jointly whenever they do anything bad or good. May we not cheat on each other and may we be an example to other couples to emulate. We stand against all other unforeseen activities of the devil that may arise in the midst of our marriage. May we overcome them all and remain united unto the end. I pray this prayer in the name of Jesus Christ. Amen. **Genesis 2:24-25; Proverbs 5:15-20; Ecclesiastes 4:9-12; Malachi 2:16; Matthew 19:6; Ephesians 5:21-31**

PRAYER AGAINST HARM THROUGH EARTHQUAKES

I thank You Father for Your word. The Bible says there shall be earthquakes in diverse places. But I will only *hear* about them and they will not affect me and what is mine. In as much as I am not involved in the sins of Korah, Dathan and Abiram, the earth will not open its mouth to swallow me, it will swallow neither my belongings nor any from my family. This prayer is stored up in my prayer bank against all such occurrences and the devastations and shocks that may follow. Your Word is true that if I pray according to Your will, You will hear me. It is written, "How beautiful upon the mountains are the feet of he who brings goods tidings, who publishes peace..." You have chosen me to carry good tidings and to publish peace, I and mine therefore shall not be the victims of earthquakes. You have said that I will hear of the rumor of earthquakes and of wars but they will not come near my dwelling. I use this prayer in my prayer bank and close all avenues for earthquakes around my area of residence. I tie down the spirit that causes rumblings and eruptions of the earth, I bind it and cast it into the abyss. My presence in my area of residence shall prevent any earthquake from happening in that area. And souls shall know that a child of God is in their midst and bow and worship his God. I pray this prayer in Jesus' name. Amen. **Numbers 16:30-32; Matthew 7:26; Matthew 27:54; Matthew 28:2**

PRAYER AGAINST EPIDEMIC/PLAGUE

Lord, I come before You this day in the name that is above all names. I recognize that the wicked one might cast his epidemic virus into the air to bring affliction upon the sons and daughters of men. My spouse and the entire members of my household shall not be touched by such a plague. You, O Lord, will envelope us and cover us with Your wings. Every available weapon that You have given to us to use to fight against our enemies such as the blood of Jesus, thc name of Jesus, the Word of God and the fire of the Holy Spirit shall readily rise up in battle against all epidemic and plagues assigned to afflict us by our enemies. We will stoutly resist the devil and he and his agents shall flee from us. Whether it is going to be air-borne or water-borne disease or contamination or pollution of the land or any form of food poisoning, it will not affect us in any way in Jesus' mighty name. We dip ourselves in the pool of the blood of Jesus, we are also baptized unto Him in that pool of His blood as we are partakers with Him in His death, burial and resurrection. And since the creator of the heavens and the earth is our God, the plague sent to afflict the world shall never hurt me and my household. I pray this prayer in the name of Jesus Christ. Amen. **Exodus 9:10; Exodus 9:23-25; Numbers 12:10; Exodus 15:26; Psalm 91:10; Mark 5:34**

PRAYER AGAINST ERRORS/BLESSING THROUGH ERRORS

Lord, prevent me from committing any errors that may cause problems in my life or the lives of others around me. Blessed Savior guide me when I am driving, or operating a machine, in the use of a gun or any other mechanism that could bring adverse effects to my life or the lives of people around me. You, O Lord are wonderful in Your doing, because the error of Uzzah became a blessing to Obed-edom and his household. As I record this prayer in my prayer bank before You, I understand that what the enemy meant for evil could turn out to be for good. Therefore the errors that others will commit will turn out to be a blessing to me, and my own errors will surely bring me favor. Through Jesus Christ, I shall not make any error that will send me, my wife and children to jail. Thank You, Lord for my answered prayer. Thank You again for Your power for victory. This prayer I pray through Jesus Christ our Lord and Savior, Amen. **1 Samuel 15:27-28; 2 Samuel 6:6; 2 Kings 1:2; Ecclesiastes 5:6; 2 Peter 2:18; 2 Peter 3:17**

PRAYER FOR FAVOR

Lord God my Maker, I am asking You to grant me favor in life. Your Word says that by strength shall no man prevail, it therefore takes favor for doors of opportunity to open for man. I recognize that nothing is accidental in Your sight, but that which You have determined in Your heart before the world began. You gave Joseph favor in Egypt, Daniel favor in Babylon, Ruth favor with Boaz, may Your favor not depart from me. May I find favor with God and with man all my entire life. Mary, the mother of my Lord Jesus Christ may not have been the only virgin in her time, but she found favor in Your sight and was elected to be the mother of the Son of God. I know that through Jesus Christ my Lord and Savior, I am elected and granted special favor to succeed and do exploits in life. May I find favor in education, sports, marriage, children, business and other aspect of human endeavor. This I ask, knowing that I have the answer, in Jesus' name. Amen. **Genesis 39:21; 1 Samuel 2:26; Psalm 30:5; Proverbs 14:9; Isaiah 60:10; Daniel 1:9; Luke 1:30; Luke 2:52**

PRAYER AGAINST FAILURE

Father, I ask that I be the head and not the tail. I also declare that I be not a failure but a very successful person in the world. In as much as I have hearkened unto Your voice to be the doer of Your Word, all the blessings written in Your Word shall come upon me and overtake me. Colleagues of mine, friends and loved ones shall not leave me behind. It shall be forward ever and backward never. I refuse to fail and also reject failure in its entirety. It shall be when I climb any hill, I shall ascend to its top very easily. It shall be success at home, success in the public service, success in education, and success in all endeavors of life. I claim success over all my dreams, those that have manifested and those that have not. One thing is sure, You made me in Your image and after Your likeness. Since You are not a failure I also cannot be a failure. The words from Your lips created all things, similarly the words from the breath You gave me has creative power. I stand by Your Word and it shall come to pass that when failure encounters me it will flee far away from me. It shall be that when failure hears of me, it shall drink a cup of trembling and take a different and separate route! This I ask in the sweet name of Jesus. Amen. **Deuteronomy 28:1-2; Deuteronomy 31:6; Joshua 1:8; Joel 2:23-26; John 31:6; 1 Samuel 2:35**

PRAYER FOR FAITHFULNESS

Faithful Father, give me a sound spirit to remain faithful in all my dealings not only with You, Lord, but also with my fellow brothers and sisters. Help me now to be faithful in a little thing and when You have blessed me, stir up my heart to remember to be faithful in much. As I stand today to record this prayer in my prayer bank before You, help me prevent the spirit of madness from coming after me in the days of my success. In the days of heavy rain and snow, let me be reminded that they are Your messengers. They are faithful to Your words and honor You by coming to wet the earth to make it bring forth and bud so as to give seed to the sower and bread to the eater. And in the day of sunshine, keep my heart at peace to know that the sun also is faithful and obedient to Your words by coming to warm the earth. I therefore through this prayer request that neither rain nor sun will make me to be unfaithful to Your words by refusing to step out and accomplish what You assigned me to do. I shall not only be faithful in tithes and offering, but also in evangelism, visitation, helping the poor and the needy, answering Your call to travel and doing whatever You ask me to do to the glory of Your name. May I be faithful to my spouse in our marriage relationship and to my children in our family. Let Your spirit of faithfulness envelope me round about and thank You Lord for this shall be my portion in the land of the living through Jesus Christ my Lord and Savior. Amen. **Genesis 4:4; Genesis 18:19; Numbers 12:7; 2 Kings 12:15; Matthew 25:21; Mark 14:6; Acts 4:36-37; Acts 10:1-2;**

PRAYER AGAINST FALSEHOOD AND LIES

Father, in the name of Jesus, I reject every spirit of deception and lies perpetrated by the enemy, the lying devil. I record this prayer against all forms of deception, through false prophets, dreams and vision, and through ignorance in interpretation of the Word of God. Lord, let lies and deception be exposed and defeated. Manifest Yourself, Lord, to those who take the Word of God for granted and make merchandise of people because of their greed. Prove to them that You are the only wise God and there is none beside

You. May Your mighty hand arrest those false apostles, deceitful workers who transform themselves into the apostles of Christ, and also those ministers of satan who transform themselves into ministers of righteousness. May the seed of deception not be sown in the heart of any member of my household particularly my children by their colleagues in their places of study. May those that double money and are dubious not succeed to deceive mine and claim their valuable treasures. I thank You, Lord, for using this prayer to prevent all forms of deception, in the Mighty name of Jesus. Amen. **Genesis 3:4; Matthew 4:9; Luke 21:8; John 8:44; Galatians 6:7; Ephesians 4:14; 2 Timothy 3:13**

PRAYER FOR FRUIT BEARING

Dear Father, I thank You for Your love for me. My request to You is that I abide in the vine so as to produce more fruit. Lord, help me not to get detached from You. It is Your command that every tree that does not bear fruit should be cut down and thrown into the fire, I therefore ask that You have power over my heart to keep me attached to You, the Vine so that I can continually bear fruit. Father in the name of Jesus, I begin to take care of those things that could make me detached from the Vine: sins of all kind, faithlessness, unproductiveness, taking the grace of God in vain, being complacent in my duty to God and compromising my faith to buy favors from men. My Lord, let not my season pass without me bearing fruit; physical and spiritual fruit alike. As I record this prayer in my prayer bank before You, I bind the spirit of dryness and decree that everything that I do shall be fruitful. Thank You Lord for answering my prayer, in Jesus' name I pray. Amen. **Proverbs 11:30; John 15:4, 16; Mark 11:13; Luke 3:10-14; Galatians 5:22-23; Philippians 1:11; Colossians 1:10**

PRAYER FOR THE GIFT OF DISCERNMENT

Most blessed Father, the author of wisdom and knowledge, I pray for the gift of discernment to enable me to know those with deceptive spirits around me. No man can discern between good and evil except by Your Spirit. Fill me with Your sound spirit: spirit of wisdom, knowledge, understanding and of revelation. I bind veiling spirits that are used by the wicked one to block the spirit of discernment. As I prepare this prayer for my bank, I am asking that discernment takes a center stage in exposing the various intents in people's hearts, as they come close for fellowship, for ministry, for worship and for friendship. I pray that all wolves in sheep's clothing, all false prophets and prophecy, and all seducing spirits be exposed. May I not be deceived, seduced and made to compromise my faith due to lack of the spirit of discernment. Thank You Lord for giving me the understanding that I need anytime through this prayer bank as I climb the ladder of promotion in Your ministry. I pray this prayer in the name of Jesus Christ. Amen. **2 Kings 5:26; Acts 16:16-18; Romans 8:27; 1 Corinthians 2:14; 1 Corinthian 12:10; Hebrews 4:12; 1 John 4:1-2**

PRAYER FOR STRENGTH FOR MY WARFARE LIFE

Father, in the name of Jesus, I stand before You today to deposit my prayer in my prayer bank against that day; the day that is determined that I will enter into battle against enemies of progress. I pray that when such a day comes, the devices of the enemies be defeated and let all their equipment malfunction. You, O Lord, will clothe me with knowledge, wisdom, understanding and power to defeat them. Their weapons shall be rendered unworkable and their chariots' wheels shall fall off from under them. I shall be clothed with offensive, defensive and protective armors. I will rise and stand therefore with my loin girded about with truth and my heart protected with the breastplate of righteousness. May my feet be shod with the preparation of the Gospel of peace and clothe me with the shield of faith to be able to quench all the fiery darts of the wicked ones. I cover my head with the helmet of salvation and let the sword of the spirit be in my hand to cut asunder every witchcraft spell cast upon me. Help my mouth to release all prayers and supplications which the Spirit of God shall motivate me to pray and let me watch with all perseverance and supplication for all saints and to see how the devil's kingdom scatter. I know that I am an overcomer and have overcome the enemies by the blood of the Lamb and by the word of my testimony. Thank You in advance for my already answered prayer, in Jesus' name I pray. Amen. **2 Corinthians 10:3-4; 2 Timothy 2:3-4; Ephesians 6:10-18; Jeremiah 51:20-24; Exodus 14:25; 1Timothy 6:12**

PRAYER FOR THE GIFT OF FAITH

Most merciful Father in heaven, I thank You for Your grace and encouragement. I believe that You can do all things and that all power belongs to You. Help me therefore to live a life of faith. Your word says that without faith it is impossible to please You and that those that come to You must believe that You are everything unto them and a rewarder of those that diligently seek You. Father, please, help my unbelief and cause me to take every word that proceeds out of Your mouth as the apple of my eyes. Since You have mentioned faith as one of the gifts of the Spirit, bestow upon me this gift and help me to develop the little faith in me to the point whereby I can move the mountain with it, and can also receive all the promises that You have for me. At any time that my faith in You is tested, help me to stand firm and also come out victorious. I therefore request the gift of faith to move all mountains, to trust You to the end, to lay down my life for the kingdom's sake and to always say "yes Lord" at all times. Thank You, Lord, for strengthening my faith in You through Jesus Christ my Lord and Savior, Amen. **Genesis 15:6; Genesis 22:8; Joshua 14:12; 1 Samuel 17:37; Job 19:25; Daniel 3:17; Mark 11:24; Romans 10:17; Hebrews 11:6-11, 33**

PRAYER FOR GOD'S CONTROL

King of all kings and Lord of all lords, take all the glory, honor, adoration, dominion, majesty and power, in Jesus' name, Amen. I stand in faith and believe and also claim all Your promises. I bind the spirit of fear, intimidation and worry. Lord, take control of my life, the life of my spouse and of my children. If there will arise any occasion, which would have brought trembling into my life, let these words readily be available in my record to defend me, "God is in control" and "I will fear no evil for You are with me." When it seems that all hope is lost and there is a concern over a situation, help me Lord to remember that You are on the throne and are watching over me. When there is a rumor of an impending danger let me rest in Your promises, and if the enemies are pursuing me as did the Egyptians at the red sea, let my desperate situation turn to confusion in the camp of my enemies and let me remember what Your mighty hand did in delivering Your people. In all, let Your peace settle in my heart and help me always to remember that You are in control. I pray this prayer in Jesus' name because I know that he that dwells in the secret place of the Most High shall abide in the shadow of the Almighty. Thank You for taking control of my life. In Jesus' name I pray. Amen. **Exodus 14:13; 2 Chronicles 20:15; 2 Chronicles 32:8; Psalm 24:1; Psalm 46:10; Isaiah 43:1-5; Matthew 28:18**

PRAYER FOR GOD'S POWER

Most glorious Father and Lord of the universe, thank You for entrusting me with Your power. Once You speak, I am assured that power belongs to You. You have declared me to be Your battle axe and weapons of war: for with me You will destroy nations and kingdoms, break in pieces the horse and his rider, the chariot and his rider, the captains and the rulers. You have also transformed me into a "defenced" city, and an iron pillar, and brazen walls. I have authority over the whole universe, to pull down and to build up, to plant and to uproot. I shall thread upon serpents and upon scorpions and none shall hurt me. I claim the power to set the captives free and to preach the Word of God with boldness and without fear. This power of the Almighty God shall be available to me wherever and whenever I stand to minister the Word of God; miracles, signs and wonders shall be my portion and souls shall be won into the kingdom of God. As I deposit this prayer into my prayer bank, I have confidence that witches that are sent to disrupt activities in churches and afflict families shall be brought down and disgraced. They shall not go free but shall confess their activities and repent. I pray this prayer in Jesus' name, Amen. **Job 42:3-5; Psalm 110:1-3;**

Isaiah 40:28-31; Jeremiah 32:17-19; Jeremiah 51:20-24; Luke 5:17; Luke 10:19; Acts 1:8

PRAYER FOR HEALING

Thank You Father, for I know that healing is bread for Your children. I have the assurance that when sickness comes the Lord will heal me. I claim mental healing, spiritual healing, emotional healing, financial healing and physical healing. May I not retain any bitterness in my relationship with others. Lord, grant me a sound mind to be able to do Your will. I shall declare without any doubt whenever I sense sickness around me: "I am healed, I am healed and I am healed", and I shall receive healing immediately. Your word says that if I will hearken unto Your words and keep Your precepts that none of the diseases that the world will suffer shall cleave to me. I truly believe this truth and have made Your holy Son, Jesus Christ, my Lord and Savior and also believe in Him, therefore none of the sicknesses of this world shall cleave to me. I apply the blood of Jesus upon my door posts and the lintel of my house for healing and protection. I apply it upon my forehead, upon my business, finances and upon my spouse and children. Use this prayer as recorded in my prayer bank and prevent sickness, whether spiritual or physical and command healing upon my body, soul and spirit. I thank You, Lord, for healing me, in Jesus' name I pray, Amen. **Exodus 15:26; 2 Kings 20:5; Psalm 23:3; Psalm 103:3; Jeremiah 17:14; Hosea 6:1; Mark 7:27**

PRAYER FOR THE SPIRIT THAT HELPS OUR INFIRMITIES

My Almighty Father in heaven, I give You praise and honor for who You are. You have shown me the way of life; in Your presence is fullness of joy, and at Your right hand are pleasures forever more. Lord it is always a good thing when I proclaim that I love You, but whenever my love for You is tested, I tend to fumble and compromise. Lord, since our father Abraham's love and faith were tested and he did not waiver, that is the reason I deposit my prayer in my prayer bank today against that day that my love for You and faith in You will be tested. Lord, on that day may Your Spirit also help my infirmities, so that even if I do not know what to pray as I ought to pray, let Your Spirit make intercession for me with groaning which cannot be uttered. Let this Spirit search all hearts and reveal every plan of the enemy concerning my family and me. I use this prayer point to fight against all contrary spirits that satan might release against us. Such spirits as: discouragement, fear, feebleness, intimidation, death, sickness and many other spirits as may be unleashed against me by my adversaries shall be defeated. I declare victory through my Lord and Savior Jesus Christ, Amen. **Roman 8:26; Hebrews 11:6; 2 Timothy 1:7; Joshua 1:6-7; Psalm 37:3-7; 1 Corinthians 4:20**

PRAYER FOR HELP/SUPPORT

Daddy, I recognize and declare that my help is in the name of the Lord. Help me out of all the problems that might come my way tomorrow. Send the necessary support, ministry, spiritual, financial and personal so that nothing shall be lacking in time of need. Daddy I know that there are people who are very intelligent but have no support to further their education. There are many who are good in sports but are suppressed for lack of helpers. There are those with beautiful voices who have even written their own songs but cannot go further for lack of finance and support. I declare that my heaven shall not be iron, or my earth brass. I prophesy to the mountains, to the hills, to the rivers, to the valleys and to the dry land to release my blessings that are in them. I declare open heaven and open door which no man can shut. I deposit this prayer in my prayer bank against the day I will need help or support, I confess that such help will readily be available. My case shall be different because You are on the throne working for me, and because You are on the throne, I can rightly say, "it is well." Thank You Lord for sending Your Spirit to make intercession for me when I do not know what to pray for, and how to pray in times of weakness. Thank You for sending Your angel to fight my battle even when I am fast asleep. Thank You, Lord, because I know You are always there for me. In Jesus' name

I pray, Amen. **Psalm 124:8; Psalm 118:13; Matthew 15:25; 1 Chronicles 12:20-22; Joshua 1:15; 1 Kings 5:18**

PRAYER FOR HELP TO MAINTAIN HONESTY

Dear Lord, keep me from the pollutions that come as a result of dishonesty. The sin of Achan shall not find its way into my dwelling neither shall the sin of Ananias and Sapphira his wife be my portion and my family's. I shall worship the Lord with all my substance and I shall pay all my vows in the presence of all His people. Lord, keep this prayer open before You so that any time I go astray You quickly bring me back by reminding me of the effects of dishonesty. Take far from me deliberate sins and help me to speak the truth even in the smallest matter. As I deposit this prayer in my prayer bank, let it keep reminding me that I am Your ambassador in this world. I bind, reject, refuse and resist every spirit of dishonesty. Help me have an honest conversation with my spouse, children and other members of my family. Help me present Your word with honesty and truth. I refuse to bear false witness against anyone, even against my enemy. Let accountability and integrity be my standard and may I not forget that I will one day stand before You to render the account of my stewardship unto You. Let Your sound Spirit of honesty take control of my heart. Thank You, Lord, for answering my prayer. In Jesus' name I pray, Amen. **Leviticus 19:35; Proverbs 11:1; Joshua 7:21; 1 Samuel 12:4; 2 Kings 5:16; Acts 5:1-2; Romans 13:13; 1 Timothy 2:1-2**

PRAYER FOR HUMILITY

My Father, my Lord and my God, send the spirit that You gave to Your Son, my Lord and Savior Jesus Christ upon my heart. Remove arrogance and pride far from me. I know You will surely bless me but in the midst of that blessing, may I remain humble. May I not esteem myself better than others, but always consider others better than myself. May I humble myself to search the scriptures and may I not claim that I already know. May I humble myself to pray and seek Your face and not rely on my own understanding. May I humble myself and listen to others when they preach or teach and may I not conclude that I know better than them. Help me to listen to my spouse and my children alike and not to term them inferior or without knowledge. I bind the spirit of pride and arrogance and cast it out of my life. I resist the temptation to look down on someone You created in Your image. Use this prayer in my prayer bank to keep reminding me to remain humble in the midst of promotion and success. Thank You Lord for answering my prayer, in Jesus' mighty name I pray. Amen. **Daniel 4:29-34; Proverbs 15:33; Proverbs 22:4; Matthew 23:12; Isaiah 14:12-15; Philippians 2:5-11; 1 Peter 5:5**

PRAYER AGAINST IGNORANCE

My Father, My Lord, and My God, I pray this day that the eyes of my understanding be enlightened to behold the things that are written in Your law. You have made it clear in Your word that the memory of the just is blessed. I reject and bind the spirit of ignorance and cast it completely away from me. I decree, I declare, I announce and proclaim the wisdom of God, the knowledge of God, the understanding of God and the power of God. Since goat begets goat, cow begets cow, therefore the Spirit of the Living God, which is full of knowledge and wisdom, begets me. I cannot and will not be blind, I cannot and will not be deaf, and I cannot and will not be ignorant of God's plan for my life. This prayer that I deposit in my prayer bank before you shall keep me from the attack of the spirit of ignorance throughout my entire life. By Your information I shall be transformed and not be destroyed for lack of knowledge. I shall be empowered not disenfranchised. I shall be enlightened not perplexed and entangled. I shall be the delight of the Lord not His desolation caused by ignorance. My donkey shall in no wise see, know or understand more than me. God's purpose and God's plan for my life shall not be obscured. I command the malevolent cloud of ignorance to dock far away from me. I put a seal upon this prayer and cover the express answer with the blood of Jesus, in Jesus' precious name I pray, Amen. **Exodus 18:21; John 20:24-25; Luke 24:30-32; John 21:3; 2 Peter 2:14; Luke 12:15;**

PRAYER AGAINST INFIRMITY

1 Corinthians 6:19-20, Father in the name of Jesus, my body is the temple of the Holy Spirit and the Spirit of the Almighty God dwells in me; therefore I am not my own, I was bought with a price; my body therefore is to be used to glorify God.

1 John 4:4, I am making my stand known and clear that greater is Jesus Christ in me, than satan that is in the world.

Hebrews 1:7, Dear Lord as you make your angels spirit, make me your minister a flame of fire, I have become a flame of fire, Holy fire in my bones, fire in my marrows, fire in my mind, fire of God surrounding me. From the crown of my head to the sole of my feet, I am untouchable. I pray against bone sickness, heart disease or cardiac problems, against kidney failure, against bladder problems and all other forms of infirmities. The fire of God in my eyes shall prevent blindness from coming upon me. The fire of God in my ears shall melt every wax or hearing impediment that the enemy will bring upon me. The fire of God in my body system shall fight and destroy every seed of cancer, diabetes, high blood pressure, heart disease and all kinds of skin disease. Once more, I declare that I have no fellowship with the unfruitful works of darkness but reprove them. In addition to the fire, Lord, I apply the blood of Jesus in all aspect of my life, and in the doorpost of my house. Thank You, Lord, for taking away the spirit of infirmity from my dwelling, in Jesus' name I pray. Amen.

PRAYER AGAINST INVESTMENT LOSSES

Father, in the name of Jesus, I know that You know the beginning from the end. You know what might happen to my investments tomorrow, and as you helped Isaac to get a hundredfold in the midst of a famine that consumed the land, help me to overcome losses in the days of investment downturn. As I have made a covenant to pay my tithes and give my offerings according to Your command, I believe that the devourer will not devour my investments. I open this account in my prayer bank solely to make deposit against losses, and I know that Your word is abiding. So then, it is not me that will, nor me that run but You, God, that show mercy. Thank You in advance for protecting my investments in the days of famine ahead. Help me to continue to reap a hundredfold as long as I have not forsaken Your word nor denied Your name and let me be like the tree planted by the rivers of waters. May I continue to bring forth my fruits in due season and my leaves never wither and may all my endeavor prosper. Thank You for my answered prayer, in Jesus' name I pray. Amen. **Genesis 26:12; Deuteronomy 28:11; 2 Chronicles 31:10 ; Haggai 1:6, 11; Malachi 3:11; Hebrews 11:1**

PRAYER FOR JOB/WORK

Dear heavenly Father, Your Word says that anyone who does not want to work should not eat. I am willing to work to be able to support my family and the works of Your house. In the name of Jesus, I reject the spirit of joblessness. There may be a time when there would be scarcity of jobs in the land, the ground may likely be dry, but when I step out, may jobs readily find me. May I step my feet on fertile ground and may I reap a hundred fold in the midst of famine. I shall not at any time suffer unemployment. Employers may not hire, but I shall be hired in a well-paying job. This prayer is stored up in my prayer bank against the season of economic depression in our land. My vow therefore is that as long as the Lord will provide me with a job, I will not fail to pay my tithes with thanksgiving unto the Lord. Thank You, Father, for honoring my prayer concerning this matter, in Jesus' name I pray. Amen. **Genesis 26:2-3; Matthew 20:1-2; Matthew 21:28; John 5:17; 1 Thess. 4:11; 2 Thess. 3:10**

PRAYER FOR LEADERSHIP ABILITY

Shepherd of Israel, thank You for providing a clear and purposeful leadership unto me from my birth until now. Your faithfulness is from generation to generation. As You did swear unto Abraham Your friend, You led him and guided him through the desert and provided water and food in the wilderness for him and all his substance, blessed be Your name for ever and ever more, Amen. Thank You dear Daddy because I have confidence that You will also lead me all the days of my life, Amen. As a person clothed with flesh, I am not immune to distractions and diversions. I therefore deposit this prayer in my bank before You that You, O Lord, allow Your rod and staff to comfort me. Lead me to the green pastures and to the waters that run slowly. Restore my soul and also lead me in the path of righteousness for Your name's sake. Let me not fear any evil even when I walk through the valley of the shadow of death, let my spirit always see Your presence with me and be strengthened. When the enemies of progress seem to block my way and stand against me, may You open a new high way which no man can shut. Lead me and give me patience in following You. Lead me and impart Your spirit of leadership upon me so as to be able to lead Your people. You made it clear to Your disciples that a student is not greater than his teacher, therefore Lord, give me a leader's mindset, a leader's knowledge, a leader's mentality and leadership spirit so that my followers will learn from me and become great leaders of tomorrow. Thank You, Lord, for being a good Shepherd to me and an example that I must follow all my life. I pray this prayer in Jesus' name I pray. Amen. **Exodus 13:21; Psalm 23:2; Psalm 25:9; Isaiah 30:21; Isaiah 42:16; John 10:27**

PRAYER AGAINST MISFORTUNE

Father in the name of Jesus, I thank You for keeping me and preserving all that I have committed into Your able hand against danger, mishap or misfortune. A wall will not fall on me or my spouse or children. The ship that transports my wares shall not be destroyed by storm or fire. The plane that I enter shall not crash. My house shall not be engulfed by fire, nor shall my children be involved in any kind of accident. As I deposit this prayer in my prayer bank, let it also be recorded in Your book of remembrance that You did promise to show me kindness and not evil. You did say that those who gather against me shall fall for my sake, and that no weapon formed against me shall prosper. My enemies will not laugh at me and ask "where is your God that you trust?" Let not those who trust in You be put to shame. Let Your angels always surround me, drive with me when I am driving, dine with me when I am eating and sleep with me when I lay down to sleep. Let my words stored up in this prayer bank wake up for my defense and cast every misfortune out of my life and house, in the most excellent name of Jesus, Amen. **Exodus 14:25; Judges 21:2-3; 1 Samuel 30:3-8; Jonah 1:5; Luke 13:4; John 11:33-36**

PRAYER AGAINST MONITORING SPIRIT

Most merciful Father in heaven, thank You for Your security and protection over me. It is by Your grace that I am alive today. You, through Your wisdom and power, have defeated the devil and all his agents and have used the blood of Your dear Son as a shield upon my life. As I stand to deposit this prayer in my prayer bank before You, I bind Satan and all his agents and also destroy all the monitoring equipment used to monitor my movements or lure me to fall. If those monitoring agents are human, I curse them to be blinded, if they are crystal balls, I command the thunder of God to strike and destroy them, if they be magical mirrors, I direct the bullets of God at them and pray that they be shattered. Whoever and whatever being used to monitor my life and movements, Lord disfigure and completely dismantle them and wreak havoc severely anywhere they get their power from. Thank You, Lord for the victory I have today through Jesus Christ my Lord and Savior. Amen. **Numbers 13:1-2; Joshua 2:1; Joshua 7:2; Judges 1:24; Judges 18:2; 2 Samuel 15:10; 2 Kings 6:13; 2 Kings 2:7**

PRAYER FOR PATIENCE

My Father, my Lord and my God, thank You for Your leadership. My prayer is that You sustain me and grant me patience to walk with You as I work for You. The road is long, the distance is far but with patience, following You will be satisfying. Do not allow evil to entice me out of Your way and do not let me go ahead of the cloud. Help me to move with the cloud as the children of Israel in the wilderness. Give me the divine enablement to understand things as You put them in Your order in case I am tempted to go ahead of You. Use this prayer that I store up in my prayer bank to speak to my spirit and tame my spirit to succumb to Your will. Give me patience in tribulation, patience with my spouse and children, patience with my neighbors, and patience with one another in the ministry. Grant me patience when things do not go my way, when expectations are not met and when I am disappointed by a fellow man. Cause me to know that with the disappointment by man, You have a better plan for me. Uphold me to be patient to the end in order to receive my crown, in Jesus' name I pray, Amen. **Numbers 9:18, 19, 22; Isaiah 40:31; Matthew 24:13; Luke 8:15; Romans 15:4-5; James 1:3-4; James 5:10-11**

PRAYER FOR PEACE

My Lord and my God, I have often asked, if there could be peace in a troubled world. But Your answer to me has always been in the affirmative. Daddy, Your Word has shown me that I first need to have peace with God before I can have the peace of God. Now, O Lord, help me to have peace with You through Jesus Christ my Lord and Savior. May I receive Him into my heart, may I daily seek His face, may I receive assurance of forgiveness through the confession of my sins. May I worship the Father daily in the name of the Son and in the power of the Holy Spirit, Amen. And now, O Lord, may the peace of God that passes all understanding be with my spirit, soul and body. May I not be afraid of sudden fear. Let Your peace live within me, go with me and stay with me. Thank You, Lord, because You know that there can never bc any progress without peace. I am confident that there shall be peace in my marriage, with my children, with my neighbors and at work and in my ministry. My prayer bank concerning peace shall never be empty and I will never lack peace in my lifetime. When there shall be news of impending earthquakes, tornado, tsunami or any form of danger, may Your Word whisper a word of peace into my heart, "son, it is well with your soul." Thank You for answering my prayer and giving me sustainable peace, in Jesus' name I pray, Amen. **Numbers 25:12; Psalm 29:11; 2 Peter 3:14; John 14:27; John 16:33; Hebrews 12:14**

PRAYER TO POSSESS MY POSSESSIONS

Dear heavenly Father, thank You because You are my possession in the land of the living. Help me to hold onto You. May I not miss the Kingdom for I know that if I possess the kingdom all other things in this life are mine. As I deposit this prayer daily, You will be my defense when I need one, You will be my healer when I need a doctor, You will be my provider whenever I need provision. From coast to coast my blessings shall flow. Your covenant with me is that You will shake the heavens, the earth, the sea and the dry land, and the treasures of all nations shall flow in my direction. Your Word says that Your cities shall be spread abroad through prosperity. Therefore the covenant of possessing the gates of my enemies is established and sealed forever. As I deposit this prayer in my prayer bank, I believe that my possession is mine. I bind every familiar spirit that will seduce me to let me miss my possession in God, which is Christ Jesus. I refuse to yield to lies and falsehood but stand by Your word that in Mount Zion there shall be deliverance and there shall be holiness and my house shall possess our possessions. My house shall be a fire and a flame and the houses of my enemies shall be stubble and they all shall be consumed. Thank You, Lord, for reminding me that my labor of love will not be forgotten but that I shall be rewarded in due season. I pray this prayer in Jesus' name. Amen. **1 Kings 21:3; Psalm 119:111; Isaiah 61:7; Obadiah 1:17; Ezekiel 44:28; Matthew 6:33; Acts 20:32**

PRAYER FOR PROMOTION

My Lord and my God, thank You for letting me know You. I did not choose You, Lord, but You chose me that I should go and bring forth fruits, and not just fruits, but fruits that will remain. I also recognize that promotion does not come from north, south east or west, but from You. I believe Your Word that I will be the head and not the tail. I know that You have the power to catapult me to a height of honored men in Your sight. I recognize that there are also pride and other devices that come with promotion, but I trust that while You move me from glory to glory You will also take control of my spirit so that pride and arrogance will not creep in. Let Your gifts in me make a way for me and also bring me before great men. I desire that You promote me to be able to defend the gospel openly. I know that a man of low status cannot speak in the open, but with the promotion that You will promote me I also shall speak openly concerning things that pertain to Your kingdom. My financial promotion will help sponsor missionaries and open doors of ministries in all the countries of the world. My spiritual promotion shall set the captives free and bring the doubters on their knees before Your throne. Thank You because with Your Word in my mouth, I shall be diligent to bring sinners to repentance. Thank You, Lord, for your preservation in elevation, in Jesus' name I pray. Amen. **Genesis 45:8; Deuteronomy 28:13; Psalm 75:6; Proverbs 4:8; Proverbs 14:34; Proverbs 18:16; Proverbs 22:29; Daniel 3:30; Matthew 23:12**

PRAYER FOR PROTECTION AND SECURITY IN OLD AGE

Father, in the name of Jesus, thank You because my old age shall be a blessing and not a curse. I shall still be fruitful in my old age according to Your word. My children, children's children and the third, fourth and fifth generations shall bring gifts to celebrate with me. I know that You are the same yesterday, today and forever, therefore as You blessed Abraham with good age without blindness, I claim that favor that at my old age I will still have my eyes to see my great-great-grandchildren. You have said that the glory of old men is their gray hair; therefore I shall fulfill my days and be steadfast to the end. Thank You, Lord for granting my request, I deposit this prayer in my prayer bank that sicknesses like high blood pressure, diabetes and Alzheimer's disease, Parkinson's and loss of sight shall never come near my dwelling. I am thanking You, Lord in advance, for Your faithfulness and Your mighty hand of protection in my old age, in Jesus' name I pray, Amen. **Genesis 15:15; Psalm 71:9; Psalm 92:13-14; Isaiah 46:4; Joel 2:28; Titus 2:2-3**

PRAYER FOR PROTECTION DURING SUDDEN TRAVEL

Lord, I pray that if it happens that I make a sudden trip, an unprepared journey which I did not prepare for, You O Lord, will lead, guide me and provide help on my way. May You not allow me to fall into the hands of the wicked ones; thieves, robbers, con-artists and those that pickpocket, neither will You allow me to lose any of my belongings. But You, O Lord will send Your angels to keep the way for me and bring me safely to my destination. You will also grant me favor in all that I might desire on my way as I go. Let it come to pass that this prayer in my prayer bank takes care of every danger that would have happened to me on my trip. If anyone marked for destruction is in the vehicle, train, plane, ship or any other means of transportation that I shall use, may my presence in that vehicle prevent evil from coming to all. I bind all demons that cause accidents, all territorial spirits and assigned agents and declare a hitch-free trip all the time. I pray this prayer in the name of Jesus because I know that He will always go with me. Amen. **Genesis 19:22; 1 Samuel 21:8; 2 Kings 4:29; Zechariah 8:21; Luke 1:39; Luke 14:21; Exodus 12:31-33; 1 Samuel 16:1**

PRAYER OF PROTECTION IN TIME OF PERSECUTION

Dear Lord, I commit my life into Your able hand. I am asking You to protect me and shield me from my persecutors. You have already made it clear to me that in the world we shall have persecution, but that I should rejoice because You have overcome the world for me. As You have made me an overcomer according to Your word, I am asking You, O Lord, to be there for me when that trying time comes. You said that if a man's way pleases You, You will make his enemies to be at peace with him. I acknowledge all my sins before You, confess them and turn away from them unto You. And because I am made righteous through Jesus Christ my Lord and Savior, all my persecutors shall acknowledge You as Lord and King and shall bow and worship You. I also pray that You give me the spirit of endurance to go through persecution as a good soldier of Jesus Christ. A persecutor Saul was converted to Apostle

Paul, therefore arrest my persecutors and cause them to repent and surrender to the Lordship of Jesus Christ. Let the blessedness of enduring persecution be my portion in the name of Jesus Christ. Let this prayer wake up in the day it is needed most and dismantle the weapons of my persecutors. Thank You Lord for I have already seen victory ahead of me, in Jesus' name I pray. Amen. **1 Kings 19:2-3; Isaiah 53:7-8; Daniel 3:20; Nahum 1:9; Matthew 5:10-12; John 16:33; Acts 7:60; Luke 23:34**

PRAYER FOR RECOGNITION

Faithful Father, may all my labor for You not be in vain. Let a day come that You will look into Your record and remember me and also cause men to recognize me. As You search in Your record, let it be discovered one good thing that I have done in Your sight and use it, Lord, to open the doors of blessings for me. I know that we are not saved by works, but let my faith in You produce good works which will further bring more people into Your kingdom. My Father, my Lord and my God, I am asking You to reject the accusation of the accuser who will try to accuse my wrong doing before You. Before he tries to accuse me before You, let me first remind You why he lost his position and left Your throne. He was made perfect and covered with all precious stones. He had a better position than I have now but lost it because of pride. He instigated rebellion against You, Lord, and also plotted to overthrow You. He boasted much about himself and was full of pride. He therefore lost his heavenly abode for me and was cast into this dark pit. Daddy, You know that he is a liar and the father of all liars, therefore whatever accusations he brings before You against me is a lie. I present the blood of Jesus as my defense, and I overcome him by the blood of the Lamb and by the word of my testimony. I pray that You reject his accusations and recognize my labor of love in Your vineyard. Thank You Lord because at the end I will be with You to inherit the position that he lost while he and his angels will forever have their place in hell. Again, since we are not justified by works but by faith in Your only Son, Jesus Christ, let my faith in Him bring me to the position of recognition before You and man. Thank You, Lord, for lifting me above all my equals, in Jesus' mighty name I pray. Amen. **Ruth 2:5-6; Esther 6:1-10; Proverbs 18:16; Proverbs 22:29; Acts 10:4**

PRAYER CONCERNING RELOCATION

Dear Father, thank You because You know all things. You know that a day will come when I will need to relocate to a new place. Lord, let that move be according to Your plan. The devil will not manipulate me to move so as to destroy me. Neither will I move without direction from You, Lord. I begin to cover the new place with the blood of Jesus; the road, the means of transportation and other things that will help me to relocate. I will not relocate my spouse, children and family only to lose them or bring harm to them in a new place. I will not relocate and later regret it. All relocations shall be according to Your plan, vision and purpose. May the vision, reason and the purpose for the relocation be made plain by Your Spirit, and may I not relocate and forget You. I block every spirit of deception, lies and manipulation that will make me to relocate to where I will encounter problems. I use the authority in the name of Jesus to block any dream concerning relocation which is not from You. May Your Words in this prayer bank arise to my defense, and may I live to continually praise the beauty of Your holy name, in Jesus Christ name I pray. Amen.
Matthew 10:23; Genesis 12:1; Genesis 13:10-11; Genesis 26:1-3; Genesis 45:5

PRAYER TO REMEMBER TO PAY MY VOWS

Dear faithful and covenant keeping Father, I am asking You to help me to keep my own covenant and vows that I made to You. Many a time the enemy tries to confuse me and to bring the spirit of forgetfulness upon me so as to prevent me from fulfilling my obligations and redeeming my vows unto You. But You are stronger than my heart and more powerful than the devil. Clothe me with Your fear and trouble my heart daily to keep my vows. Father, in the name of Jesus, I refuse to compromise and I reject any invitation by satan to sin against You with my tongue. Let Your Spirit that helped Abraham to pay his vow, and also Israel as a nation to keep the word of their vow and also helped Jephthah not to rescind the words of his vow, keep me and continue to remind me to be faithful in all things big or small, toward You. I know that You are able to do all things. Please, Daddy, help my heart to accept the fulfillment of its obligations towards You, and through this I shall be abundantly blessed through Jesus Christ our Lord and Savior, Amen. As I deposit this prayer in my prayer bank before You, I ask that it will stand as a reminder every time to influence my heart to do what is good by fulfilling my vows, in Jesus' name I pray. Amen. **Genesis 28:20; Jonah 1:16; 1 Samuel 1:11, 27-28; Ecclesiastes 5:4-6; Psalm 116:14**

PRAYER FOR A RIGHT PARTNER

Lord, may I not be married and still remain lonely. Give me a spouse that will quench my taste of loneliness. Let the partner You, O' Lord give me help me to meet the needs of my ministry and comfort at home. My partner should be a good thing that brings favor from the Lord. A witch or wizard must not cross my path as a potential partner. Even if I am being manipulated or hoodwinked, may I never marry a witch. My spouse should be like a fruitful vine planted by the side of the house. My partner will do me good and not evil all the days that we are together. My voice shall be heard in the street because of my partner and as You, Lord, will be the one who joins us together, nobody shall put us asunder, in Jesus' name I pray. Amen. Use this prayer that I deposit into my prayer bank daily and the overflowing devotion to help us in our marriage. If the enemy shows up to test our relationship and faith in You, if any of us starts acting contrary to Your word or expectations, let our account be visited and grant us victory through Jesus Christ our Lord and Savior. Lord I am putting Your Word back to You that because You hate "putting away", we shall live together and prosper. I pray and ask in the name of Jesus. Amen. **Genesis 2:18; Proverbs 18:22; Psalm 128:3; Proverbs 31:12-23; Matthew 19:5-6; James 1:17**

PRAYER FOR SECURITY AND PROTECTION

Father, in the name of Jesus, I thank You who have been with me all my lifetime and I appreciate You who have delivered me from all my enemies. This day I pray that You continue to extend Your hand of protection over me especially when I am weak in the flesh. You did say that the battles that Your children are going through are Yours and that we should hold our peace; therefore, let God arise and let His enemies be scattered. I deposit this prayer in this prayer bank against the day my strength will fail me. It happened to Your servant David, but there were faithful men around him so that he was not cut down by the giants and put Your name to shame. Let such faithful men be around me and help me through Your spirit so that Your name will not be ridiculed among the heathens. I stand upon Your promises one of which is, "behold I am with you always, even unto the end of time." When I am weak, there is assurance that You are with me according to Your word. Thank You, Lord, for honoring Your word, in the mighty name of Jesus I pray. Amen. **2 Samuel 21:15; Isaiah 35:3-4; Joel 3:10; Romans 14:1; 1 Corinthians 15:43; 2 Corinthians 12:9-10; Hebrews 11:34**

PRAYER AGAINST SICKNESS

Dear Father, I stand on Your authority upon my life as a child of the Most High God and lock my door against the spirit of sickness from coming into my dwelling. You are the greatest physician, and you know and own every organ in my body. You know how to preserve them from the attacks of the enemy. I bind all the Egyptian plagues from entering into my body and my dwelling place. Such sicknesses as cancer, leprosy, issue of blood, internal bleeding, blindness, ulcers, heart attacks, etc. are perpetually bound and kept out of my life and home. You, O Lord, have promised not to put any of the Egyptian diseases upon me, in the name of Jesus, I reject them and take my stand against them from coming into my body. I sprinkle the blood of Jesus at my door posts and at the lintel of my house. I also sprinkle the blood of Jesus in the air, water and the land as this will prevent air pollution and disease, water pollution and disease and sand contamination. I bind food poisoning and all forms of eating in the dream. Any sickness that attacks as a result of sin shall not see me as I confess my sins daily before You. Any sickness sent by the witches or enemies to afflict me shall not come because I am a worshiper of You. I also bind and resist all spiritual sicknesses, weakness, prayerlessness, spirit of sleep and slumber, eating and merry making in my dreams. This prayer in my prayer bank through the Word of God shall block sickness from getting into me and my household, in the name of Jesus. Amen. **Exodus 15:26; 2 Kings 20:1-6; Isaiah 38:1-5; Matthew 8:16-17; Mark 16:18; John 11:3; James 5:14-15**

PRAYER AGAINST SIN

Lord, keep me away from every presumptuous sin. Your Word has taught us a lot about sin and the effects of it. The Israelites did not move for seven days because of Miriam's leprosy, which was as a result of sin. This means that sin slows progress, kills vision and also throws the sinner out of Your kingdom. The Israelites also suffered defeat in battles because of one man, Achan. So many things happen as a result of sin, I therefore ask You Lord to keep me from deliberate sin. Lead me not into temptation but deliver me from all evil. Lord, I refuse to compromise my faith, because I know that a day is coming when my faith shall be put to test. Keep me away from strange men/women, from lust, from fornication and adultery and from lies, and from all manner of things that are contrary to Your words. Expose them and give me the strong will to overcome them all. I bind sin by association, sin through marriage, sin through business undertaking, and sin through deception of satan. May I not regard some sins to be minor and some to be great, but help me see sin for what it is, whether big or small, sin is sin. Thank You, Lord, for giving me victory over sin, in Jesus' precious name I pray. Amen. **11 Samuel 11:1-4; Hosea 10:13; Matthew 7:17; Acts 5:1-5; Romans 1:29-32; Galatians 5:19; James 1:15; 1 John 3:9**

PRAYER AGAINST SPIRIT OF ARROGANCE AND PRIDE

Most glorious Father in heaven, I submit myself to Your will and Your ordinances. I break the power of arrogance and pride in me. I welcome Your humble Spirit into my life. Sanctify me through Your word and make me a vessel of honor so that I will minister life and not death to my hearers. This day, I record all these prayers into my prayer bank trusting that You, O Lord, will use it to break the yoke of pride and arrogance in me. It shall watch over my life and bring me to order when I would have wondered astray. Let me learn to say, "It's all about you, and not me," all the time. Guide me particularly at the time of success, and may I learn to give You all the glory. Holy Father, remind me that a man can receive nothing except it is given him from above. And may I acknowledge the giver more than the gift. In whatever position I may find myself tomorrow, help me to esteem others more than myself. Keep reminding me why Lucifer fell and let me walk with You in fear and humility. Thank You, Lord for Your love for me, this I pray in Jesus' mighty name. Amen. **Luke 18:10-14; Proverbs 8:13; Proverb 16:18; Proverb 29:1, 23; James 4:6; Philippians 2:5-11**

PRAYER AGAINST SPIRIT OF COMPLACENCY

Father, in the name of Jesus, I stand this day to deposit my prayer into my prayer bank against evil birds that my enemies might send after me. I bind and destroy the power of all the seed-devouring birds. I bind and blind the eyes of all the monitoring birds sent after me. I bind and resist the power of all the birds sent to eat up the sacrifices that I offer unto the Lord. I put my selected stones in my catapult and use them against all the birds that eat up my anointing and my calling off my head; all the flesh-eating birds are destroyed. I begin to rise and shine because my light has come and the glory of the Lord is risen upon me. This prayer in my prayer bank shall expose every hidden nest built by monitoring birds in my roof and the equipment used by evil birds to record my conversations. I use every spiritual trap available to me to catch evil birds and destroy them as I also pray the favor of God upon my soul. I decree that no weapon formed against me shall prosper. I pray that in the place of ignorance, knowledge shall be found, in the place of weakness, strength shall be found. Lord, help me understand the dreams You show me and whatever I bind shall remain bound, those that I allow shall be allowed, this I pray in Jesus' name. Amen. **Joel 3:10; Isaiah 60:1; 1Timothy 6:12; 11 Corinthians 10:3-6; Romans 8:37; Isaiah 54:17; Galatians 2:20**

PRAYER AGAINST SPIRIT OF DECEPTION

Dear Heavenly Father, thank You this day for the opportunity You granted me to be Your child. Those that must remain as Your children are those that have believed and received Your only Son, Jesus Christ. I reject every lying word that the devil speaks to deceive me to compromise my faith. I resist him in every way and cause him to flee. I rebuke him and I stand against him and his deception. Lord, I shall be obedient to Your voice at all times and shall keep Your commandments. I bind every spirit of deception, lying tongues and enticing prophecy. I come against any spirit that seduces and manipulates people in order to deceive them and take them out of the will of God for them. The prayer that I deposit in my prayer bank shall stand for my defense and any day anybody will try to deceive me, let that person be exposed. May I also not be used as an agent to deceive others. I use the name of Jesus and come against every lying spirit that might seek opportunity to use me to tell lies to others. I know that to whom I yield my body, a servant of that person I am. I have decided to yield my body to the Holy Spirit; I am therefore a servant of the Holy Spirit. Lord Jesus, bless me with the gift of discernment of spirits to enable me know the spirits in those that work with me. Thank You Father for divinely enabling me to continue in Your Word as this will help me to know the truth that will also set me free. Thank You, Lord, because I am free from all deceptions, in the name of Jesus. Amen. **Proverbs 1:10; John 8:44; Mark 16:18; Acts 5:2; Joshua 1:7; 1 Samuel 15:15**

PRAYER AGAINST SPIRIT OF DELAY

Father, in the name of Jesus, I bind every spirit of delay. It shall not stand in my way to hinder my progress. I confess and declare this word upon my life, "forward, ever and backward, never." I use the authority in the name of Jesus and attack the spirit of delay and cast it into the lake of fire. I release blindness against the spirit of delay so that it will be blinded and will not see me forever. Lord, as the clock ticks, the set time to favor me has come. My marriage shall be timely, children shall come timely, jobs shall come timely, house shall come timely; and everything pertaining to me shall come at a time You purposed in Your heart for me. Guide my spirit O Lord that I may not make decisions in haste. Every decision I make shall be according to your plan. The devil shall be late to come to me. It shall be that before he arrives my blessings have already been bestowed upon me. The spirit of delay shall not steal those precious things you have bestowed upon me. I will keep and maintain them for use to the glory of Your name, Amen. Lord, make me very watchful to be able to know what Your will for me is. I bind the spirit of distraction that follows the spirit of delay, help me Lord, to stay focused and continue to guide my spirit in every way, in Jesus' name I pray, Amen. **Genesis 45:9; 1 Samuel 13:8-12; Exodus 32:1-2; Mark 13:33-37; Psalm 40:17; Psalm 70:5; Habakkuk 2:3; Isaiah 46:13;**

PRAYER AGAINST SPIRIT OF DRUGS, DRUNKENNESS, PROSTITUTION, LIES, STUBBORNNESS AND STEALING

Holy Father, thank You for loving me with an everlasting love and also drawing me unto You with Your loving kindness. If You, O Lord, were to count iniquity, no man would be saved, no, not one, but so that You may be justified when You speak, that there is forgiveness in You, You have thoroughly washed me with the blood of Your Son, Jesus Christ and have cleansed me and made me whiter than snow. Now I can say with rejoicing in my heart, the Lord is for me, what can any man do unto me? Thank You for putting Your Spirit in me, which has helped drive away all the evil spirits that once held me captive. As I deposit my prayer in my prayer bank, I stand against the spirit of drugs, drunkenness, prostitution, lies, stubbornness and stealing. I also stand against all the spirit of oppression, self-pity, inferiority complex and the spirit of the past from haunting me. I declare myself more than a conqueror through our Lord and Savior Jesus Christ. Thank You Father for helping me and making me an overcomer, in Jesus' name I pray. Amen. **1 Chronicles 4:9-10; Genesis 27:41; Genesis 37:4; Judges 6:15; 1 Samuel 19:9-11; Luke 8:2**

PRAYER AGAINST SPIRIT OF ENVY

Father God, I declare this day that You will not bring me into fellowship with those that envy me. Your word has made it clear that envy is one of the works of the flesh and whoever envies is a murderer. Every one called a brother or a sister or a friend or a neighbor or even a colleague who shall harbor evil intentions and the spirit of envy in order to destroy my life shall be exposed and removed out of my way. I also pray that You, Lord, clothe me with a sound spirit to not envy anyone for any reason but rather give praise to You at all times. Thank You Lord for answered prayer, in Jesus' name I pray. Amen. **Genesis 37:10-11; Psalm 37:1; Proverbs 3:31; Proverbs 14:30; Mark 15:10; 1 Corinthians 13:4; Galatians 5:26**

PRAYER AGAINST SPIRIT OF FEAR

Great God of wonders, let it be known that You alone are God in heaven above and on earth beneath. There is no searching of Your wisdom and power. This day I kneel before you depositing this prayer into my prayer bank against the spirit of fear and torment. Many have been seduced and deceived to deny You. Many have lost faith in You and have committed suicide because of what the liar and the father of all liars told them about their future. But my foundation is on You. I am not afraid of tomorrow because it was not by my power that I went through yesterday. I am secure no matter what vial the wicked one might pour upon the earth. Give me the grace to resist him and cast him out of my sight. Will it be the fear of death, sickness, joblessness, or barrenness? I will fear no evil for You, O

Lord, are with me. I shall travel to all parts of the globe and declare the works of the Lord, and shall not die because Your Spirit shall travel with me. I have your name to declare, I have your Words to preach and I have souls to win into Your kingdom. I will not allow the spirit of those who went back in Gideon's army to come upon me; I shall fight to the end and defeat all Your enemies and mine. Spirit of fear, I bind you in Jesus' name, we are not friends but adversaries. You spirit of fear, beware of me as I am a child of the Living God. I shall be a terror unto you and shall rule over you. You will encounter me and tremble, in the daytime and in the night. I shall finish my race and I will receive my crown. I will fulfill all that the Lord assigns me to do without further regard to you. Thank You, Lord for giving me the opportunity to prepare in advance against that day, for I have enough strength stored and ready to launch out by faith. I pray and live by faith, trusting that Jesus my Savior is alive and He has helped me overcome the spirit of fear. In Jesus' name I pray. Amen.
Isaiah 43:1; John 14:1; Philippians 4:6; Psalm 23:4; Psalm 118:6; Roman 8:15; 1 John 4:18

PRAYER AGAINST SPIRIT OF FORNICATION / ADULTERY

My Father, to You alone I give all the praise. I thank You for who You are and for Your work of redemption. Holy Father, keep me daily from the evil spirit of lust and immorality. Help me to daily declare my body as Your sanctuary. I've been bought with a price; I am not my own, may the spirit of Jesus dwell in me. I know that the seducer may attempt to knock me off my perch and my flesh may be enticed, but with my prayer in my prayer bank, I will draw strength from You. Cause me to always see every elderly woman/man as my mother/father, middle-aged woman or man as my sister or brother, and a younger woman or man as my daughter or son. Prevent me from any carnal affairs with any sheep of Yours that I am shepherding. Protect me from all forms and manner of bestiality, pornography and immorality that I am constantly surrounded by. Never

allow me look at a woman or man lustfully, neither should I entertain any evil thought in my heart. Thank You for helping me to overcome this spirit of whoredom in the mighty name of Jesus. Amen.
2 Samuel 11:3-4; 2 Samuel 13:12-14; Acts 15:20; 1 Corinthians 6:13, 18; Colossians 3:5; 1 Thessalonians 4:3

PRAYER AGAINST SPIRIT OF JEALOUSY

Most blessed Father, I thank You for maintaining me from my childhood until now in Your mighty hand. Your Word says that he that dwells in the secret place of the Most High shall abide under the shadow of the Almighty. If it has not been You, Lord, men would have swallowed me up. One thing is certain; You that had begun a good work in me will be faithful to complete it. I am not afraid of what man shall do unto me because You are always there for me. I pray that you also bless those that will become jealous of me so that they will take their minds off me. You did bless Esau for the sake of Jacob, and I believe that if Jacob had returned from Laban, his uncle a blessed man and met his brother, Esau, in wretchedness, his brother would have killed him. But to appease him You blessed him also. I am asking that You keep those that will be envious of me busy and give them the spirit of forgetfulness. May I also not envy someone in his or her success. Help me with strength to work hard and to compete with men and women of great status. Help me use the time I would have devoted to jealousy for things beneficial to me and the Body of Christ and to sing praises unto Your name. I deposit this prayer in my prayer bank with you and use it to neutralize the spirit of jealousy and envy, in Jesus' name I pray. Amen.
Genesis 4:8; Genesis 37:1-20; Matthew 27:18; Proverbs 6:34; Song. 8:6

PRAYER AGAINST SPIRIT OF LABORING IN VAIN

Genesis 1:8, "And the Lord remembered Noah..." Father in the name of Jesus, There shall be a remembrance of me, my household and all my labor of love. I shall not be abandoned nor forgotten neither will I labor in vain.

Isaiah 3:10, "…It shall be well with me; I will eat the fruit of my doing…"

Psalm 1:3, "And I shall be like a tree planted by the rivers of water, my fruits shall come forth in due season, my leaves will not wither, and all that I do shall prosper."

Esther 4:16 I shall speak of God's favor in everything that I do and recognition by women and men of high standing.

Blessed Father, may the beauty of the Lord God be upon me, establish thou the works of my hands. Let me be a shining light. Let my labor be recognized and rewarded. Fruitfulness, recognition and promotion are all I claim. Lord, bring my star out of the dark cloud and position it where it will shine forth for the whole world to see. Every fault of mine shall be turned into a blessing; for such are the portions of those that wait on thee. My growth shall have no boundary and I shall excel in strength and favor. As I deposit this prayer into my bank with you daily, I know that the spirit of laboring in vain will neither see me nor come near me. I pray this prayer in the name of the only Son of God, Jesus Christ the righteous. Amen. **Psalm 78:46, Psalm 128:2; Proverbs 14:23; Eccl. 2:24; Eccl. 5:19; Isaiah 65:23-24; 1 Cor. 15:58; Phi. 2:16.**

PRAYER AGAINST SPIRIT OF LIMITATION

Mighty Deliverer, King of kings and Lord of lords, let it be known this day that You are God that holds the whole universe with the words of Your mouth. Arise and show Yourself strong because of Your name. You are the God of all flesh, is there anything too hard for You to do? Out of nothing You spoke and it was created, You commanded, and it was established. I know that I can do nothing of myself, but I can do all things through Christ who strengthens me. I therefore deposit this prayer into my prayer bank that I am strong

through Him. I am not weak, I am a winner, and I am not a loser. You are everything to me, and I cannot limit or question Your power. Spirit of limitation, you have no hold on me, My God is all in all and I am fearfully and wonderfully created. I am a marvelous creature of God. It shall come to pass that whenever the fear of limitation and faithlessness comes near me, this prayer from my prayer bank shall rise up, fight and defeat it. And because I know my God, I am strong and can do exploit. I further make the following declaration that I am rich, I am healed, I am blessed beyond the curse, I am successful and I can stand in time of trial. I confess that I was made in His image and after His likeness, and therefore, I am who He is. I pray this prayer in the name that is above all names, Jesus Christ of Nazareth, Amen.
Psalm 46:1-5; Psalm 121:1-8; Revelations 12:13-16; Joshua 1:5-9; Isaiah 40:28-31

PRAYER AGAINST SPIRIT OF LUST

Dear heavenly Father, thank You this day for allowing Your Spirit to indwell in me. I know that there is nothing that You cannot do. As for me, I do not know how to take control of my body, because I lust daily and this lust works against Your Spirit in me. I also know that if the lust in me conceives, it will bring forth sin which will lead to death. I therefore desire that my soul, my heart, my mind and my entire body be brought in subjection to the obedience of Your Son, Jesus Christ. I stand this day to deposit this prayer in my prayer bank requesting that Your Spirit in me will continually yield towards righteousness, love, peace, joy, good works, goodness, mercy, faith, hospitality and faithfulness. I stand this day in opposition of the spirit of lust and I attack the very foundation with which it stands. I attack all its pillars and cause them to crumble. I bind all its agents and command the spirit of holiness upon me. I believe that I will lust after Christ and not evil. I pray this prayer in the overcoming name of Jesus. Amen. **Galatians 5:24; 2 Timothy 2:22; Titus 2:12; 1 Corinthians 10:6; 1 John 2:16-17; Proverbs 6:25**

PRAYER AGAINST SPIRIT OF REJECTION

(You have to use the spirit of acceptance, heir of God and adoption to counter the spirit of rejection)

Father, in the name of Jesus, I declare today that my faith in Jesus has opened the door of acceptance for me in the sight of God and man. I am accepted by those who once rejected me. I declare that I am a child of God and wherever the Spirit of the Lord is, I am accepted. As a child of God, I am loved and beloved by all who love Him. I claim the spirit of adoption whereby I can proudly say, Abba, Father. I am an heir of God and a joint heir with my Lord and Savior Jesus Christ. I am accepted in the beloved to offer praises unto His name. In the home, I am accepted by my spouse and children. In the church, I am accepted by the brethren. When I am among friends, I am accepted and welcomed. Anywhere I go in the world that is good, I am accepted. But I shall be rejected in the camp of the witches, in the voodoo covens and in the kingdom of satan. I record this prayer in my prayer bank before You so that You will consider me as a precious ornament, as someone to be desired and sought for, and I shall be called, a favored child. My parents will love me, my spouse will continually admire me. Friends will cherish me and I will be adorable before men and women of goodwill. I know that You were rejected for my acceptance. I pray this prayer in the name that is above all names, the precious name of Jesus Christ. Amen. **Judges 11:2; Romans 8:15, 23; Romans 9:4; Galatians 4:5; Romans 8:17; Galatians 3:29; Ephesians 1:6**

PRAYER AGAINST SPIRIT OF SADNESS

Dear heavenly Father, I thank You for answering my prayers and restoring my joy. It is certain that I was created to praise the beauty of Your holiness. There are millions and millions of angels before Your throne singing daily to glorify Your name, in Your presence is fullness of joy, and at Your right hand are pleasures for ever more. Thank You for counting me worthy to be among the living, restore unto me this day, the joy of Thy salvation and cause me to rejoice and be glad in You. If there are things in life that try to steal Your joy from my heart and bring the spirit of heaviness and sadness upon me, Lord, turn my sadness into joy and put the song of praises on my lips. I stand this day before You to deposit this prayer in your prayer book and in my prayer bank. Let it come to pass that the veil of sadness is completely torn off my face as You clothe me now with the beauty of Your countenance. I pray this prayer in Jesus' name believing that the spirit of sadness and sorrow has no place in me. Amen. **1 Samuel 1:18; 1 Kings 21:5; Isaiah 61:3; Mark 10:21-22**

PRAYER AGAINST SPIRIT OF SETBACK

Father, in the name of Jesus, I stand here before You this day by faith declaring that I am the head and not the tail according to your words concerning me. Colleagues of mine shall not leave me behind. I reject that spirit that was in the woman with the issue of blood. I resist and refuse all kinds of bleeding, spiritual, financial, economic, social and political. I take my strong stand against the spirit of setback. I use every weapon at my disposal, the name of Jesus, the blood of Jesus, the Word of God and the fire of the Holy Spirit to neutralize and paralyze every spirit that tries to take me one step backward. One thing is sure, You made me in Your image and after Your likeness. You are not a failure, and therefore I am not and will not be a failure. You are blessed forever, I, too, am blessed forever. By the words of Your mouth all things were created, I believe also that the words of my mouth have creative power. I stand by Your Word concerning me, and whatever anyone says or thinks about me does not erase what You think or say about me. You say that You know the thoughts that You think towards me, the thoughts of peace, success and prosperity and not of evil, to give unto me a hope and a very successful future. You also assure me that You will give me the keys of the kingdom of heaven and the power to bind and loose on earth with a confirmation of binding and losing in heaven. Whatever therefore that I bind is bound and whatever I loose is loosed. It shall come to pass that when failure sees me it will flee. I stand strong in You today and deposit these prayers in my prayer bank before You and I am sure that I am free from the spirit of setback. I pray this prayer in the name of Jesus Christ who is the head of all powers and principalities. Amen. **Matthew 9:20; Joel 1:4; Exodus 14:15; Haggai 1:9-11; Genesis 19:26**

PRAYER AGAINST SPIRIT OF SLEEP AND SLUMBER

Dear Father in heaven, thank You for your love and kindness towards me. As I kneel before You, help me to pray like the Psalmist prayed: "Why art thou cast down, O my soul? And why art thou disquieted in me? Hope thou in God: for I shall yet praise Him for the help of His countenance," (**Psalm 42:5.**) I am rejoicing today because You have taken the spirit of sleep and slumber away from me and caused me to awake to my responsibilities. When my enemy will be cast down, Thou, O Lord will raise me up and I shall triumph over them all. I bind the spirit of sleep and slumber; I rebuke it and resist it. As I deposit this prayer in my prayer bank, I understand that you will use it to protect me against wreckage of nerves, worries and intimidation. Every spirit of heaviness, dullness, and weariness is rebuked, resisted and cast out. I shall be up and doing, no spirit of slothfulness, tiredness and laziness shall weigh me down. Thank You, Lord for my answered prayer, in Jesus' name I pray, Amen. **Isaiah 56:10; Exodus 14:24-25; Romans 11:8; 13:11; Ephesians 5:14; Matthew 13:25**

PRAYER FOR THE SPIRIT OF SOUL WINNING

Most blessed Father, make me a practical instrument for Your use. Use me O Lord to win souls into Your kingdom. No matter my other daily activity, help me make soul winning a priority. I know that anything that any man does is dependent upon his vision, interest and his desire in it. Give me a burning desire for soul winning so as to empty hell and make Your kingdom full. Keep the spirit of soul winning burning in me and give me no rest if I slack and get overwhelmed with other events or activities as I grow. Keep kicking my heart and reminding me that the heart-cry of God is for souls. It is because of the redemption of souls that Jesus had to come and die and not for mere activities and administration works. Count me as one of the wise men before You because he that wins souls is wise. And let me be a shining star before You forever because as many that turn others to righteousness shall shine as stars forever. Thank You Lord as You continually use this prayer in my prayer bank as a mark to keeping me in remembrance of soul winning all the days of my life. I pray this prayer in the name of Jesus my Lord and Savior. Amen. **James 5:20; Proverbs 11:30; Daniel 12:3; Matthew 28:19-20; Mark 16:20; 1 Corinthians 9:19**

PRAYER AGAINST SPIRITUAL BLINDNESS

Dear Lord, You made it clear in Your Word that the light of the body is the eye. I reject spiritual blindness and also reject physical blindness. Since a blind man cannot lead a blind man, I cannot lead Your people when I am blind, then we both shall fall into a pit. Therefore Lord, let me see both in the realm of the natural and in the realm of the spiritual, especially regarding Your glory so as to reveal the same to Your people. As I record this prayer in my prayer record, I take authority in the name of Jesus and attack every spirit of blindness and all such spirits that darken vision. Lord, Isaac, through the blindness of his eyes gave the blessing he wanted to give to Esau to Jacob. Therefore I record this prayer in my prayer bank and bind every sickness associated with blindness. I ask that the God of our Lord Jesus Christ give me the spirit of wisdom, and revelation in the knowledge of Him. And that the eyes of my understanding be enlightened that I may know what is the hope of His calling, and what the riches of the glory of His inheritance are in the saints, and what the greatness of His power toward us is. Thank You, Lord, for honoring my prayers. This I pray in Jesus' name. Amen.
Isaiah 6:10; Isaiah 29:10; Mark 4:12; John 12:40; Romans 11:25; Ephesians 1:17-23

PRAYER FOR SPIRITUAL GIFT

My Lord and my God, thank You for the gift of Your only Son, Jesus Christ who came from heaven to die and redeem me from my sins. I am praying for spiritual endowment and outpouring of Your gift to enable me to operate my ministry gifts effectively. I recognize that these are gifts that You promised Your Church before You went back to heaven and generously poured upon Your disciples on the day of Pentecost. I come in agreement with Apostle Peter that these gifts are for us, our children and children's children and for those afar off who will later believe in Your name. I am a believer in Your name and therefore desire these gifts for the benefit of the Body of Christ. I now open a spiritual gift prayer bank and deposit every anointing that comes with every gift into the bank. Whether it be words of wisdom or knowledge or faith or gift of healings or of working of miracles or prophecy or discernment of spirits or of tongues or interpretation of tongues. Or whether it has to do with ministry gifts and offices such as: apostolic, prophetic, evangelistic, pastoral and teaching, give me the understanding and the grace to make it a worthy ambassadorial representation of Your glory before people, this I pray and ask in the name of Jesus Christ, Amen. **Isaiah 56:5; Jeremiah 24:7; Ezekiel 11:19; Matthew 25:15; Romans 12:6; 1 Corinthians 4:7; 1 Corinthians 12:8-11; Ephesians 4:8, 11**

PRAYER FOR SPIRITUAL GROWTH

Dear Father, help me to grow in grace and in the knowledge of Your Son, Jesus Christ. I reject any spirit of stagnation. I ask You, O Lord, to fill me with all understanding whenever I study Your Word. I recognize that without spiritual growth there can never be other growth in all aspects of my life; ministry, finance, social and political. Help me O' Lord and bestow upon me all the necessary ingredients that will help me grow spiritually. May I also grow in love and understanding with my spouse, children and other people that come around me. This prayer bank shall stand as a reminder every time I seem to have spiritual stagnation through lack of fer-

vent prayer and study of Your word, may I be fired up from within and in my mind. Thank You, Lord as You renew my visions, dreams, sense of humor, spiritual understanding and revelation knowledge, especially when I study Your Holy Book. Let me find joy in reading Your words and educate me more on what it takes to be a champion of faith and of works. I pray this prayer in Jesus' name knowing that if I grow, the harvest is Yours. Amen.
2 Peter 1:5; 2 Peter 3:18; 2 Timothy 2:15; 1 Thessalonians 3:12; 1 Thessalonians 5:21; Ephesians 4:13; Hebrews 6:1

PRAYER FOR SPIRITUAL HUNGER

Dear Lord who satisfies my hungry soul with fatness, let it be recorded this day in Your record that I have made a determination to seek after You all the days of my life. As the deer pants and longs for the water brooks, so pants my soul after You. Lord, cause me to hunger daily for You as I would hunger for natural food. Take away laziness and sleep from me and cause me to have no rest until I have read, meditated, and received a Rhema from You. Help me to study in order to show myself approved unto You and to be a workman/workwoman that does not need to be ashamed, but rightly dividing the word of truth. I stand against the spirit of weakness, discouragement, entanglement, busybody and diversion. I resist the devil and all his agents and refuse to bow to unnecessary pressures of life and wicked devices of the enemy. According to Your promise, anyone who hungers and thirsts after righteousness shall be filled. I ask that You, in Your mercy, fill me with true spiritual hunger and cause me to be filled and satisfied. Make me to know Your perfect will for my life through the study of Your word. Thank You Lord for granting me my request, in Jesus' name I pray. Amen. **Matthew 5:6; Acts 17:11; Psalm 42:1; Jeremiah 33:3; Philippians 3:10**

PRAYER FOR STRENGTH

Dear heavenly Father, I desire to begin this prayer with a song that says: "guide me through, Lord Jesus, guide me through. Guide me through, Lord Jesus, guide me through. There is a race to be run, there is victory to be won, give me power every hour, to be through." Since no man can prevail by his physical strength, let Your spiritual strength which was released from heaven unto us in the day of Pentecost rest upon me and set me upon my feet for the task that You set before me. I need physical strength to be able to sleep and wake up. I need spiritual strength for global evangelization and to overcome the devices of my enemies. I know that a day will come when the wicked one will bring discouragement to try to weaken me by attacking my mind and my health, let this prayer in my prayer bank appeal to You and cause You to remember me according to Your faithfulness unto Israel Your elect in the days of his weakness. And as Caleb at eighty-five requested and claimed the mountain which You promised him when he was young and full of life, so also shall I claim all my mountains even at a hundred because I am also a carrier of good news. As You encouraged Joshua not to faint but to be strong and courageous through the meditation of Your word, I receive encouragement today through the meditation of Your word and will forever remain strong and courageous to finish the task that You committed into my hand. Thank You for answered prayer, in Jesus' name I pray, Amen. **Nehemiah 8:10; Psalm 46:1; Isaiah 26:4; Revelations 3:8; 1 Samuel 2:9**

PRAYER TO STRENGTHEN MY PRAYER LIFE

Dear covenant keeping God, there is none like You in heaven above and on earth beneath. I submit my life into Your able hands and ask You to wake my spirit to pray without ceasing. You made it clear that if I will humble myself and pray and turn from my wicked ways and seek Your face, then You will hear from heaven and You will heal my land. Lord, I ask that You humble me and steer up my spirit to pray. I acknowledge my sins before You because I know that there are times I ought to be praying but I am sleeping or doing things that are contrary to Your will. One thing is sure, You O' Lord love me with everlasting love and with Your loving kindness have You drawn me. I know that whenever I am weak, You are strong and my weakness cannot prevent Your strength. When I am in doubt, You are faithful and my doubting cannot stop Your faithfulness.

Neither can my disobedience hinder Your Word from being active, nor my laziness and complacency prevent the move of Your power. Blessed Father, help me overcome my weakness and keep my prayer life active. May I pray without ceasing. Even when I know not what to pray, may Your Spirit make intercession for me with groaning. Thank You, Lord, for waking my spirit to pray daily, and for reminding and strengthening my heart, through this prayer bank, to do the right thing, especially when I am weak and seem to forget to pray. Thank You and thank You again for Your love, mercy and help, this I pray through Jesus Christ my Lord and Savior, Amen.
1 Chronicles 16:11; 2 Chronicles 7:14-15; 1 Thessalonians 5:17; Matthew 7:7-11; Matthew 26:41; Luke 18:1-8; John 16:24; Ephesian 6:18; James 5:13

PRAYER FOR UNDERSTANDING

Lord God Almighty, as I kneel before You this hour, I am asking You to fill me with understanding. By Your wisdom, Lord, You founded the earth and by understanding You established the heavens. I know through Your word that without understanding of Your purpose and plan for me, I shall never be established. Lord, it was You that blessed the children of Issachar with the understanding to know the times and what Israel ought to do. I also believe that with understanding I shall be able to know the times and what I'm supposed to do and when in Your ministry. I therefore ask You to fill me with understanding of the dreams that You give me, their interpretations and applications. I also ask You to enable me know the sign that You give concerning what might happen next, to know the people that come around me, and Your plan for me. I reject the spirit of confusion and blindness. I store up this request in my prayer bank before You so that in all my ways I will acknowledge You and will not lean on my own understanding. As I make my daily declarations, fill me with wisdom, knowledge and understanding every day to be able to know and lead the people that You commit into my care. I pray this prayer in the name of Jesus because He alone is the wisdom of God.

Amen. **Deuteronomy 4:6; 1 Chronicles 12:32; Psalm 119:104; Proverbs 2:6; Proverbs 4:7; Matthew 2:2; 2 Timothy 2:7**

PRAYER AGAINST THE UNITED SPIRITS (DEMONS' CONFEDERACY)

Dear Father, dear Son, dear Holy Spirit, let it be known this day that the church of Jesus Christ has agreed to come together in one accord, one Spirit, one baptism, and one fellowship and communion to take a stand against the spirit of disunity in our midst. We drop the bomb of disunity into the kingdom of darkness; they have to be judged with thunder, with earthquake with great noise, with storm and tempest, and the flames of devouring fire. Lord, send Your lightning to strike and discomfit the gathering of all the demonic forces. As I deposit this prayer in my prayer bank, it shall come to pass that every day the ground will pull from under wherever the agents of satan shall plan to gather to fight against Your church. In the air, let the air be too hot for them to congregate. In the water, let the sea get to its boiling point and send them drowning. On land, let the earth begin to quake until they bow and worship the Living God in heaven. I also take a stand against demonic confederacies against me and my family. I resist them, I rebuke them and I bind and destroy all their activities; in the air, on the land and in the sea. I pray this prayer in the one and only name of Jesus Christ, my Lord and Savior. Amen. **Matthew 12:25; Acts 2:1; Acts 4:24-32; Ecclesiastes 4:9-12; Matthew 18:19**

PRAYER AGAINST UNTIMELY DEATH

- Through child bearing,
- Through car accidents
- Through plane crashes,
- Through boat mishaps,
- Through motorcycle or bicycle accidents,
- Through sports
- Through bullets of war,

- Through collapsed buildings;
- And other spirits of violent death.

Lord, You did promise to satisfy me with long life and prosperity. You said there shall be no death of infants in my household. You did promise that my children shall surround my table and that I shall see my children's children. Therefore untimely death has no power over me and members of my household. I reject untimely death by any form of accident. This prayer is stored up against that day the enemy will raise his ugly head to try to cause havoc in my life and that of my family. At such a time let the air be too hot and peppery and become uncomfortable for the prince of powers of darkness to operate. The water shall be at a boiling point and will not permit the spirit in it to use it as a base to operate. All channels that the wicked ones operate to cause accidents and cut people's lives short will be closed. The sun by day shall be as a scorching, eviscerating, blinding laser beam to shoot the devourer down. I sprinkle the blood of Jesus in the air, land and sea. As I pray daily depositing my prayers in my prayer bank, let a wall of protection be built around me, and as long as I live, let me continue to worship in Your presence. Thank You, Father for the victory that overcomes the world, as I keep our faith in the one and only name of Jesus Christ, Amen. **John 11:26; Psalm 91:16; Psalm 118:17; Job 1:18-19; Isaiah 65:20; Luke 13:1-5**

PRAYER OF VICTORY OVER TEMPTATION

Dear Father in heaven, thank You for assigning Your angels to keep and protect me, particularly in times of temptation. I am registering this prayer against any form of temptation that might come my way as I continue my life journey. Daddy, I know that temptation itself is not a sin but falling into its trap is terrible and also leads to death. Father, I know that Your Son, Jesus, was tempted yet without sin. This was so because He knew the purpose why He came and stayed focus on it. I pray that You reveal to me in advance before it knocks and also show me the way out of it. The Bible has revealed many kings who lost their kingdoms through the power of temptation and sin. But You have made it abundantly clear that with each

temptation You will also make a way of escape. Let Your words, Lord, in the Bible and my prayer bank before You empower me to resist every temptation that comes my way. For I know, Lord, You do not tempt with evil, neither tempt You any man. But I am tempted when I am drawn away of my own lust and enticed. I therefore bind the spirit of lust that drags man into temptation and entices him to sin. I pronounce the spirit of lust, barren so as not to conceive and bear sin that will eventually lead to death. May I overcome temptation so as to receive the crown of life which the Lord has promised to those who love Him and keep His words. I thank You Lord for my answered prayer, in Jesus' name I pray. Amen.
Genesis 3:4-5; Genesis 39:7; Matthew 4:1-11; 1 Corinthians 10:13; Hebrews 2:18; Hebrews 3:13; James 1:2-3, 12

PRAYER FOR VISION

Abba Father, Your Word declares that where there is no vision, the people perish. I pray this day that You make me a visionary leader in the execution of Your calling. I pray that You open my eyes of understanding to behold the things that are written in Your law. I request that in due season, my vision be made clearer in every aspect of my life. Cause me to see events as they build up in the spirit realm before they manifest in the physical so as to stop those events that need to be stopped and to allow those that should be allowed. I bind every spirit that veils and blinds spiritual sights so that I do not see what danger is ahead of me. As I deposit my prayer concerning vision into my prayer bank, I declare that I shall never be a blind leader so that those You give me to lead and I will not fall into a pit, together. I also pray and ask that You make those You have chosen to follow me to understand the reason You chose me to lead them. Lord, expose every witch who shall disguise and camouflage herself to be another person. Reveal her true personality and identity and let her not have any hiding place in our midst. Thank You, Lord, for my answered prayer, this I pray in Jesus' name. Amen. **Genesis 15:1; Amos 3:7; Habakkuk 2:3; Acts 16:9; 1 Corinthians 2:10; Proverbs 29:18**

PRAYER AGAINST WASTE

Father God, thank You this day in the name of Jesus. Thank You for providing for me and my family all necessities of life. All glory to You also for the privilege for me to use Your blessings to thank You. I know that as my Father, You love me and it is Your desire for me to use Your blessing upon me and prosper there from. I bind the spirit of waste, I resist it and I rebuke it and I cast it out of my life and my household. As I record this prayer in my prayer bank, I stand against the loss of time, gold, diamond, jewels, property, money and anything You Lord, have given me to use for Your glorification. I close every loophole and any indirect way the enemy would like to pass through to make me wasteful. I stop the waste from dependent relations: my spouse, children or any relatives. Thank You, Lord for helping me to stop this spirit from operating any further in my household, and thank You for the victory that I have today, this I pray in the name of Jesus Christ, Amen. **Isaiah 49:17-19; Isaiah 58:12; Isaiah 61:4; 1 Peter 4:11; 1 Kings 17:14; 2 Kings 4:6**

PRAYER FOR WISDOM

Dear Lord, the author of all wisdom, knowledge and understanding, I stand before you today to deposit this prayer into my prayer bank concerning wisdom for living. Your Word makes it clear that wisdom is the principal thing, therefore I request that You bless me with wisdom; wisdom in communication, wisdom on how to handle disputes, wisdom in investment and how to manage my finances, wisdom in all things. It is clear that out of the ten virgins that came to await the arrival of the bridegroom, only the five wise ones made it in, but the other five failed for lack of wisdom even though they were all virgins. You have instructed me to ask for wisdom if I lack it, Lord, I ask that You envelop me at all times with wisdom and help me to conduct Your business with discretion. I give You thanks because I know that You are faithful to keep Your promises. I know that if I will ask anything in the name of Jesus You will give it to me so that my joy may be full. Thank You, Lord, for answered prayer, for in Jesus' name I ask, Amen. **1 Kings**

3:9; 2 Chronicles 1:10; Psalm 104:24; Proverbs 9:1; Isaiah 11:2; James 1:5; Matthew 25:2

PRAYER AGAINST WITCHCRAFT OPERATION

Lord, God Almighty, thank You for sending Your Son Jesus Christ to come and shed His blood to redeem man from all the powers of darkness. Lord, I pray against all the powers of witchcraft in my family, in Your church and near my dwelling. Wherever I shall live, let there be spiritual traps all around my house. Those traps shall be all over the roof of my house, all around the building itself and even the very foundation which it stands on. Those traps shall capture and expose all witches and their agents. There shall not arise any spirit of rebellion in my family influenced by the spirit of witchcraft. I destroy every spell cast to subject me and my family to the influence of witchcraft. I sprinkle the blood of Jesus in the air, sea and the land and make those places uncomfortable for witches to operate. Let the wings of all the flying witches be cut off, and let their transportation system be dismantled. I release the blood of Jesus to flow in camps and all their meeting places. I deny them a place to congregate. Any witch that will rise up to challenge me, privately and publicly, let them meet an open disgrace and repent so that they will know that heaven and earth belong to You, Lord. Any witch that refuses to repent let the word of God that says that we should not allow a witch to live go after them and annihilate them. May the blood of Jesus, the name of Jesus, the Word of God and the fire of the Holy Spirit destroy and devour the power of witchcraft in the church and in the world and set their captives free. I pray this prayer in the name that is above all names, in Jesus' name I pray. Amen.
Exodus 22:18; Isaiah 54:15-17; Matthew 18:18; Mark 3:27; James 5:5; 1 John 4:4

********* ********* ********

PRAYERS FOR COMFORTING THOSE IN DISTRESS

PRAYER FOR THE BEREAVED

Dear heavenly Father, blessed is Your name. As it is written, in everything give thanks, I give thanks unto You today because of who You are, and because of what You do and will continue to do. You created man in Your own image and breathed through Your nostrils the breath of life and man became a living soul. It also pleases You to take man home at the completion of his work on earth, for this place is not our home. Thank You Father, because there is hope of eternal life because when the trumpet shall sound the dead in Christ shall arise first and we that are alive and remain shall be caught up together in the cloud, and there shall we ever be with You forever. Having this hope therefore, comfort our hearts not to weep like those that have no hope. I pray for the family that one of their own has departed into heaven. I pray that You comfort their hearts and remind them that the one that sleeps in the Lord is not lost but shall awake in the last day into the resurrection of joy. Comfort and remind them that the departed shall not go through any pains again but has entered into eternal rest. Thank You, Lord, for comforting us at this very hour of pain and desolation. In Jesus' name I pray, Amen. **Psalm 116:15; Ecclesiastes 7:1; John 14:1-3; 1 Corinthians 15:19; 1 Corinthians 15:51-58; 1 Thessalonians 4:13-14; Hebrews 4:9-11**

PRAYER FOR COMFORT

Dear Father, in the name of Jesus, thank You for giving me the opportunity to come and comfort my fellow brother or sister at this critical time. Thank You for Your love and for the finished work that was wrought in us at the cross of Calvary by Jesus Christ our Lord and Savior. As You, O Lord, have instructed us to comfort each other with Your word, I pray for the comfort of the Holy Spirit at this critical time of need and difficulty for this household. I pray that they should not lose hope but realize that You are able to do exceedingly and abundantly above all that they think or ask according to Your power that is working in them. I pray Your words keep reminding them that in this world we are bound to have tribulations, but that we should also rejoice because You have overcome the world for us. I pray that the hope of eternal life be released upon every member of this household to enable them come to terms with the fact that there is a better place and a better life than here. Thank You, Lord for your love and for answered prayer. This I pray in Jesus' name, Amen. **Isaiah 51:3; Matthew 9:22; Isaiah 12:1; John 14:18**

PRAYER OF CONSOLATION

Everlasting Father in heaven, I stand before You this day to pray for those in tribulation, in need and in sorrow. Reach out, O Lord unto them so that they may know that You are the God of all flesh though they may not know You and Your Holy Son, Jesus Christ. I pray this day that You send help and support and bind up their wounds and heal their bruises. Good Father, for the loss that they have already suffered, make necessary provisions through Your angels to reach them even as I stand praying. Through the consolation of Your spirit let them come to understanding and acknowledge You as their Lord and Savior, in Jesus' name I pray. Amen. I also pray for Your own children that are going through difficulty at this very hour. Let Your mighty hand of comfort reach out unto them and console them by taking away their heavy burdens from off their shoulders and the yokes off their necks. Let those burdens and the yokes be destroyed because of Your anointing upon their lives. Let them see You in their dreams as You go before them and lead out of their tribulations into a place of safety. Speak to them that their weeping has come to an end, and that although they have been given the bread of adversity and the water of affliction, their teachers shall not be removed. And that they also shall hear the words of their teachers behind them saying, "here is the way, walk ye in it." Then shall they rejoice and glorify Your name. Thank You, Lord, for consoling Your people, in Jesus' name I pray. Amen.
Psalm 119:50; Isaiah 30:19-21; 2 Corinthians 13:4; Romans 15:4

PRAYER TO COUNTER THE WISHES OF THE ENEMIES

My Father, my Lord and my God, blessed be Your Holy name for all things You have done. Thank You for You have the whole world in Your hand, as You have never released any of Your children into the hands of their enemies to afflict them. I use every spiritual weapon available to me; the name of Jesus, the blood of Jesus, fire of the Holy Spirit and the Word of God to bind all the forces of darkness and destroy all the weapons of those that fight against me. You have said that not a single hair on Your children's heads will fall without You knowing the reason. I am therefore confident in Your Word that not a single hair shall fall off my head and the heads of all those who trust in You, without You knowing the reason. I also pray according to Your word which says that we should pray for those who persecute us and afflict us. My prayer therefore is that my enemies do not die without repentance. Let them live and join me in spreading the Good News of the kingdom of God. Turn their names from Saul the persecutor of the way, to Paul the defender of the way. I pray this prayer knowing that what the enemy thought for evil, You Lord have turned for good to the glory of Your name. I pray this prayer in Jesus' name. Amen. **Exodus 15:9-10; Numbers 23:23; Isaiah 54:15-17; 1 John 4:4; Luke 10:19**

PRAYER DUE TO DELAY IN CHILD BEARING

My Father, faithful Father, blessed Father, all knowing Father, Father to the fatherless, husband to the widows, it is written, "forever, O Lord, Thy word is settled in heaven." You that keep covenants, even a covenant unto Your people Israel that there shall not be found among Your people any that shall be barren, neither shall their vine cast off their fruits before time. Therefore, whose report shall we believe? It is the Lord's. The Bible says this concerning Elizabeth, "And, behold, thy cousin Elizabeth, she hath also conceived a son in her old age: this is the six month with her, who was called barren." This was the confirmation of Your word by Your prophet that a barren woman shall be a happy mother of children. Lord, I do not call this barrenness but a delay, because there is no barrenness among Your people. At this time of delay, help Your people (daughter and son) that are going through it to be at peace and also keep their faith. Lord, I prophesy that by this same season that this prayer is read and prayed, next year, this woman/man shall be a happy mother/father of children. They shall be lively children that will know You and praise the beauty of Your holiness. Is it not written that those that fear Your name shall still bear fruit even in old age? Therefore, there is hope for this woman/man because they trust in Your word. Thank You because the confidence that we have is that if we pray according to Your will, You hear us and also grant us our petition. Blessed be Your name, Lord, in Jesus' name I pray. Amen. **Genesis 1:28; Genesis 21:1-2; Deuteronomy 28:4-5; 1 Samuel 1:9-16; Luke 1:36; Luke 22:42**

PRAYER FOR DELIVERANCE (ESCAPE)

Most Holy Father, thank You because as the keeper of Israel, You will neither slumber nor sleep. I thank You much more, for the death of Your Son on the cross was not in vain. It was for my salvation and deliverance. Your mighty hand is upon me because You have anointed me to preach deliverance unto them that are bound. As You prayed for Peter when the devil went after Him and You told him that when he was healed, he should strengthen his brethren. It is the same way that You delivered me to strengthen my brethren. Your word in my mouth is not in vain, the blood of Jesus was not shed in vain, the Holy Spirit was not sent in vain and the name of Jesus was not given in vain. Father, in the name of Jesus, I use these weapons that You freely gave to us to destroy every power that put Your people in captivity and in bondage. I shell and destroy the power of sin and shatter the dungeon and the coven built by the enemy to imprison Your children. I declare that if the Son has set them free, they are free indeed. Through the shed blood, I pronounce them delivered and also make them sit with Him in heavenly places far above all principalities and powers and every name that is named, not only on earth but also in heaven. And by this deliverance I can rightly say that Your people shall possess their possessions.

And finally, I say unto these that are liberated, go and sin no more. This I pray through Jesus Christ our Lord and Savior. Amen. **1 Samuel 19:10; Ezra 9:8; Psalm 55:8; Psalm 124:7; Obadiah 1:17; 2 Chronicles 20:15**

PRAYER FOR FORGIVENESS

Dear heavenly Father, thank You for counting me worthy to stand before You and pray this prayer for Your children (this family). They were shapen in iniquity and in sin did their mothers conceive them. But You, O Lord, have not considered all these, but with Your steadfast love have blotted out, as a thick cloud, their transgressions and cleared the cloud of their sins. You have put forth Your hands and embraced them. Cause them also to forgive others as our Lord Jesus taught us to do. As they receive this assurance of forgiveness, may they forever stand and minister in Your presence. May they never be remembered of their past which You already have cleansed them of and have counted them worthy to minister in Your presence. In Your presence in fullness of joy, and at Your right hand are pleasures forever more. I pray that You create in them a clean heart, and renew the right spirit within them. Make them to hear joy and gladness and uphold them with Your free spirit. I pray this prayer in Jesus' name believing that they are healed and restored. Amen. **2 Samuel 12:13**; **Psalm 51:5-12**; **Psalm 78:38**; **Psalm 103:4**; **Isaiah 44:22**; **Ephesians 1:7**

PRAYER FOR THE GIFT OF MIRACLE

My miracle working God, the Rock of my salvation, I ascribe all glory unto Your name, Amen. If it had not been You, O Lord, who was on my side, men would have swallowed me up. I would have been a reproach and a wanderer to and fro in the land of the living. When I call to remembrance all Your faithfulness to me and how You delivered me from the violent waters that had almost dragged me into the sea, Your praise will not depart from my mouth. You also miraculously saved me from head-on collisions which would have taken my life. Your daily provision for me and my family is

beyond my explanation. First of all I am asking You to bless Your ministers with the gift of miracle and the anointing to bring people to Your kingdom. Let salvation be preached from the altar and let the hearers mourn for their sins and repent and give their lives to You. Let them make You the Lord of their lives. Except the people see signs and wonders they will not believe. Let therefore our preaching not be with the enticing words of man's wisdom, but with the demonstration of Your power and Your Spirit. Lord, bring miracles of finance, favor and of health. Let not Your people spend the blessing You bless them with in the hospital. Bless them with miracle children, homes, jobs and connections. Thank You for answering my prayer as we continually sing this song: "He's a miracle working God, He's a miracle working God; He's the Alpha and Omega, He's a miracle-working God." I am praying this prayer in Jesus' name knowing that He is faithful that promised. Amen and Amen.
Genesis 21:19; Exodus 14:16; 2 Kings 7:1; Mark 7:37; John 6:1-13; Acts 3:6-7

PRAYER OF LIFTING FOR THOSE CAST DOWN

Father Divine, my rock, my shield, my strength, my redeemer, my hope, and my dwelling place, take all the glory, honor, adoration, majesty, dominion and might, Amen. Lord, touch Your people with strength as I release them into Your able hand. Clothe them all around with Your shield of faith to enable them quench the fiery darts of the wicked and to triumph over sin that weakens them and make their prayer lives dull. This is a critical moment in their lives and that of their families. It is a time that the wicked one has gone all out to test the faith of those that worship You. As he tries the faith of Your people, let them come out pure and clean as gold tried in the fire seven times and purified and made to stand the test of times and seasons. At any time that the enemy tries to pull them down in order to destroy them, Lord, for Your name's sake, arise and protect them. Let not the weakness of their flesh translate into weakness in their spirits. I also take consolation in Your word that says, "Let the weak say I am strong." I, therefore, openly declare that I am strong as they individually also declare, they are strong! Thank You for clothing

us with Your strength. I pray this prayer in Jesus' name. Amen.
Exodus 15:2; Isaiah 40:31; Nehemiah 8:10; Mark 11:22

PRAYER FOR PEACE

Dear Father, our Lord and Savior, thank you for this day that You have made that we should rejoice and be glad in it. Thank you for sending Your Son, Jesus Christ, the Prince of Peace, to bring peace from heaven into our hearts here on earth. Help us to keep the peace and remind us to know that the kingdom of God is not meat and drink, but righteousness and peace and joy in the Holy Spirit. Lord, bring peace upon our nation, and upon our state. Let Your peace reign in Your church and in the homes of those that love peace and earnestly pray for it. I pray particularly for this family or couple that the enemy has been fighting. I bind the spirit of confusion, intimidation, trouble and fighting in their lives. I command, as Jesus spoke peace to the troubled waters and there was calmness, that peace be still in their home and surroundings, Amen. Thank You, Lord, for honoring Your anointing in me, and answering this prayer for Your own glory so that our joy may be full. May the peace of God that supersedes all understanding be with us; body, soul and spirit, in Jesus' name I pray. Amen.
John 14:27; Psalm 29:11; Roman 8:6; Psalm 119:165

PRAYER FOR RESTORATION

Thank You Father for fetching these ones back from their wanderings. Their hearts had departed from Your precepts and they had failed to say "Good morning, Daddy." But today You have searched and brought them back unto Yourself. You have called them Your children and have begotten them this day forward. When they kneel down trembling in fear, Your word says to them, "I love you my beloved children, do not tremble but go and change your garments, bathe yourselves and come and take your rightful place, for I have restored you." The veil of blindness is put away from them and now they can see Your glory. The wax of deafness is removed from their ears and they can hear Your tender voice clearly. As they read and study the scriptures, they can hear You minister into their hearts the understanding and joy that once were lost. Their dreams are true revelations of You, and their visions are Your plan and purpose for them. Thank You, Daddy, for who You are, and thank You again for counting them worthy to be called Your children. I pray this prayer believing that these ones are permanently restored. In Jesus' name I pray. Amen. **Isaiah 57:18, 19; Hosea 14:4; Romans 11:5; Jeremiah 3:21-22**

PRAYER FOR OPEN DOOR

Dear heavenly Father, the maker of all things, the Creator of mankind who hangs the earth upon nothing but the Word of His mouth. You that open and no man can shut, and shut and no man can open. Let it be known unto all people that the Creator of heaven and earth is not a man that He should lie, neither the son of man that he should fail. You have the power to kill and to make alive, to wound and to heal. Arise and show Yourself strong on behalf of Your people. Move in a very special way so that the whole world will come to acknowledge You as God. Let all the doors that You have opened remain opened and let no man be able to shut them, and those You have shut should remain permanently shut and no man should be able to open them. May Your people prosper where others have failed, and may they not labor in vain. Let the door of ministry be opened for them to walk in, from nation to nation and from kingdom to kingdom. I bind the powers of hindrances that might try to block their ways by making them stagnant and unproductive in ministry. I take authority over every spirit of blockage and setback. May the doors of marriage, business, prosperity, favor, etc. that You have opened for Your people remain permanently opened. I pray this prayer in Jesus' name. Amen. **Genesis 22:17; Genesis 26:12-14; Psalm 1:3; Psalm 24:7-8; Revelation 3:8**

PRAYER AGAINST WITCHCRAFT TRANSPOSITION, MANIPULATION, FAMILIAR SPIRIT AND SPIRITUAL HUSBAND/WIFE

Most Holy Father, the Maker of the heavens and the earth, mighty in power, mighty in battle, the Great I AM THAT I AM, to You be the glory for ever and ever more. Amen. Let Your Spirit bear witness with my spirit that I am a child of God. I bind every transposition of any kind that the witches might want to use to deny me of my right in life, my admission into the school of my choice, the titles to my property and my certificates after my studies. I reject, refuse, resist and destroy all the activities of the witches. Whenever my name is mentioned, let fire burn. Whenever my exam number is invoked, let thunder strike. I destroy their seducing and manipulating power, their charm and spell, their tricks and all other devices used by the witches to deceive people. I also destroy the special code assigned to my name and exam number to be used against me. I release the fire of God to destroy the kingdom of witches, wizards and all dark powers. I bind incestuous spirit, dog spirit, pig spirit, peacock spirit and the spirit of the last days. I destroy all blood sucking and blood tapping agents and command the fire of God to burn around me and my bed at all time. I pray that any blood of mine that falls into their hand shall turn to acid and burn them. I become a flame of fire when I am sleeping, in my home, hotel room and any other place. I completely block them from coming and going and blind their eyes from seeing me. I bind all the activity of spiritual husband/wife. I declare that my body is the temple of God and the spirit of God dwells in me. Who therefore shall try to seduce me to commit fornication with him/her shall be exposed and defeated, in Jesus' name. I cover myself with the blood of Jesus and clothe upon myself the whole armor of God. As I deposit this prayer in my prayer bank, I am calling unto the Lord so that He will answer me and show me great and mighty things that I do not know. Reveal clearly to me everyone that I work with and reveal me to those that You send to work with me. Thank you for giving me victory. I pray this prayer in the name of Jesus Christ. Amen. **Genesis 27:18-29;**

Genesis 30:37-39; Judges 14:15-18; 1 King 3:16-27; Isaiah 29:6-8; Hebrews 1:7; 1 John 4:4

WARFARE PRAYER AND THE ARMOR OF GOD

Our Almighty Father in heaven, I come to You in the name of Jesus. I ascribe to You all glory, honor, adoration, dominion, majesty, power and might. You are the beginning and the end; You are our rock, our hope, our strength, and our dwelling place. Thank You, Father, for the gift of Your only Son, Jesus Christ who came and died and set me free from all curses, generational spirits, and powers of enslavement and captivity. I confess before You this day, all sins, known and unknown, generational, ancestral, personal, and parental. I confess before You all lies, cheating, and pollution. I wash myself in the pool of the blood of Jesus. I am washed, cleansed, renewed, sanctified and restored through His blood.

I now dress myself with the totality of the armor of God, defensive, offensive and counter offensive. I declare that Jesus is the truth, and I gird my loins with that truth. I am not going to this battle by my righteousness but by the righteousness of God through Christ Jesus, therefore I tie the breastplate of righteousness around my chest, around my back and shield my front. I put on my helmet of salvation by declaring that I am saved because He died to save me.

I take in my left hand the shield of faith which is my defense, and by faith I am seated with Jesus in heavenly places far above all powers and principalities; and in my right hand, I take with me the sword of the spirit, which is the Word of God, and I now declare emphatically thus:

It is written, touch not my anointed and do my prophet no harm; it is written, I have overcome the devil because greater is Jesus in me than the devil that is in this world. It is written, the name of the Lord is a strong tower; the righteous runs into it and is saved. It is written, I shall not die but live to declare the works of the Lord. It is written, the battle is not mine; the Lord will fight for me and the Egyptians that I see today, I will see them no more forever. I command the Spirit to help my infirmity even as I pray in case I do not know what to pray. As I pray in the Spirit, set a watch over me that no bullet of the enemy shall penetrate to harm me.

I now destroy all the powers of darkness and burn down the kingdom of satan, setting all his agents a fleeing. With my feet shod with the preparation of the gospel of peace, I go to his prison houses and release those souls in captivity and set them free; I command a new spirit into them and plant the love of God in their hearts. I bind all demonic forces and resist them from regrouping. I release the blood of Jesus into the air and dislodge all the spiritual wickedness from their habitations and from their strongholds.

I claim total victory to live and to continue to worship You, my Lord and Savior. Thank You, Father, as I put a seal upon this prayer and send it express to the throne of grace, and by faith I receive immediate answer now in Jesus' mighty name. Amen and Amen.

FINAL BENEDICTION

One who reads his or her Bible regularly and also applies the ideas embedded in this book and follows the recommendations, taking to heart that Jesus Christ, King of kings and Lord of lords is alive and grants our fervently presented prayers, shall never lack and shall inherit the kingdom of God. Amen.

HOSANNA!!! SAVE US NOW, LORD!!!